GAUGUIN

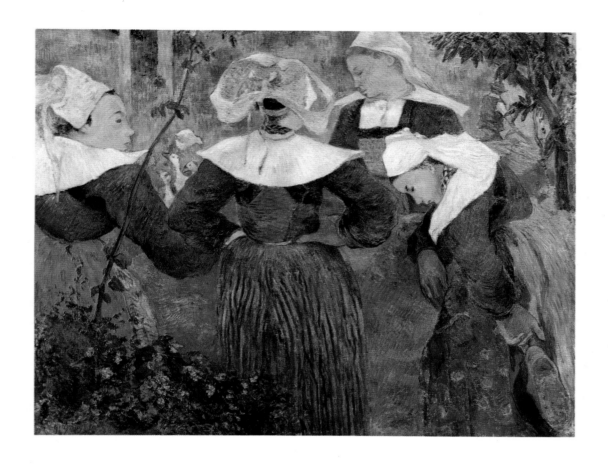

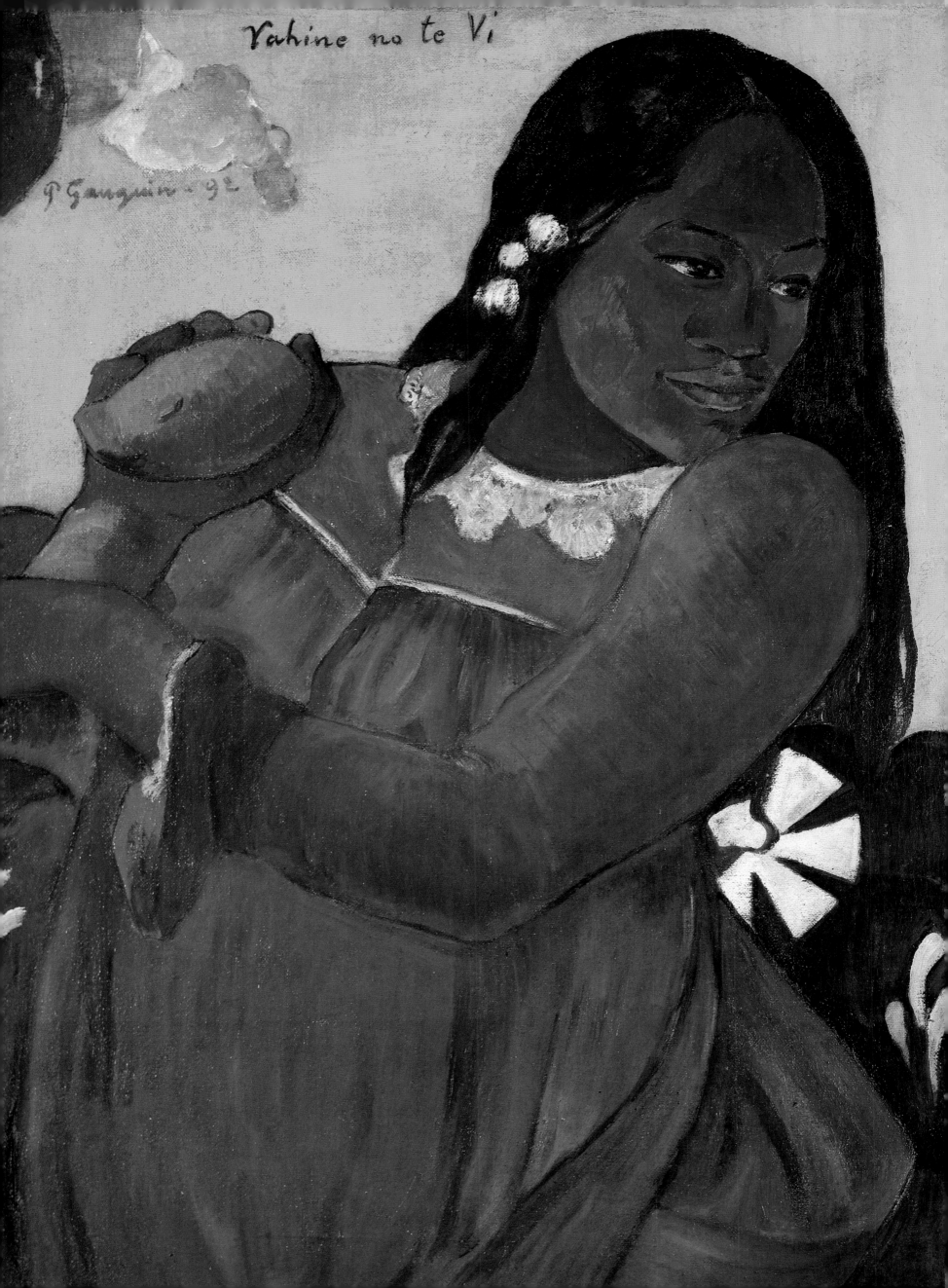

GAUGUIN

LESLEY STEVENSON

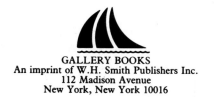

GALLERY BOOKS
An imprint of W.H. Smith Publishers Inc.
112 Madison Avenue
New York, New York 10016

Published by Gallery Books
A Division of W H Smith Publishers Inc.
112 Madison Avenue
New York, New York 10016

Produced by
Brompton Books Corp.
15 Sherwood Place
Greenwich, CT 06830

ISBN 0-8317-3767-0

Printed in Italy

FOR LINDSEY WITH LOVE

Page 1: *Four Breton Women*, 1886, Bayerischen
Staatsgemäldesammlungen Munich

Page 2: *Vahine no te Vi (Woman with a Mango)*,
1892, Baltimore Museum of Art

Contents and List of Plates

Introduction 6

Landscape 26
The Seine at the Pont d'Iéna, Snow 28
The Market Gardens at Vaugirard 30
Study of a Nude or Suzanne Sewing 32
Flowers, Still Life, or Interior of the
  Artist's House, Rue Carcel 34
Vase of Flowers 36
Garden in the Rue Carcel 37
Still Life with Oranges 38
Madame Mette Gauguin 40
Blue Roofs (Rouen) 42
Entrance to a Village 44
Sleeping Child 46
Oestervold Park, Copenhagen 48
Provençal Landscape (after Cézanne) 49
Cows in a Landscape 50
Still Life with Mandoline 52
Women Bathing 54
The Breton Shepherdess 56
Four Breton Women 58
Still Life with Profile of Laval 60
By the Sea, Martinique 62
Mango Pickers, Martinique 64
Tropical Landscape on Martinique 66
Martinique Landscape 67
Breton Girls Dancing, Pont-Aven 68
Young Bretons Bathing 70
Boys Wrestling 72
Self-Portrait (Les Misérables) 74
Vision after the Sermon or Jacob
  Wrestling with the Angel 76
Portrait of Madeleine Bernard 78
Still Life, Fête Gloanec 79
Still Life with Three Puppies 80
Van Gogh Painting Sunflowers 82

Night Café at Arles 84
The Alyscamps 86
Old Women at Arles 87
Landscape near Arles 88
Grape Harvest at Arles, Human
  Anguish 90
Still Life with Fan 92
The Schuffenecker Family 94
La Belle Angèle 96
Nirvana, Portrait of Meyer de Haan 98
Bonjour Monsieur Gauguin 100
Self-Portrait with Halo 102
Christ in the Garden of Olives
  (Agony in the Garden) 104
Woman in the Waves (Ondine) 106
Yellow Christ 108
Green Christ (Breton Calvary) 110
Naked Breton Boy 112
Yellow Haystacks 113
Haymaking 114
Portrait of a Woman, with Still
  Life by Cézanne 116
Landscape at Le Pouldu 117
The Loss of Virginity or the
  Awakening of Spring 118
Tahitian Landscape 120
Suzanne Bambridge 122
The Meal 124
Ia Orana Maria (Hail Mary) 126
Man with an Ax 128
Te Tiare Farani (The Flowers of
  France) 129
Aha oe Feii 130
Vahine no te Vi (Woman with
  a Mango) 132
Portrait of Atiti 133
Nafea Faa Ipoipo? (When will

you Marry?) 134
Manao Tupapau (The Spirit of the
  Dead keeps Watch) 136
Arearea (Pranks) 138
Ta Matete (The Market) 140
Pape Moe (Mysterious Water) 141
Merahi Metua no Tehamana
  (The Ancestors of Tehamana) 142
Hine Tefatou (The Moon and
  the Earth) 144
Ea Haere Ia Oe? (Where are
  you Going?) 145
Self-Portrait Wearing a Hat 146
Mahana no Atua (Day of the God) 147
Peasant Women from Brittany 148
Upaupa Schneklud 150
Paris in the Snow 151
Self-Portrait (at Golgotha) 152
Te Tamari no Atua (The Birth of
  Christ, Son of God) 154
Nave Nave Mahana (Wonderful Days) 156
Te Rerioa (The Dream) 158
Nevermore O Tahiti 159
Where do we come from? What
  are we? Where are we going? 160
Faa Iheihe (Tahitian Pastoral) 162
Three Tahitians 164
And the Gold of their Bodies 165
Still Life with Sunflowers 166
Girl with a Fan 168
Riders on the Beach 169
Contes Barbares (Primitive Tales) 170
The Offering 172

Index 174

Acknowledgments 176

Introduction

Possibly more than any other artist, Gauguin has been the subject of a wide variety of myths about the role of the artist and the creative process. The construction of a legend surrounding the man and his work is partly due to an attempt to place him at the beginnings of modernist art, in recognition of the formal innovations in his work. His exotic personality, the subject of a number of films and novels, lends itself to the creation of a fiction. Yet the development of myths surrounding the artist and his production began during his lifetime and much of it was manipulated by Gauguin himself. It is important, therefore, to place Gauguin within the context of late nineteenth-century art, in order to see to what extent he developed out of and relied on the work of the previous generation of avant-garde artists, and how many of his formal developments were in fact only possible because of the institutional changes which the Impressionists, among others, had helped bring about in the art world of the 1860s and 1870s. Unlike earlier artists Gauguin made a much more conscious use of publicity to promote his art. He became increasingly aware of the need to court critics and other literary figures, who could act as intermediaries between his paintings, carvings and ceramics and his public. Indeed so heavily did he rely on these writers to make his art accessible to the public, that their judgments and assessments are now often viewed as sacrosanct and the twentieth-century view of Gauguin has to an extent been distorted by this relatively uncritical acceptance.

Gauguin became increasingly aware of the need to promote his art and himself wrote a number of texts, some of which were intended for publication while others were personal and private records of his work. In these writings he encouraged his reader (and viewer) to regard his art within fairly tight constraints: the written text complemented the visual image in an unprecedented way. Because these literary interpretations of his works seem definitive, they have subsequently been viewed in isolation from the circumstances of their production. It is in fact clear that Gauguin's motives were financial as well as artistic, as he tried to create a place for himself within the Parisian artistic avant-garde.

Rather than conforming to the myth of an artist concerned only with his art, working in isolation from civilization and distancing himself from the decadence of contemporary France by going to Tahiti, Gauguin turned continually to Paris for a support which was both cultural and economic. While he worked on the other side of the world, his paintings and carvings were shipped to the French capital for display in the galleries of dealers and he continued to exercise great control over their presentation. The Gauguin we now know is a product of his consummate skill at using the existing infrastructure to his own advantage.

Impressionism

Eugène Henri Paul Gauguin was born in Paris on 7 June 1848. A year later his family moved to Peru, and the sights there seem to have remained with him for the rest of his life, predisposing him to a taste for the exotic. After the death of his father, Gauguin, his sister and mother returned to France and he was sent to Orléans to be educated. In Paris his mother worked as a seamstress and became friendly with the financier Gustave Arosa (1818-83), whose influence on the earlier part of Gauguin's career was to be decisive. In 1865 Madame Gauguin named Arosa as the guardian of her children. She died two years later, when Gauguin was at sea as a merchant seaman.

Back in Paris in 1872 Gauguin began work as a stockbroker on Arosa's recom-

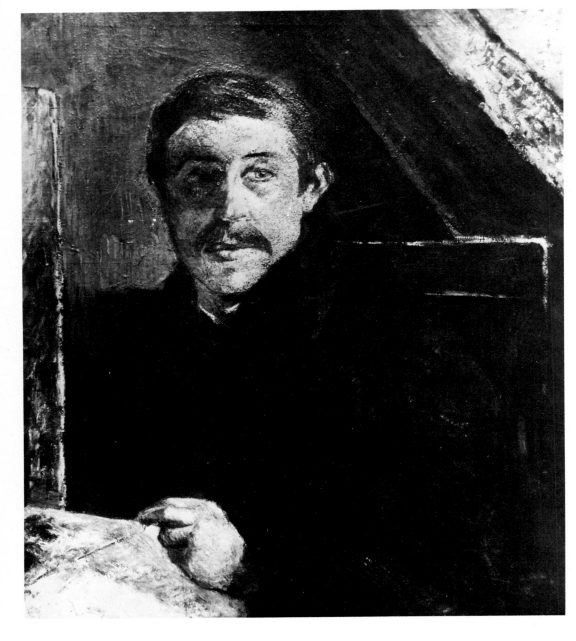

mendation. At about this time, he began painting in his spare time with one of his colleagues, Emile Schuffenecker (1851-1934). Together they began to study in the evenings at a large informal studio, the Académie Colarossi. By the time he was introduced at Arosa's home to Mette Sofie Gad (born 1850), a young Danish woman whom he married at the end of 1873, Gauguin was already an accomplished landscape painter in the manner of the Barbizon school. The early *Landscape* (page 26) is reminiscent of Corot in its soft grays and large expanse of sky. In Arosa's home he would have been able to study a collection of contemporary paintings by artists such as Courbet, Corot, Delacroix and Pissarro. At some point in the early 1870s he was introduced to Pissarro (1830-1903) by his guardian, and was no doubt encouraged in his art by the older painter.

Arosa's taste in art seems to have been determined not only by a wish to invest in affordable works, but also by a genuine enthusiasm for paintings quite different from those to be seen at the fashionable Salon. In the early 1870s the art world in Paris was dominated by this annual official exhibition of art, which was supported by the French state. Despite a few attempts to circumvent the monopolistic control which the Salon exercised on artists' lives throughout France, the government encouraged a type of art which was lacking in any kind of innovation in terms either of technique or subject-matter. By turning over a large exhibition space each year to works preselected by a jury composed of conservative artists and representatives of the French state, who were eager to preserve the status quo, and by buying and commissioning works from artists who produced acceptable paintings and sculpture, the French government was instrumental in shaping public taste in the 1870s. In the days before dealers were commonplace, when artists depended on public exposure at the Salon in order to generate sales and therefore on the influence of the much-hated jury, painters and sculptors tended to compromise their art in order to gain acceptance at the Salon. They produced huge works to attract the attention of a weary public, executed in a highly finished style with attempts at photographic exactitude, and their subject-matter was usually drawn either from ancient history or from sentimental genre scenes representing everyday life.

In 1874 a group of young artists, some of whom who had already had a degree of success at the Salon, decided to form them-

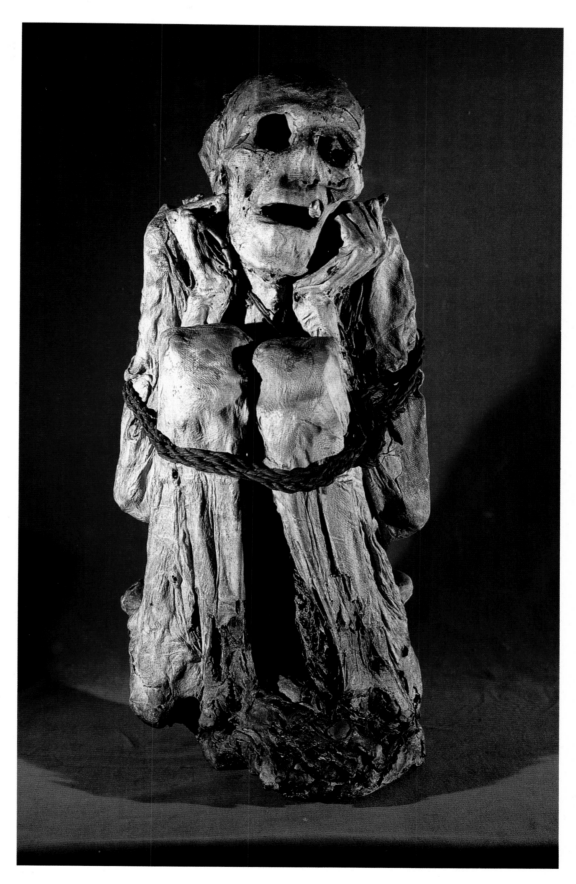

selves into a limited company and mount an independent exhibition in order to try to loosen the Salon stranglehold. One of the guiding forces behind the show was Camille Pissarro, who was joined by Monet, Renoir, Cézanne, Sisley, Berthe Morisot and Degas among others in what came to be called the first Impressionist exhibition. As well as its importance in representing a determined break with the in-

stitutional structure of the Salon, the exhibition was notable for assembling a collection of paintings which were technically very different from those to be seen at the Salon.

Although this was the first time that these artists had exhibited together as a group, the basis of what is now regarded as the impressionist style had been developed as much as five years previously, when

7

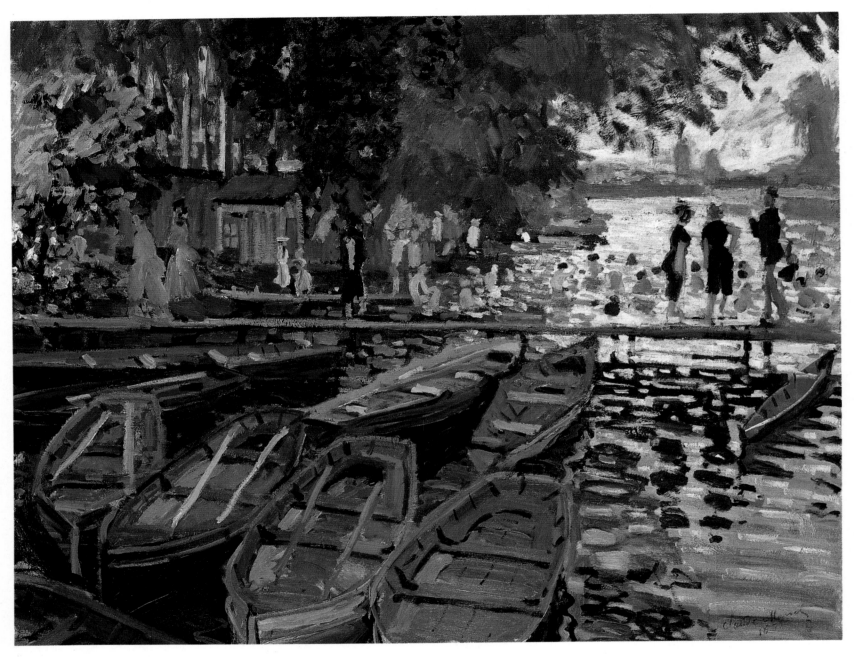

Monet and Renoir worked together at La Grenouillère on the River Seine. In the summer of 1869 the two artists positioned their easels side by side in the open air and produced a series of small canvases depicting the popular bathing resort. In Monet's *Bathers at La Grenouillère* we find the artist analyzing color in a much more systematic way than previously, noting that the local color of an object is affected by the light in which it is observed and by reflections from its surroundings. He introduced color into shadows, and the water in the foreground ripples with a wide variety of tones, an effect helped by a much looser brushstroke in which dabs of paint are clearly visible. Because of this and of the much smaller canvas used in working out of doors, the effect was one of greater informality in comparison with the highly wrought canvases found at the Salon, their subject-matter drawn from areas of little relevance to an urban population.

In the following five years Monet continued to refine and develop this style in works such as *Impression Sunrise* of 1872, which was shown at the 1874 exhibition. In this canvas he represented the effect of sunrise on water at the port of Le Havre in a remarkably free style, in which the figures on the small ships are reduced to a few summary daubs of pigment. This lack of smooth finish led the critic Louis Leroy to suggest in a satirical journal that 'wallpaper in its embryonic state is more finished than this seascape' and by extension to dub the entire group 'impressionists', which mocking title stuck and which the limited company was finally to adopt and use for later exhibitions.

Gauguin doubtless showed some interest in these independent exhibitions but in 1876 he chose to send a landscape to the Salon, apparently the only painting he ever exhibited there as he is only listed in one catalog. By 1879, when he and his wife and three children were enjoying a period of prosperity, he had begun to invest in works by members of the impressionist circle, no doubt following Arosa's example. While it was by no means unusual for financiers to buy and deal in paintings and sculptures, they normally favored works by successful Salon artists, which guaranteed a relatively higher return than those by unknown artists. It seems that, while there was a financial motive to his purchases, Gauguin was already interested in these works for their artistic merits and may well have used them as a means of self-instruction.

By the mid-1880s his collection boasted works by a number of major impressionist painters, including Renoir, Sisley, Degas, several Pissarros, a Manet and in particular six Cézannes, which Gauguin regarded as the jewels of his collection and which he refused to sell even when in desperate need of money. These included a number of works painted around 1880, including the

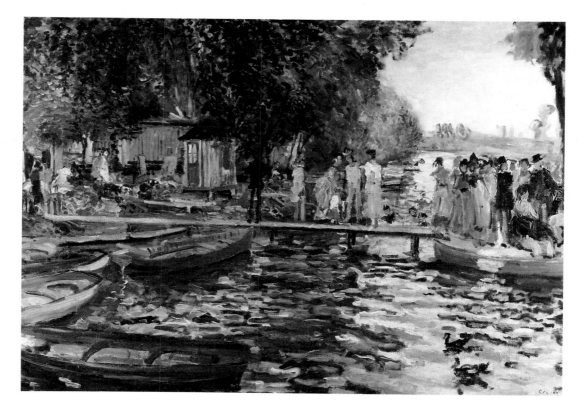

Mountains at l'Estaque and the *Castle at Médan*, both of which were to serve as direct influences on Gauguin's art.

In 1879 Gauguin was listed in the catalog of the Impressionist exhibition as loaning three landscapes by Pissarro. More importantly, he had been invited by Degas and Pissarro to exhibit with the group but so late was the invitation that his name was not included among artists in the catalog and he submitted only one work, a marble bust of his eldest son Emil. However the fourth Impressionist exhibition was very different in character from the earlier ones. By this time Cézanne, Berthe Morisot, Renoir and Sisley had withdrawn and some of the founding members had defected to the Salon, while Degas had introduced some of his protégés, such as Mary Cassatt and Gauguin, which was to cause further rifts in the original group.

In 1880 Gauguin exhibited with the Impressionists again, this time submitting eight works, one of which was a marble sculpture of his wife, *Portrait Bust of Mette Gauguin*. His paintings also included a still life, while the remainder were all naturalistic landscapes, such as the *Market Gardens at Vaugirard*, (page 30) which still shows clearly the influence of Pissarro's work. It is remarkable that he could muster eight highly competent paintings while continuing to work in the financial world.

The following year, 1881, the Impressionists' dealer Durand-Ruel bought three paintings from Gauguin for a total of 1500 francs, at a time when the annual wage of an artisan was between 900 and 6000 francs. Gauguin exhibited his most confident and varied set of works at the sixth group show, including two sculptures and eight paintings, and received his first positive review, from the critic Huysmans, for a robust *Study of a Nude* (page 32). Huys-

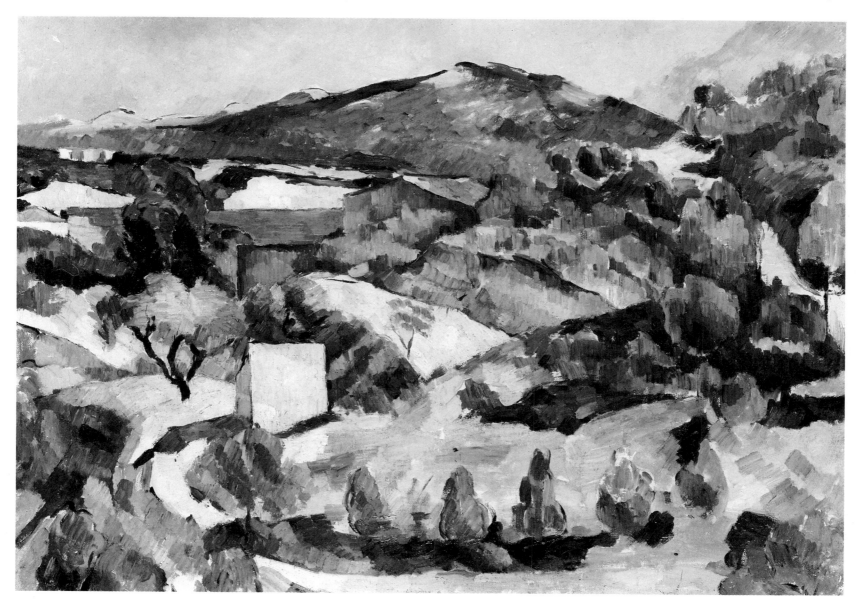

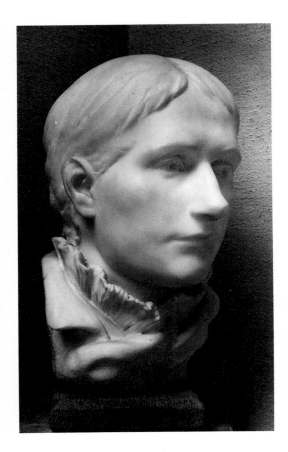

tions of her flesh rather than the smooth pink skin of the Salon nudes.

That same summer he joined Pissarro at his home in Pontoise and worked under the older artist's guidance. They were joined by Cézanne, and both Gauguin and Pissarro profited from watching him work. By this time the doubts troubling Monet and Renoir about the limitations of the impressionist style had begun to assail Pissarro, and he tried to solve them by reference to Cézanne's technique. While works such as *Impression Sunrise* were admirable in their analysis of the effects of light, to take such a method to its logical conclusion led to an almost total disintegration of the picture surface and a lack of any kind of pictorial unity. Cézanne recognized this and in his works of 1880-1 began to structure his picture in a much more systematic way. He adopted the device of grouping his brushstrokes together in a coherent fashion, sloping them diagonally across the surface of the painting; the end result is a highly integrated picture, but which lacks the apparent spontaneity of the impressionist works of the 1870s. In works such as the *Castle at Médan*, however, the freshness of outdoor painting is preserved, partly owing to the juxtaposition of emerald and vermilion. This and other paintings represent a significant development; Cézanne retained the scientific advances of impressionism, while abandoning any pretence at completing a canvas at a single sitting.

Whether or not Gauguin actually discussed these ideas and their implications with Cézanne seems doubtful; the older artist was notoriously jealous and suspicious, perhaps rightly as far as Gauguin was concerned given what Gauguin wrote in a letter to Pissarro on his return to Paris:

mans praised him for daring to depict a contemporary woman and for not hesitating to show the puckering and imperfec-

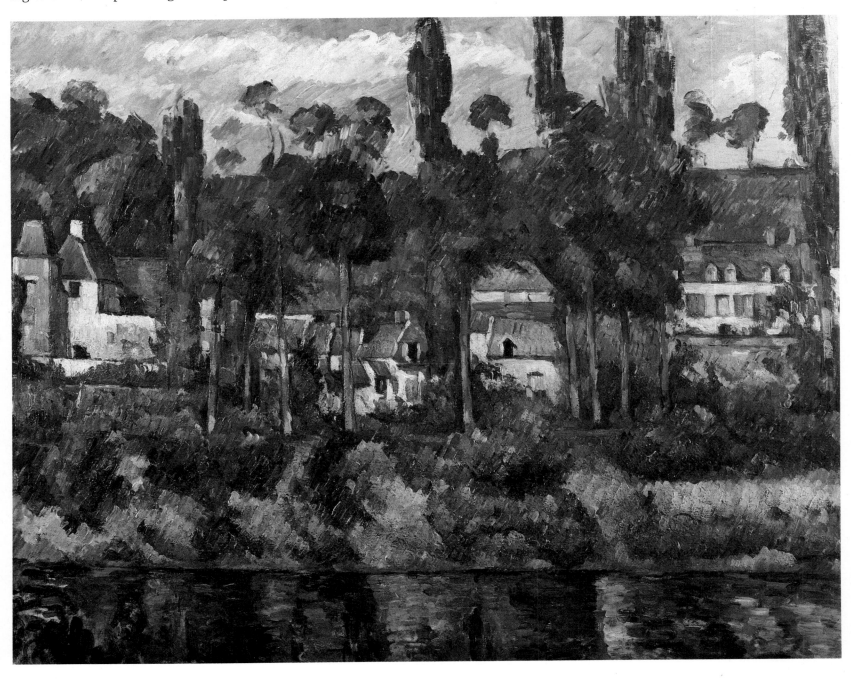

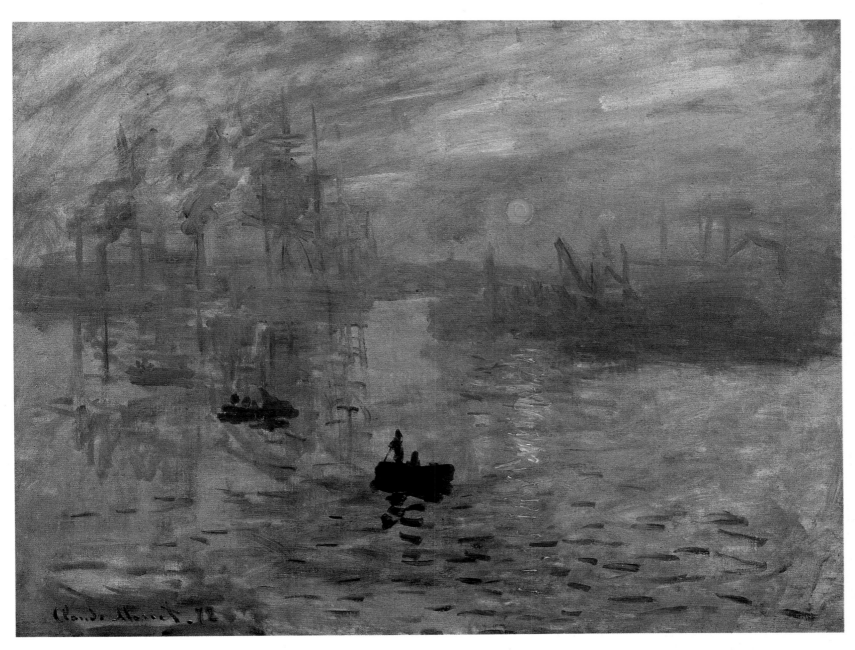

Has M. Cézanne discovered the exact formula for a work that would be accepted by everyone? If he should find the recipe for concentrating the full expression of all his sensations into a single and unique procedure, I beg you to try to get him to talk about it in his sleep by administering one of those mysterious homoeopathic drugs to him and come directly to Paris to share it with us.

Gauguin obviously learned a great deal from his collection of Cézanne canvases, the majority of which were painted in the closely hatched style of the early 1880s, and both he and Pissarro adopted for some time Cézanne's method of ordering picture space.

Gauguin's submissions to the seventh Impressionist exhibition were his most ambitious and varied to date, comprising a number of landscapes, four still lifes and several figure studies, including a bust of his son Clovis and three paintings of his children. The inclusion of figure studies in 1882 demonstrates that Gauguin was taking a lead from both Degas and Mary Cassatt, who had exhibited a number of pictures of children in the previous group show.

In 1883 Gauguin faced severe financial hardship. He lost his job, as an indirect result of the collapse of the Stock Exchange at the beginning of the previous year, and was forced to consider making his living full-time as an artist. Whether or not he would have chosen to relinquish a well-paid position for the hazardous life of an artist, had he not been forced to do so, is difficult to say. Certainly he seems to have met with some resistance from his wife who was loath to surrender the comfortable existence they had enjoyed at the end of the 1870s, particularly since their fifth child was expected at the end of 1883. In addition Durand-Ruel, who was worried about his own investments, decided to hold a series of one-man shows in 1883 rather than the usual group exhibition.

This infuriated Gauguin, who by now had come to depend on the exposure of the Impressionist show in order to generate sales, and saw his work being passed over in favor of the older, more established Impressionist artists. After the birth of Pola Gauguin the family moved to Rouen, in January 1884, where it was hoped it would be cheaper to live. In July 1884 Mette Gauguin took the baby and their daughter Aline to her family's home in Copenhagen, and Gauguin was forced to join her in November. That each viewed this as a fairly protracted visit is evident from the fact that Gauguin took with him his prized collection of impressionist paintings, most of which remained in Denmark and were gradually sold by his wife whenever she was short of money.

The period spent in Copenhagen does not seem to have been a happy one; Gauguin was employed as a traveling sales representative for a tarpaulin company and his wife gave French lessons but there were constant worries about finances. This was not helped by his antipathy towards the Danish, and his in-laws in particular, and a feeling of frustration at his isolation from the cultural hub of Paris; he was particularly annoyed at missing a large Delacroix retrospective exhibition. His letters to Pissarro and Schuffenecker ask hungrily for news of the art world. In the two years since becoming a more or less full-time artist, however, Gauguin's output had risen dramatically, and in 1885 he painted around 50 canvases compared with about a dozen in the years when he was exhibiting with the Impressionists. More importantly, the period spent in isolation in Copenhagen seems to have been crucial for his artistic self-assessment, and his letters reveal a much more analytical and pre-

meditated approach to his art. While the paintings of the time are still impressionist in style and subject-matter (for example, *Oestervold Park*, (page 48), his correspondence betrays increasing dissatisfaction with rigorous naturalism.

Gauguin wrote to Schuffenecker from Copenhagen, 'Colors, although less numerous than lines, are still more explicative by virtue of their potent influence on the eye', and, 'Above all don't perspire over a picture. A strong emotion can be translated immediately: dream on it and seek its simplest form.' Gauguin was beginning to edge toward theories which were to be fully explored when he aligned himself with the literary Symbolists. And yet his theory and practice were widely divergent at this time. He produced a large

number of landscapes, many of them in the style of Pissarro, and borrowed extensively from Cézanne. He painted a fan in Copenhagen in which the main motifs were taken with little alteration from Cézanne's *Mountains at L'Estaque* (*Provençal Landscape*, page 49). Much of Gauguin's subject-matter at this time was determined by what he knew Durand-Ruel could sell in Paris and his fan painting also demonstrates an artist with an eye to the market. In May 1885 Gauguin exhibited at the Society of Friends of Art in Copenhagen but in his letter he was dismissive about the art world in that city; certainly his work received little critical attention. The following month he returned to Paris taking his six-year-old son Clovis with him, apparently finding the claustrophobic family life in Copenhagen beyond endurance and tired of his in-laws' lack of comprehension.

The following year Gauguin was one of the main contributors to the eighth and final Impressionist exhibition. He showed a total of 19 paintings, the majority of which were landscapes including recent works from Rouen and Copenhagen, and a wood relief. By this time, the impetus which had fueled the first group show 12 years previously had all but disappeared. Out of the original members only Pissarro remained committed to the idea and sent work to all eight exhibitions; and the introduction of new members such as Seurat and Signac signaled a change in identity in these shows. Moreover, the stranglehold of the Salon had been somewhat eroded and the jury was becoming more tolerant of freer painting styles. A number of the original Impressionists had exhibited there in recent years, most notably Monet and Renoir, although others such as Cézanne continued to submit works only to be rejected. In addition the number of alternative outlets and exhibitions had increased and private galleries had become more popular, as the bourgeoisie favored buying its art from sympathetic dealers rather than commissioning directly from the artist. In this sense the institutional hurdles which had made an independent exhibition a virtual necessity in 1874 had been overturned.

Brittany
In July 1886 Gauguin decided to leave Paris and spend the summer in Brittany, where he hoped it would be cheaper to live. Guidebooks recommended various areas in Brittany as being suitable for artists, combining pleasant scenery, temperate climate (for painting landscapes) and

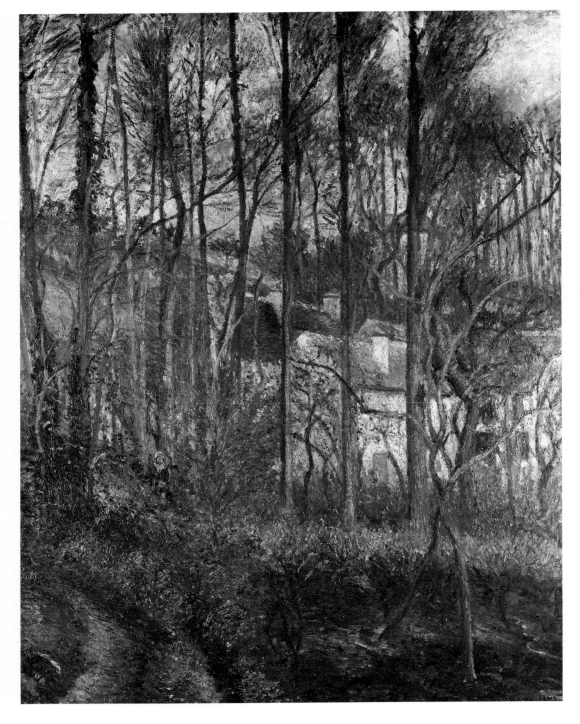

peasants who were only too willing to pose in their picturesque costumes. Gauguin settle in Pont-Aven, a small port only four miles from the sea, which was singled out for praise in various tourist guidebooks and artists' handbooks. In the mid 1880s its population was only about 1500 but this was augmented each summer by a steady stream of tourists, many of them art students on vacation from Paris. Like them, Gauguin stayed at the Pension Gloanec, which was particularly recommended as a 'true bohemian home' where one could have two good meals a day plus cider and for which he paid only 65 francs per month.

Shortly after his arrival, Gauguin wrote to his wife in Copenhagen that there were hardly any French visitors in Pont-Aven but some Danes and lots of Americans. His letters show that at first he was delighted with what he perceived as the quaint, simple way of life in the relatively isolated area of Brittany. He was later to write to Schuffenecker:

I love Brittany, I find something savage, primitive here. When my clogs echo on this granite earth, I hear the dull, muffled powerful note that I seek in painting.

It would seem that for some time Gauguin was seduced by the image of Brittany as a place where innocence remained, but in fact the 'savage' aspects he found there were largely the result of wishful thinking. Nonetheless the original impact of that relatively unsophisticated culture was quite momentous and one which he went to great lengths to recapture, eventually crossing the world to Polynesia in what was ultimately to prove a frustrating and fruitless quest. By the final quarter of the nineteenth century the image of a picturesque and slower way of life in Brittany was largely a fiction, but one which was all-pervasive. The kind of abounding sentimentality found in Dagnan-Bouveret's popular Salon painting *Pardon in Brittany* (page 14), depicting a religious festival in a meticulous style, was one of a number of

such images which confirmed this view of the 'primitive' way of life to be found in Brittany. Certainly the remote coastal area was not as industrialized as the capital but it was expanding rapidly and its industries, including tourism, were one of the success stories of the Third Republic. By the time Gauguin went there in 1886 the popular image of Brittany was largely anachronistic, but one to which he clung for some time until disillusionment set in. Consequently the work he produced in Brittany is highly selective – he turned with renewed interest to figure painting and exploited the decorative aspects of the costumes worn by the women there (the men are largely ignored), as in *Breton Girls* (page 68). He also focused on the religious festivals much as Dagnan-Bouveret did, despite the fact that by the 1880s they seem to have become virtually a tourist attraction.

Gauguin returned to Paris in October after a productive summer, but the images of Brittany remained with him and he drew

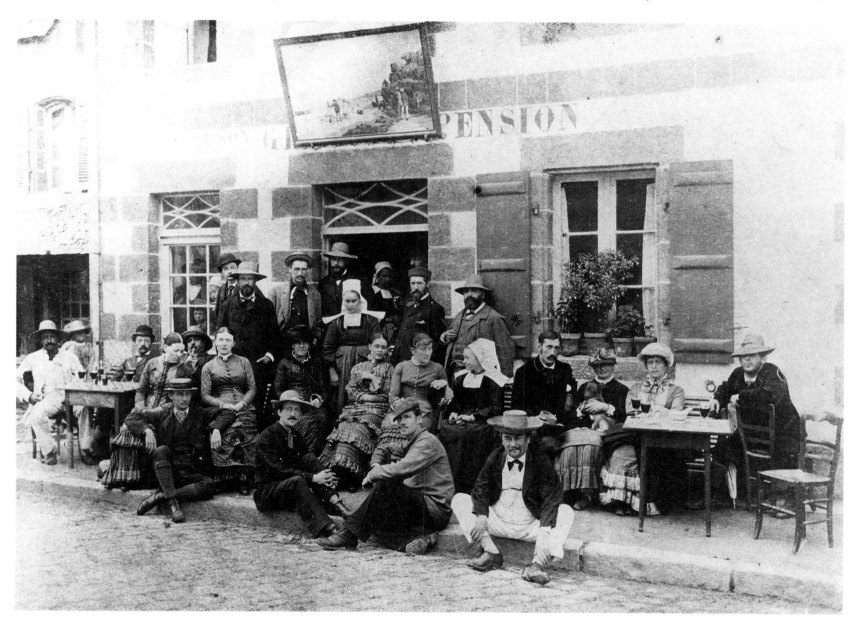

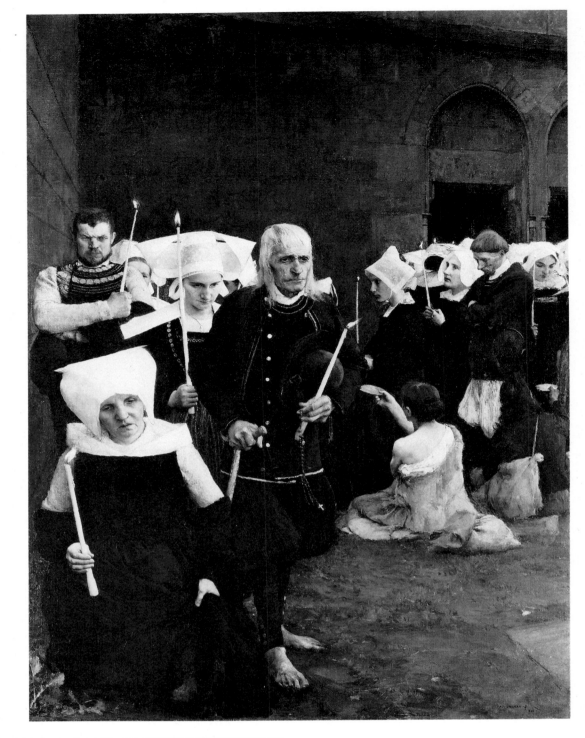

on them for subject-matter back in the capital. *Four Breton Women* (page 58) was painted in Paris towards the end of that year, based on the little pastel drawing *Breton Girl*. That winter Gauguin ventured into the new medium of ceramics and made a number of pots under the guidance of Chaplet. He simplified and pared down Breton imagery to suit the medium, as in *Vase with Breton Girls* in which he recycled the image yet again.

In the following spring the longstanding lure of a simpler and more 'savage' way of life led Gauguin to leave Europe. On 10 April 1887 he left France for Panama, accompanied by the young artist Charles Laval. They arrived in Panama by the end of the month but the elaborate plans Gauguin had made for going on from Panama to Tobago were upset because of lack of funds. Laval was forced to turn out some academic portraits on commission, but Gauguin preferred not to compromise his art and endured 15 backbreaking days digging the Panama Canal 13 hours a day. After being laid off he went with Laval to Martinique, which had been in French possession since the seventeenth century. The works he produced there (*By the Sea, Martinique*, page 62, *Mango Pickers, Martinique*, page 64) employed jewel-like colors and demonstrated a fascination with the tropics which was to haunt Gauguin once back in Paris.

Towards the end of 1887 a number of Gauguin's recent Martinique paintings

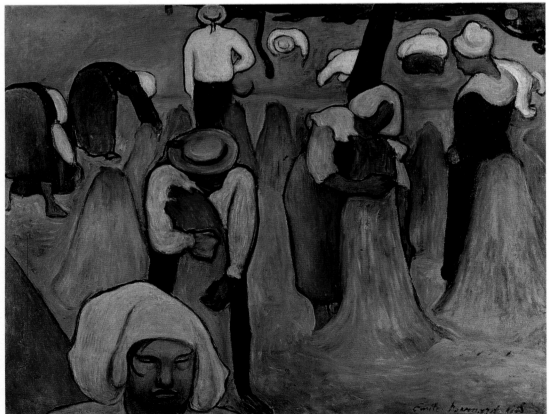

were on display at Portier's gallery in Paris, where they were admired by Vincent Van Gogh (1853-90) and his brother Theo (1857-91) who was employed as an art dealer in Paris. Through Portier, who lived in the same apartment block, they arranged a meeting with Gauguin, and Theo Van Gogh offered to take on five ceramics and four paintings, one of which he sold for 450 francs. During the following year Theo Van Gogh bought a number of Gauguin's works and, in the summer of 1888, offered him a regular monthly income of 150 francs in exchange for one painting if Gauguin would join his brother Vincent in Arles in the south of France.

At the beginning of 1888 Gauguin returned to Pont-Aven, remaining there until October when he went to Arles. This was a remarkably productive period in which he produced some of his most important works, several of which Theo Van Gogh sold in Paris. In August 1888 Gauguin was joined by the young artist Emile Bernard (1868-1942), whom he had met briefly two

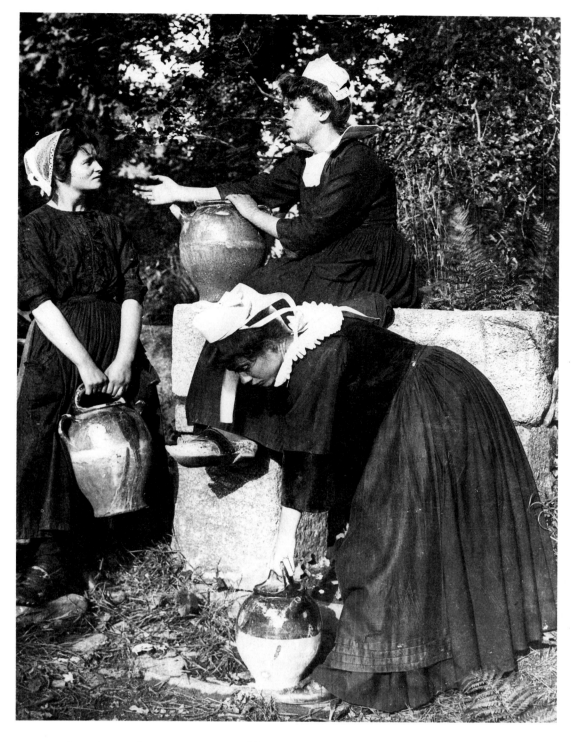

Left: This oddly contrived photograph of Breton women at the well demonstrates the willingness of the Bretons to pose for the camera or the artist.

Below: *Vase with Breton Girls*, 1886-7, an example of Gauguin's ceramic work using a popular Breton motif.

men like the critic Huysmans (*Study of a Nude*, page 32) were most concerned with 'truth' and 'objectivity'. They imagined that the worth of an artist was to be measured by the fidelity with which he reproduced a vision of the external world.

The Symbolists, under the influence of German Idealism, developed a quite different view of the basis of knowledge and hence the role of the artist. They held that reality existed only in the viewer's mind and the objective, external world was simply an 'Idea' in the beholder's mind. They laid great stress on the role of the imagination, which was held to offer a much more profound and complex vision of reality. The artist's function became one of identification, of selecting the essence of the subject and revealing its inner meaning. This process of selection meant that the painter had to simplify and synthesize his forms and colors and arrange them in such a way as to convey certain ideas to the viewer. His role was no longer one of chronicling reality but rather of arousing feelings and emotions in the viewer.

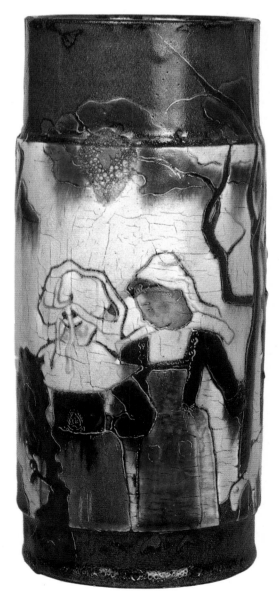

years earlier. Bernard was accompanied by his mother and sister Madeleine (1871-95), whom Gauguin admired greatly. Although Bernard was 20 years his junior, his coming to Pont-Aven that summer seems to have acted as a catalyst for Gauguin, forcing him to reconsider his art in the light of the younger artist's theories. A painting such as Bernard's *Buckwheat Harvest* may well have influenced Gauguin's work, particularly the key work of the summer of 1888, *The Vision after the Sermon* (page 76). The startling use of red in Bernard's work may have encouraged Gauguin to adopt the nonnaturalistic vermilion ground in the *Vision* and the simplification of the peasant women, in which their clothes are reduced to flat blocks of color, is very similar. Through Bernard, Gauguin became acquainted with the latest literary theories in Paris, and was introduced to members of the literary avant-garde, who were his first real champions and who laid down many of the theories about his work which have come to be regarded as definitive.

Symbolism

In 1886 Jean Moréas published the *Symbolist Manifesto*, in which he declared that Symbolism had replaced all previous cultural movements. At first the movement was essentially a literary one, dominated by men like Albert Aurier (1865-92) who was friendly with Bernard, but gradually the ideas of literary Symbolism became wider in their application after Aurier found aspects in Bernard's, and particularly in Gauguin's, art which seemed to echo what the group was striving for in literature. Initially the movement grew out of a dissatisfaction with the naturalism which had dominated much artistic thought in the earlier part of the nineteenth century, and which was reiterated not only in the novels of men like Zola but also in the paintings of the impressionist circle. Naturalism or Positivism, from which it took its theoretical underpinnings, held that the only dependable basis of knowledge was the observation of material reality. Zola, the impressionists and

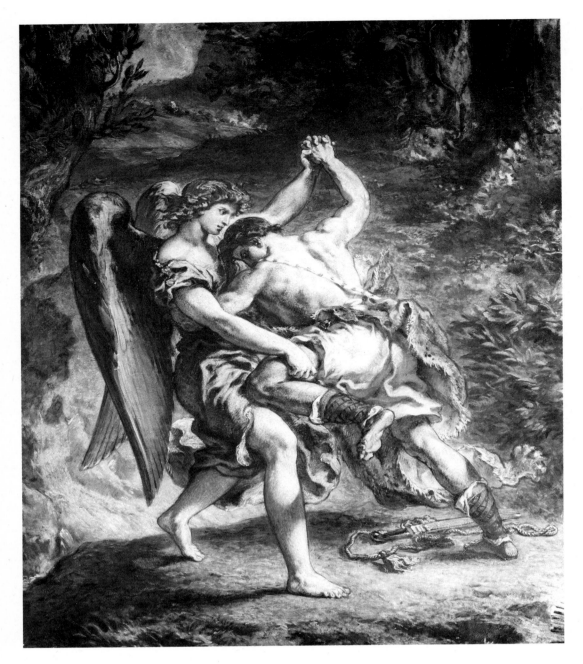

Left: A detail from Delacroix's fresco *Jacob wrestling with the Angel*, 1849-61, painted for a church in Paris, which may have inspired Gauguin in his depiction of the same theme (page 76).

As many of these ideas were at first expressed in literary and hence theoretical terms, they were not immediately adopted wholesale by painters like Bernard and Gauguin. Rather, their influence was more subtle. In a sense, Gauguin had already been edging towards some of the ideas himself. He had shunned Parisian subject-matter, which was inextricably linked with Impressionism with its emphasis on contemporary subjects, and turned to a much wider variety of motifs. He had begun to work in a synthetic fashion, in works such as *Four Breton Women* (page 58) and *Vase with Breton Girls*, painting away from the subject. And he had written to Schuffenecker from Pont Aven on 14 August 1888:

A hint – don't paint too much directly from nature. Art is an abstraction. Study nature then brood on it and treasure the creation which will result. . .

After Bernard arrived in Pont-Aven the two artists discovered a common interest in avant-garde literary theories, they developed a symbiotic relationship, swapping ideas and learning from each other's work. In a sense Bernard merely confirmed and consolidated Gauguin's theoretical position. When Bernard introduced Gauguin

to Aurier he performed him a great service; for the first time Gauguin's work was provided with an interpretation which hurled it into the midst of the artistic avant-garde in Paris, and placed him firmly at the head of a group of the most innovatory artists of the time.

Shortly after meeting Bernard in August 1888, Gauguin began one of his most important works of that year, the *Vision after the Sermon* or *Jacob Wrestling with the Angel* (page 76), a theme which had already been treated by Delacroix. In this work Gauguin can be seen putting many of the new theories into practice. In trying to convey the effect of a religious experience on the simple peasant women, he abandoned traditional western perspective and naturalistic color. He wrote to Schuffenecker on 8 October:

I have painted a picture for a church; of course it was refused (by the priest), so I am sending it to (Theo) Van Gogh. . . This year I have sacrificed all, execution and coloring, for style, intending to compel myself to do something different from what I usually do.

Naturally Symbolism met with some resistance from orthodox impressionists, and Gauguin was regarded as an opportu-

nistic charlatan by some of his original friends. Pissarro wrote an unusually bitter letter to his son Lucien:

I do not criticize Gauguin for having painted a vermilion background, nor do I object to the two struggling warriors and the Breton peasants in the foreground, what I dislike is that he stole these elements from the Japanese, the Byzantine painters and others. I criticize him for not applying his synthesis to our modern philosophy which is absolutely social, anti-authoritarian and anti-mystical. That is where the problem becomes serious.

However in Aurier's important article 'Symbolism in Painting – Gauguin', published in 1891, he dealt with the *Vision* at some length and placed it at the start of the Symbolist movement in painting. He emphasized the painting's daring formal qualities and the bright red ground, which he saw as marking a decisive break with naturalism. Throughout the twentieth century, critics who wish to regard Gauguin as one of the pioneers of modern art have followed Aurier's lead in laying great stress on the formal innovations of works such as the *Vision*, to the detriment of Gauguin's earlier works and without examining his artistic intentions. Aurier wrote:

Far, far away, on a fabulous hill, where the earth appears a gleaming red, the biblical fight between Jacob and the Angel takes place. . . While these two legendary giants, whom distance transforms into pygmies, fight their fearsome fight, some women watch, interested and naive, doubtless not understanding much of what is happening on that fabulous crimson-flushed hill. They are peasants. And in the full-span of their white caps used like the wings of a seagull, and in the typical medley of their shawls and in the form of their dresses. . . one recognizes natives of Brittany. They have the respectful postures and staring faces of the simple creatures listening to extraordinary stories. . .

After his description of the work, which dealt at some length with its formal qualities and emphasized the 'primitive' qualities of the women, Aurier continued:

. . .in front of the marvelous canvas by Paul Gauguin, which enlightens the mystery of the Poem. . . which reveals the unutterable charms of the Dream. . . and the symbolic veils which are only half raised . . . the artist always has the right to exaggerate those directly significant qualities (forms, lines, colors, etc,) or to attenuate them, to deform them, not only according to his individual vision, (but also) . . . according to the needs of the Idea to be expressed.

Right: Sérusier's *The Talisman*, 1888, painted under Gauguin's direction, illustrates many of his most recent developments.

Below right: In Van Gogh's version of *The Night Café*, 1888, he evokes a mood of menace by the use of rushing diagonals and simplified colors.

Gauguin's reputation was gradually increasing and he came to be regarded as a leader by a number of younger artists who were based in Paris. In October Paul Sérusier (1863-1927) produced a tiny landscape, *The Talisman*, under Gauguin's direction, in which many of Gauguin's ideas were put into practice. Sérusier painted the Bois d'Amour near Pont-Aven, working quickly with paint squeezed directly from the tube and with little regard for the local colors of the landscape. According to his later description of events Gauguin asked:

How do you see this tree? Is it really green? Use green then, the most beautiful green on your palette, and that shadow, rather blue? Don't be afraid to paint it as blue as possible.

Arles

Before Gauguin went to Arles toward the end of October 1888, Van Gogh asked him and Bernard to exchange portraits. Gauguin planned to send one of his most symbolic and contrived works, *Les Misérables* (page 74), while Emile Bernard sent *Self-Portrait for his Friend Vincent* (page 22). Before dispatching *Les Misérables*, Gauguin described it in a letter to his friend, who replied:

. . . your general idea of the impressionist, of which your portrait is the symbol, is striking. I am more than anxious to see it, but I feel fairly sure that this work is too important for me to have by way of exchange . . . I must tell you that even while at work I do not cease thinking of this enterprise of starting a studio with you and me for permanent residents. . .

Van Gogh had been preparing for Gauguin's arrival in Arles for some time, and envisaged a community of artists learning from each other and swapping ideas. Gauguin's motives were probably more mercenary. Theo Van Gogh had promised him a regular monthly income in exchange for one picture and this clearly freed him from worries about sales, allowing him to develop his art without constant reference to his market. Theo was also eager to have someone nearby to support Vincent. The two months which he spent at Arles were a period of prodigious productivity for Gauguin, although he professed not to be as inspired by either the countryside or the people in the south compared with his 'barbaric' Brittany. The two artists often drew on the same subject-matter. In *The Night Café*, completed before Gauguin's arrival, Van Gogh's intention as stated in a letter to Theo had been to:

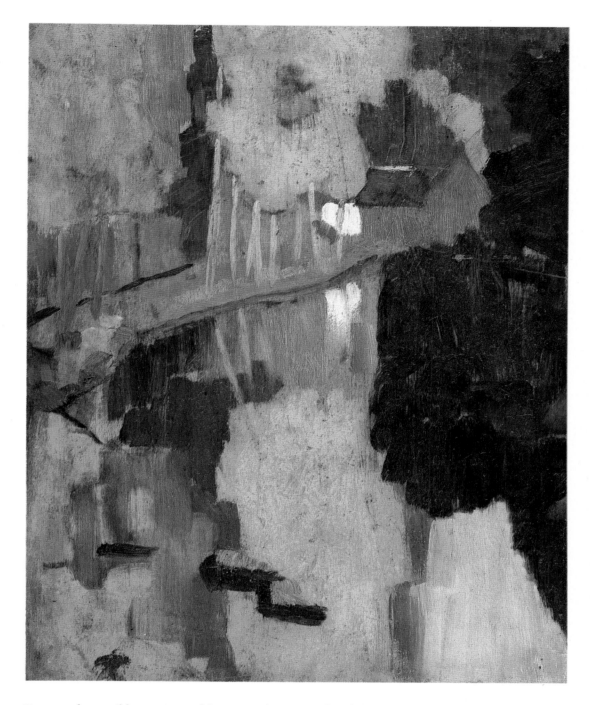

Express the terrible passions of humanity by means of red and green . . . The room is blood red and dark yellow with a billiard table in the middle; there are four chrome yellow lamps

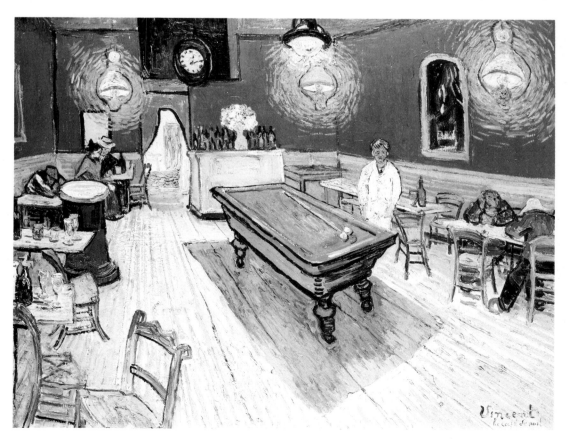

Right: Courbet's *Bonjour Monsieur Courbet*, 1854, in the museum at Montpellier. Gauguin later painted a free adaptation of the scene.

Below: Bernard's *Portrait of my Sister Madeleine*, 1888, depicts Madeleine Bernard with whom Gauguin fell in love.

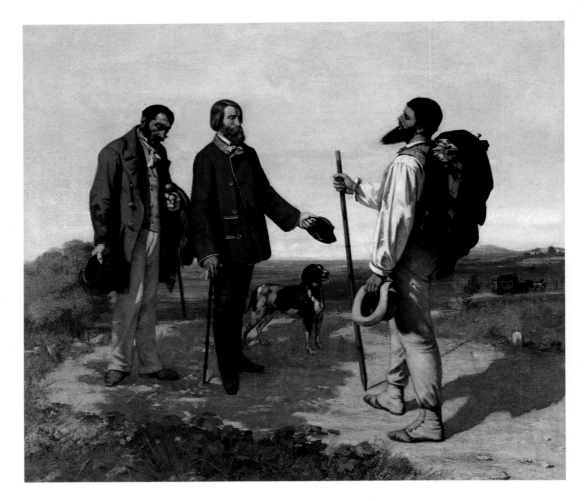

with a glow of orange and green. Everywhere there is a clash and contrast of the most alien reds and greens . . .

When Gauguin went to the same night café he painted it very differently, although making use of the same rich red and green (*Night Café at Arles*, page 84). He positioned its proprietress, Madame Ginoux, in a pose which he had already used with *Madeleine Bernard* (page 78), head resting on hand, denoting lassitude, but coupled with a flirtatious sideways glance. The table is tipped up in the same way as Van Gogh's billiard table and the objects on it appear ready to slide off into the viewer's space. The figure of Madame Ginoux is effectively cut off from the background figures by a wisp of smoke. Gauguin, however, has tried to suggest the atmosphere of the place by the portrait of a woman, while Van Gogh has striven for the same effect by

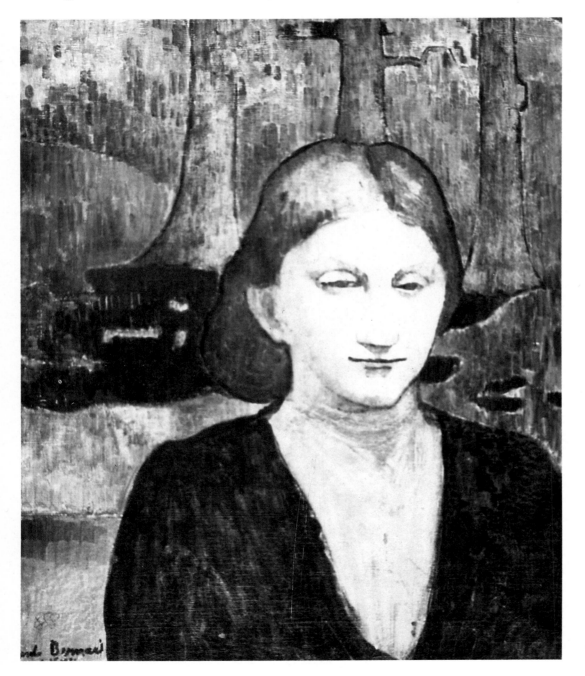

the juxtaposition of reds and greens, by the plunging perspective, the harsh lighting and the alienation of the white-coated figure.

In December Gauguin and Van Gogh traveled round the coast to Montpellier to see the famous Bruyas collection in the museum there. Gauguin later paid homage to the fine Courbets he saw by adapting *Bonjour, M. Courbet*, a double portrait of the artist and his patron, into the ironic *Bonjour, M. Gauguin* (page 100). Less than a week after the trip, a confrontation between Van Gogh and Gauguin ended in Van Gogh's threatening his friend with a knife and, later the same evening, mutilating himself by cutting off a portion of his ear. With Van Gogh in hospital, Gauguin returned to Paris with Theo and the experiment of an artistic community was effectively over.

The Exposition Universelle and the Volpini Exhibition

In February of 1889 Gauguin set off once again for Pont-Aven, where he began to plan one of his most ambitious projects to date, which he had been considering for some time, an exhibition of his work intended to capitalize on the crowds who were expected in Paris that summer to enjoy the Exposition Universelle. This was a celebration of the centenary of the French Revolution and was widely supported by the Republican government. It was a materialistic, chauvinistic display, meant not only to promote France in the eyes of other industrializing nations but also to justify and consolidate her presence in her overseas colonies.

The exhibition included many different sections, celebrating various aspects of French industry, commerce and culture, with a large section given over to French art in the specially constructed Palais des Beaux-Arts, under the new Eiffel Tower. The works there were on the whole respectable Salon pieces – Dagnan-Bouveret's *Pardon in Brittany* was included – but Cézanne, Monet and Pissarro were also represented and there were 14 Manets on display. In a sense the avant-garde art of the previous generation was becoming an accepted part of the art establishment, and Gauguin's decision to participate in an independent exhibition may be construed as an attempt to distance himself from any vestiges of impressionism in his art. None of the works which he exhibited could properly be described as impressionist in terms either of technique or subject-matter.

The place chosen for the alternative exhibition was a prime site. Schuffenecker persuaded Monsieur Volpini, proprietor of the Café des Arts next to the Palais des Beaux-Arts, to display a number of works on his walls from May until July. Eight artists, including Gauguin, Schuffenecker and Emile Bernard and a number of followers, exhibited a total of about 100 works. Gauguin was represented by 17, including ten from Brittany and four from Arles. The paintings were hung on red walls and were framed in white. In an account written in 1934, Maurice Denis wrote of his reactions to the Volpini show:

. . . the distortions of the drawings, the caricatural aspect, the flat application of the colors, everything shocks. . . Instead of windows opened onto nature, like the Impressionists' pictures, there were decorative surfaces, powerful colors outlined with savage contours. . .

Bernard's friend Albert Aurier included a review of the exhibition in his new weekly publication *Le Moderniste*, to which both Gauguin and Bernard contributed. Aurier was probably responsible for giving the show the title of 'the Impressionist and Synthetist group', in an attempt to distinguish their art from orthodox impressionism and align it with the new Symbolist ideas.

Gauguin spent most of 1889 in Brittany, but he had begun to plan another trip to the tropics. He made several visits to the Palais des Colonies at the Exposition Universelle, where natives from French overseas territories could be seen in an environment intended to resemble their homes, wearing native dress and demonstrating aspects of their life and culture. In March 1889 he wrote to Bernard:

You have missed something in not coming the other day. In the Java village there are Hindu dances. All the art of India can be seen there, and it is exactly like the photos I have. . .

The idea continued to preoccupy him and he wrote to Bernard in the summer of 1890:

What I want to do is set up a studio in the tropics. . . I can buy a hut of the kind you saw at the Exposition Universelle. An affair of wood and clay, thatched, near the town but in the country. This would cost almost nothing. I should extend it by felling trees and make of it a dwelling to our liking, with cows, poultry and fruit, the chief articles of food, and eventually it ought to cost us nothing to live. . .

This letter demonstrates the extent to which Gauguin was enticed by the official propaganda which accompanied these exhibits, which were partly intended to recruit potential colonialists. Life in the overseas territories was presented as being idyllic, the natives friendly and the living cheap. Coupled with the colorful subject-matter offered, it is small wonder that Gauguin was attracted to life in a French colony, and spent the next two years planning his escape from France.

By this time he had begun to construct an image for himself which had been germinating during his stays in Brittany and Martinique. He wrote to Vincent Van Gogh in June 1890:

Alas I see myself condemned to be less and less understood, and I must resign myself to following my path alone, dragging out an existence without family, like a pariah. . . the savage will return to the wilderness.

This vision, which Gauguin was keen to

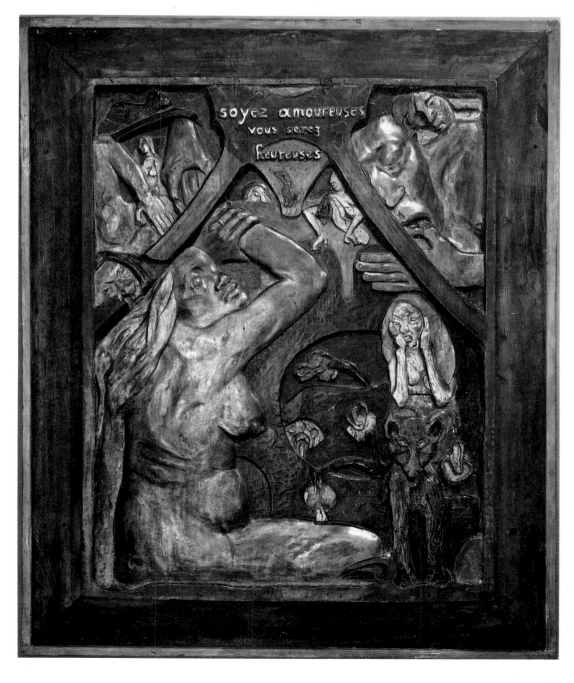

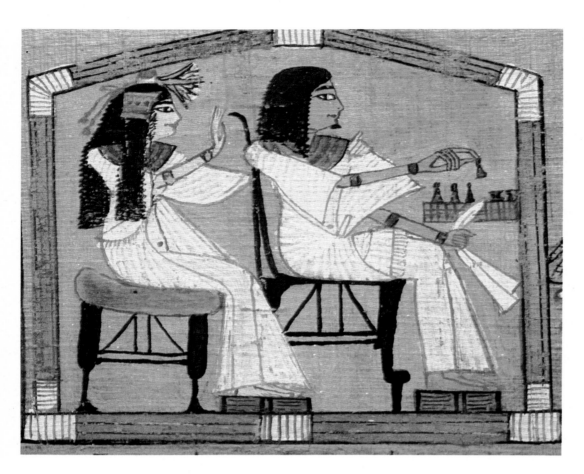

cultivate, of the artist as misunderstood outsider, was echoed in a series of self-portraits around this time. In works like *Self-Portrait with Halo* (page 102), *Christ in the Garden of Olives* (page 104) and *Yellow Christ* (page 108), the depictions of Christ are highly stylized self-portraits. The correlation between Christ's Passion and Gauguin's own artistic quest for understanding is made quite overt.

Tahiti

By 1890 Gauguin was consumed by the idea of returning to the tropics and considered a number of the French colonies, such as Madagascar, Tonkin and Martinique, before eventually deciding on Tahiti. The idea had been fueled partly by his visits to colonial exhibitions at the Exposition Universelle, partly by a dissatisfaction with the commercialism of Brittany and its failure to live up to his idea of the 'savage'. In the subsequent construction of the myth of Gauguin as a misunderstood individual who rejected civilization in order to 'render the unspoilt intensity of nature's children', the artist did as much as anyone to perpetuate such an image. Van Gogh wrote to Theo at the beginning of February 1890:

. . . he is just the sort to be off to Tonkin, he has a sort of need for expansion and he finds. . . the artistic life ignoble.

In addition the idea of the tropics as a place

of innocence was current because of the popularity of works like Pierre Loti's *Rarahu* or *The Marriage of Loti*, published in France in 1880. It told the story of a sailor's marriage to the 14-year-old native girl, Rarahu, and played on certain notions about the availability of women in the tropics, their beauty and uninhibited sexuality. Gauguin wrote to Bernard, whom he was hoping would accompany him, from Le Pouldu in Brittany in June 1890, painting a picture of an idyllic existence with limitless women:

A woman out there is, so to speak, obligatory, which will provide me with an everday model. And I can assure you that a Madagascar woman has a heart just as much as a Frenchwoman. . .

He continued:

Loti saw things as a writer, and he had his own boat and plenty of money, bread trees, wild bananas, etc. But all this is to be found in the tropical zone, coco-trees etc. . .

His image of Tahiti, like that of Brittany, was based on certain popular misconceptions, limited first-hand knowledge gleaned from the exhibits at the Exposition Universelle, and a large element of wishful thinking.

Crucial to his elaborate plans for going to Tahiti was his need to find promoters and a degree of financial backing. In a shrewd move, Gauguin began to court the avant-garde writers and critics of the day,

mainly those in the Symbolist circle. In doing this he took a calculated risk, knowing that they could promote him in some of the leading literary and artistic journals but aware at the same time that their sphere of influence was still relatively limited. Many of the works he produced at this time seem to acknowledge this new audience in an unprecedented way. A work like *The Loss of Virginity* (page 120) appears to have been painted for a small, élite, well-informed public. This manipulation of his audience was henceforth to be an important aspect of Gauguin's artistic production, and did much to shape his posthumous reputation.

The Loss of Virginity also had a more mundane source. Manet's *Olympia* had finally entered the Luxembourg Museum, which was dedicated to contemporary art mainly by living artists. The work represented all that was radical in the painting of the previous generation, and Manet had been regarded as a figurehead by the independent artists of the 1860s and 1870s. Shortly after the painting went on display in the Luxembourg Museum, Gauguin made a copy of it in oils and we know that he took a photograph of the Manet with him to Tahiti; a number of works of reclining women from around this time draw on this important source. What is surprising is that, even while he was deliberately aligning himself with the avant-garde in Paris, he still continued to seek inspiration from works which were almost 30 years old and whose original shocking impact had been greatly lessened. In a sense Gauguin never made any conscious break with the work of the 1860s and 1870s, although he tried to base his reputation on his iconoclastic tendencies. Around the same time we find him blatantly incorporating a Cézanne still life into the background of his *Portrait of a Woman with a Still Life by Cézanne* (page 118).

In order to raise money to finance his trip Gauguin held a sale of his work at the Hôtel Drouot, the public auction house in Paris, on 23 February 1891, when 30 of his paintings were sold. The sale realized almost 10,000 francs and when he wrote to Mette the following day he reported that it had been a success. The following month Aurier's article 'Symbolism in Painting' appeared in the *Mercure de France*, in which he set out to establish Gauguin as the founder and leader of a new school of painting and placed *The Vision after the Sermon* at the start of that new style, which was characterized as 'ideist, symbolist, synthetist, subjective and decorative'.

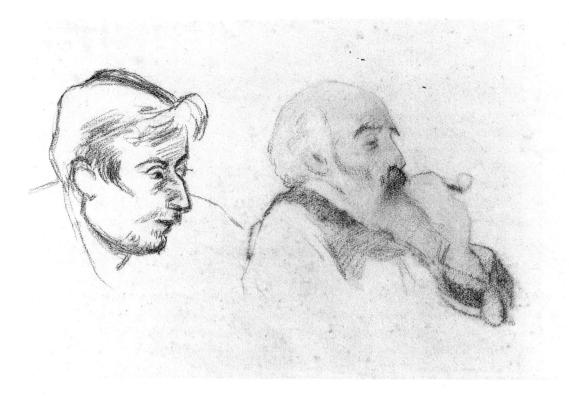

chase 3000 francs worth of his work on his return. A week before his departure a large banquet was given in his honor at the Café Voltaire in Paris, attended by Symbolist writers and critics. On 1 April 1891 Gauguin left France for Tahiti.

Much of Gauguin's posthumous reputation is built on the works which he produced in Tahiti but, just as important, the personality of the artist also became part of the subsequent cult. The idea of the artist as a maligned genius working outside western civilization in an attempt to make his art that much purer, without recourse to the conventions of realism, gained great appeal in the twentieth century when Gauguin was seen as the forerunner of much Expressionist art. By the time Gauguin left France, however, he had already been an artist for almost 20 years, had exhibited at the Salon as well as at a number of important independent shows, had acquired important patrons and supporters who were responsible for shaping his reputation, and had held a public auction of his work which he considered a success both in economic and artistic terms. The next eleven years were spent in the South Seas, with a

After seeing his wife and children in Copenhagen, for what was to prove the last time, Gauguin tried to raise some money from the Ministry of Public Education and Fine Arts, presenting his trip as an official fact-finding mission in which he wished to capture the character of the countryside and its inhabitants in his art. He was given some assistance with his passage and an undertaking that the Ministry would pur-

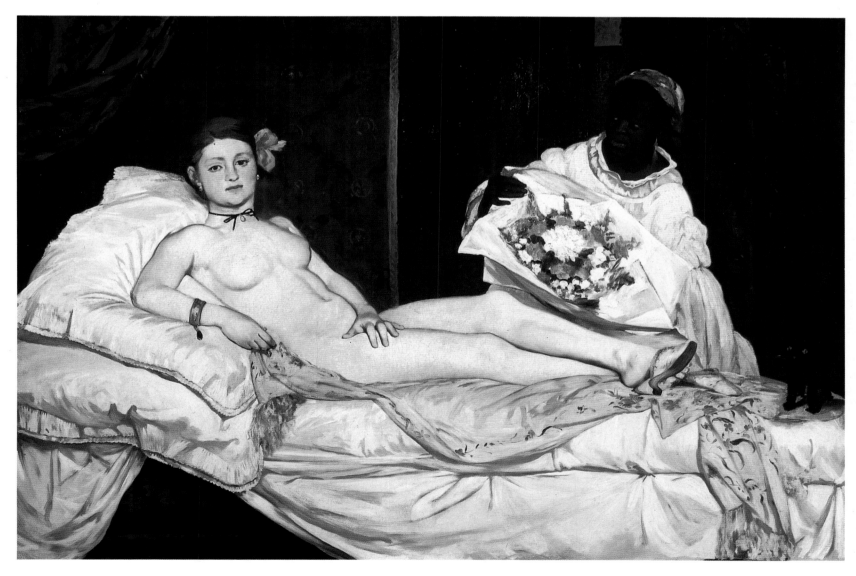

Below: Bernard's *Self-portrait*, 1888, was painted for Vincent Van Gogh.

Bottom: Detail from *Still Life with Oranges*, c. 1881 (page 38), showing Gauguin's impressionist brushstroke and his mastery of the use of complementary colors.

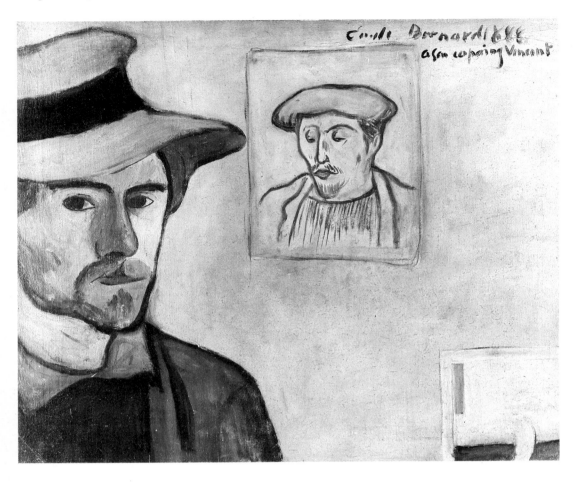

two-year break in Paris where in a sense he consolidated much of what he had already developed, but at no time did he retreat into self-imposed isolation. He was too acute a businessman to ignore his market and continued to correspond with friends, acquaintances and dealers in Paris, even when it looked as if he would never return there. He sent his wood carvings and paintings to the French capital, often accompanied by elaborate instructions for their display, promotion and sale. At the same time as acquiring a certain 'primitive' reputation for himself in the tropics, he became increasingly sophisticated in his manipulation of his public and began to write more texts, both public and private, intended to complement and explain his two- and three-dimensional work. These writings were among the greatest successes in the second part of his artistic career, and were largely responsible for shaping many of the modern notions about the role of the artist.

If, as legend goes, Gauguin went to Tahiti in order to escape civilization and to return to a simpler way of life, then he must have been greatly disappointed. He arrived in Papeete on 9 June 1891. By that time the capital of French Polynesia was a Europeanized shanty town. He wrote to Mette in July:

The Tahitian soil is becoming quite French, and the old order is gradually disappearing. . . Our missionaries have already introduced a good deal of Protestant hypocrisy [a swipe at his wife's native religion] and are destroying a part of the country – not to mention the pox which has attacked the whole race (without spoiling it too much to be sure).

Many of the Tahitians had been converted to Christianity and attended missionary schools and many wore westernized clothing. Sexually transmitted diseases had been introduced by European settlers (including Gauguin himself). Not only were the old religious beliefs gone but there was little sign of their outward manifestations; the idols and rituals which Gauguin had hoped for were almost gone. Because of the lack of any real native artistic tradition, Gauguin began to construct one for himself from a variety of sources. He took a wide variety of photographic sources with him to Tahiti. He wrote to the artist Redon in 1890 prior to his departure:

I am taking a whole little world of friends with me in the form of photographs [and] drawings who will talk to me every day.

These were not simply works like Manet's *Olympia* but also details from the Parthenon in Athens, Buddhist temples in Java and details from works in the British Museum in London. These sources were added to Gauguin's vocabulary of the 'primitive' which he had been steadily assembling from his study of Japanese prints, early Italian painting, and religious artefacts in Brittany. In addition Gauguin received regular packages from France and subscribed to leading journals which included reproductions. His use of such imagery was both selective and sophisticated.

In 1892 a colonial lawyer introduced him to one of his richest sources when he lent him a copy of J-A Moerenhout's *Voyages aux Iles du Grand Océan*, published in two volumes in Paris in 1837. This work dealt with the geography,

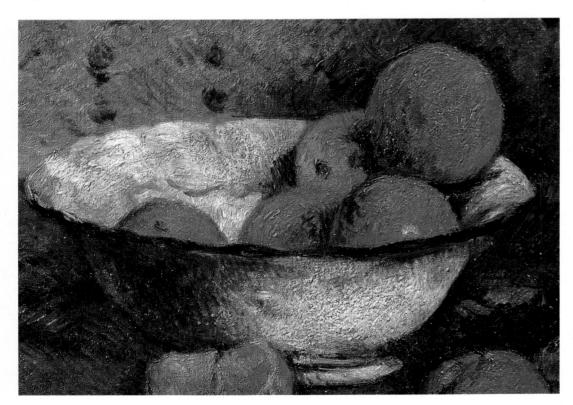

politics, language, literature, religion, customs and costumes of Polynesia and Gauguin read it avidly. He copied large sections from it into a notebook to which he gave the name *Ancien Culte Mahorie*, illustrated with original watercolors, and which was subsequently to become the basis for his most important literary project, *Noa Noa*. Many of Gauguin's ideas of the forgotten religious and pagan rituals which he elaborated in his writing, painting and carvings come from this source, augmented with reference to fictionalized accounts like the *Marriage of Loti*. Rather than documenting the life which he discovered in Papeete, with its clear evidence of colonization, Gauguin chose to ignore that aspect of life in the tropics and succumbed to the depiction of a highly personalized vision of Tahiti.

On his arrival in Papeete his original plans for seeking patronage were upset by the death of the king, Pomare V, which formed one of the stories in his text *Noa Noa*. He was forced to look to portraiture as a means of making money, and wrote to Mette, 'I think I shall soon have some well-paid commissions for portraits: I am bombarded with requests to do them'. Unfortunately, the only commission he seems to have secured was for the portrait of *Suzanne Bambridge* (page 124), for which he received only 200 francs. After a few months spent in Papeete, he decided to venture to a less colonized area and moved around the coast to Mataiea, probably accompanied by the first in a succession of young native women, Titi, who was of Anglo-Tahitian origin. Shortly after she left him he contracted a native marriage to the 13-year-old Tehamana, who was immortalized in a number of paintings and in *Noa Noa*. Because much of the flavor, if not the facts, of Gauguin's writings about this first period in Tahiti rely on *The Marriage of Loti*, there seems to be an element of one-upmanship in his account of his nubile young wife; Loti's Rarahu was 14, Gauguin married the 13-year-old Tehamana, who was to become pregnant with his child.

Throughout the latter part of 1892, Gauguin made increasingly urgent requests to France and Copenhagen as his money ran out, and he made several attempts to be repatriated. In December he sent Mette a letter in which he gave her a degree of control over a number of canvases to be included in an exhibition to be held in Copenhagen in 1893. He supplied her with translations of the titles he had given the works, but stressed that these alternative titles were only to be given to those who requested it.

It seems that he wished to lend the works a degree of mystery with their foreign names. These included *Manao Tupapau* (page 136), and he specified that it was to be sold for no less than 1500 francs, indicating the high regard in which he held it.

In May 1893 Gauguin's requests for repatriation were successful and he was granted a passage back to France, leaving Tahiti at the beginning of June. He arrived back in France toward the end of August 1893 and remained there until June 1895, when he returned to Tahiti. In Paris his painting output dropped dramatically but, ironically, it was one of the busiest periods in his life. Degas, who had long admired

his work and had bought several examples of it, prevailed on Durand-Ruel to give Gauguin a one-man exhibition. In the two months before the show opened on 4 November Gauguin was busy stretching, retouching and repairing any works which had been damaged on the voyage from Tahiti. He then had to mount all his two-dimensional works in the simple white frames which had by then become standard for him.

The catalog to the exhibition listed 44 paintings, the vast majority of which were from the Tahitian period, and a couple of sculptures. The prices fixed for the works were much higher than Gauguin normally commanded – 2000-3000 francs, but

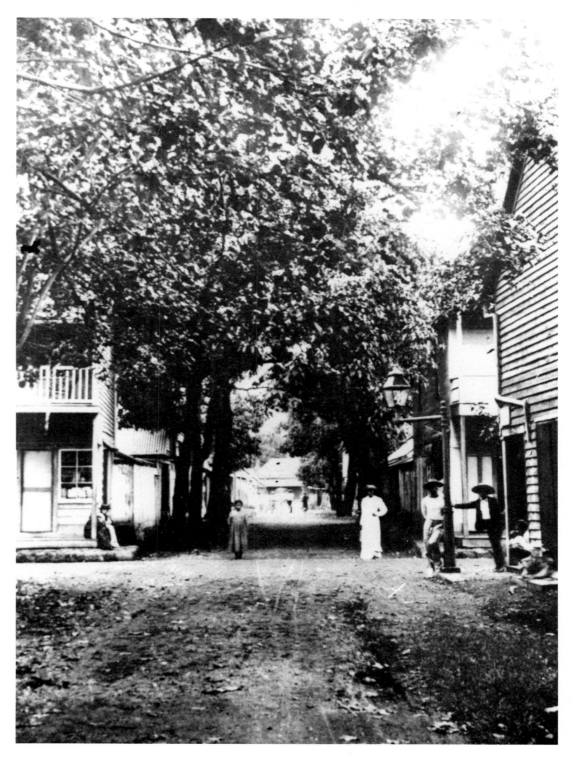

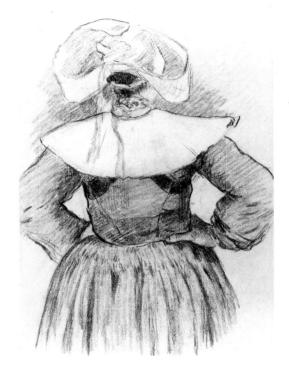

Durand-Ruel had a certain reputation to maintain. Perhaps for this reason the show was not a financial success: only eleven works were sold. However, Gauguin was pleased with his critical reception and wrote to Mette at its close:

The most important thing is that my exhibition has had a very great artistic success, has even provoked passion and jealousy. The Press has treated me as it has never yet treated anybody, that is to say rationally with words of praise. For the moment I am considered by many people to be the greatest modern painter. . .

Probably an over-optimistic account of events, this may have been a clumsy attempt to affect some kind of reconciliation with his wife, but Gauguin clearly never underestimated the importance of the critic. At the same time, however, there is no doubt that he managed to estrange

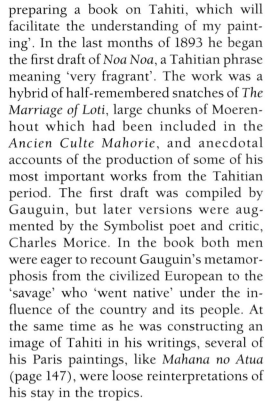

large sections of the public by his refusal to translate the titles for what were already mystifying images.

He wrote to Mette in October 1893, before the opening of his show, 'I am also

preparing a book on Tahiti, which will facilitate the understanding of my painting'. In the last months of 1893 he began the first draft of *Noa Noa*, a Tahitian phrase meaning 'very fragrant'. The work was a hybrid of half-remembered snatches of *The Marriage of Loti*, large chunks of Moerenhout which had been included in the *Ancien Culte Mahorie*, and anecdotal accounts of the production of some of his most important works from the Tahitian period. The first draft was compiled by Gauguin, but later versions were augmented by the Symbolist poet and critic, Charles Morice. In the book both men were eager to recount Gauguin's metamorphosis from the civilized European to the 'savage' who 'went native' under the influence of the country and its people. At the same time as he was constructing an image of Tahiti in his writings, several of his Paris paintings, like *Mahana no Atua* (page 147), were loose reinterpretations of his stay in the tropics.

In January 1894 Gauguin took a studio at number 6 rue Vercingétorix in Paris, which he painted in chrome yellow and decorated with a number of his own works. He installed his latest teenage girlfriend, a Singalese who called herself Annah the Javanese. In this bohemian apartment Gauguin hosted a number of gatherings, at which the majority of guests were key literary figures. In the spring he left Paris for Brittany once again and visited both Le Pouldu and Pont-Aven but in May he was involved in a brawl and his leg was broken, which left him incapacitated and unable to paint for some time.

By the winter of 1894-5 Gauguin was already planning another trip to Tahiti, and hoped to organize a sale similar to that held in 1891. In January he invited the Swedish dramatist August Strindberg (1845-1912) to one of his Thursday soirées and asked him to write an introduction to the catalog for the forthcoming sale. Strindberg refused, but Gauguin published Strindberg's letter anyway and used it in the periodical *L'Eclair* to promote the sale. Strindberg wrote:

. . .I owe you an explanation for my refusal. . .I cannot understand your art and I cannot like it. I have no grasp of your art, which is now exclusively Tahitian. . . you have created a new heaven and earth, but I did not enjoy myself in the midst of your creation. It is too sun-drenched for me. . . and in your paradise there dwells an Eve who is not my ideal. . . What is he then? He is Gauguin the savage, who hates a whimpering civilization. . .

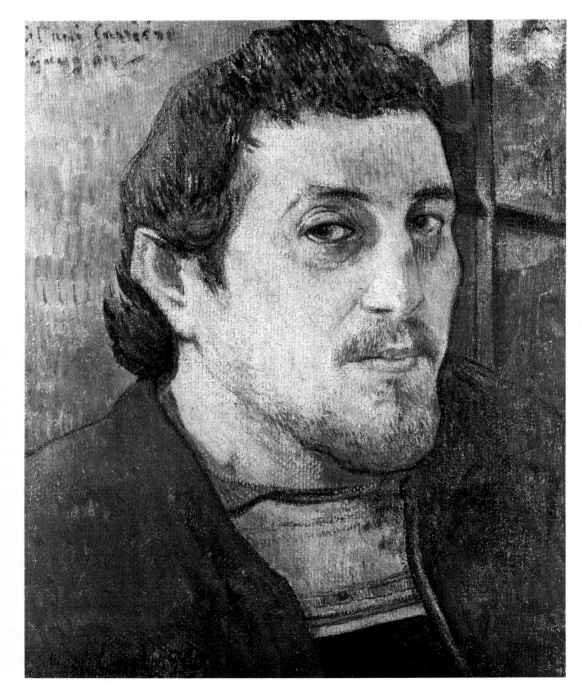

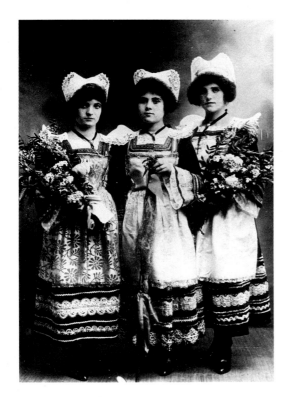

Left: Queen and maids of honor at a pardon in Pont-Aven, photographed in 1913.

Below: Paul Gauguin, photographed in Paris in 1894 before he left the French capital for good.

The letter was printed in its entirety with Gauguin's reply, in which he attempted to justify his position:

. . .I had a premonition of a revolt: the conflict between your civilization and my barbarism. Civilization from which you suffer; barbarism which is for me a rejuvenation. . . Compared with the Eve of my choice, whom I have painted in the forms and harmonies of another world, your chosen memories have perhaps evoked a painful past. The Eve of your civilized imagination makes misogynists of almost all of us; but the ancient Eve, which frightened you in my studio, might well smile upon you less bitterly one day. . . The Eve which I have painted can alone remain naturally nude before our gaze. In such a simple state yours could not move without being indecent and, being too pretty (perhaps), would provoke evil and pain.

In the event the sale was not a success. Gauguin was forced to buy in some of his own works and, after paying his expenses, made less than 500 francs. At the beginning of July, however, he set off to Tahiti, leaving France for the last time.

On arrival in Papeete he wrote to his friend, the composer and musician William Molard, 'What a change here since I left! Papeete, the capital of this Eden, Tahiti, is now lighted by electricity. . .' In November he moved to Punaauia, three miles outside the capital, where he constructed a native hut on a small plot of land, and found another 14-year-old Tahitian companion, Pahura, who was to bear him two children. By 1896 Gauguin's health was failing, the syphilis from which he was suffering caused various complications, and he had a number of heart attacks. In 1897 he seems to have staged an abortive suicide attempt but only after taking care to leave what he regarded as a definitive artistic statement in the massive canvas *Where do we come from? What are we? Where are we going?* (page 160), in which he explored the fundamental questions of existence. In 1902 Gauguin finally left Tahiti for Hivaoa, or La Dominique, where he had contemplated going as early as 1892, when he had written to Mette:

. . .I shall go the Marquesas, to la Dominique, a tiny island which has only three European inhabitants, and where Oceania is not yet swamped by European civilization. . .

In Hivaoa he found yet another 14-year-old girlfriend who was to bear his child. His health became progressively worse and, in the middle of an appeal against a custodial sentence for libelous remarks about the police, he died, on 8 May 1903. In his last letter to Charles Morice, written about a month before his death, he continued to justify and explain his position:

I am stricken to the ground, but not yet vanquished. . . You were mistaken once in saying that I was wrong to say I am a savage. It is true nevertheless, I am a savage. . . The work of a man is the explanation of that man. . . Artists, having lost all of their savagery, having no more instincts, one could even say imagination, went astray on every path . . . they act only as a disorderly crowd, they feel frightened like lost ones when they are alone. That is why solitude must not be advised for everyone, since one must have strength to bear it and to act alone.

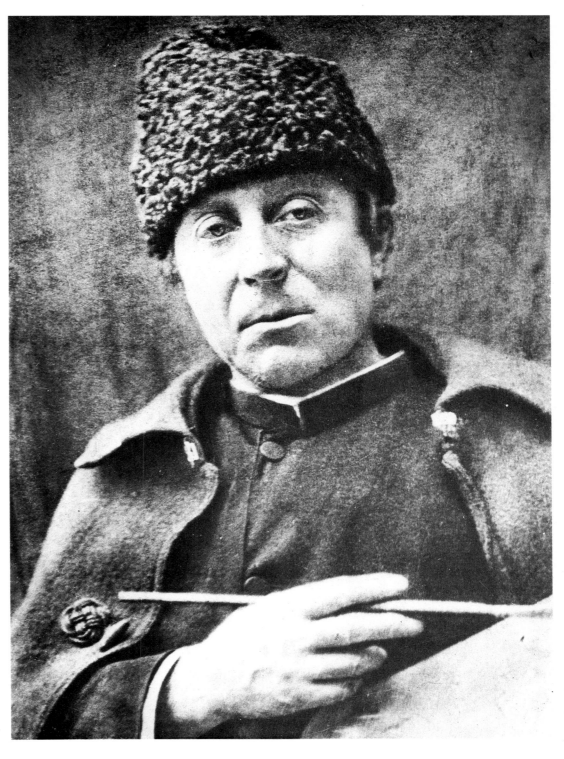

Landscape, 1873

Oil on canvas
19⅞×32⅛ inches (50.5×81.6 cm)
Fitzwilliam Museum, Cambridge

This is one of Gauguin's earliest works, signed and dated 1873; it was produced while he was still a stockbroker and painting only in his spare time. It is a competent work, painted using a fairly limited palette of grays, browns and blues, with a large area of the picture given over to an atmospheric treatment of the sky. The work is executed on a fine-grain canvas, and its surface is smooth in finish, with areas such as the well in middle distance outlined in dark lines. The low horizon and the small, anecdotal figures, which give the viewer some sense of scale, lend a Dutch feeling to the work. In conception, however, the painting is perhaps closest to the work of Corot, some of whose landscapes were included in the collection of Gustave Arosa, Gauguin's guardian.

The work may also owe something to the landscapes of Camille Pissarro, who was to exhibit at the first Impressionist show the following year and with whom Gauguin became acquainted around this time. The broad massing of planes and the heavy earth colors are reminiscent of Pissarro's work from about 1870. This is hardly yet an impressionist landscape, however; it has none of the free handling which characterizes the canvases of Monet or Renoir from this period – indeed the brushstrokes are hardly visible. Nor has Gauguin represented the local colors of the landscape using the primary palette of the mature impressionist style, but has retained the rather heavy earth tones of the previous generation of artists. This is the kind of landscape which would have been perfectly acceptable to a Salon jury, and may be similar to the canvas Gauguin exhibited at the Salon in 1876. In 1873 when he painted *Landscape* Gauguin was still working within a fairly safe, established tradition, as befitted his amateur status.

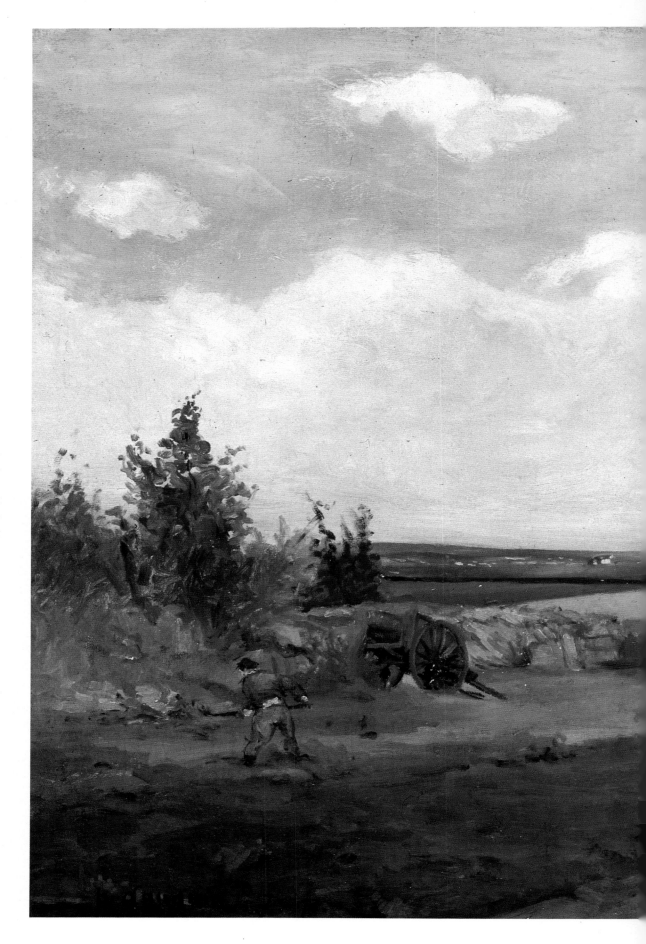

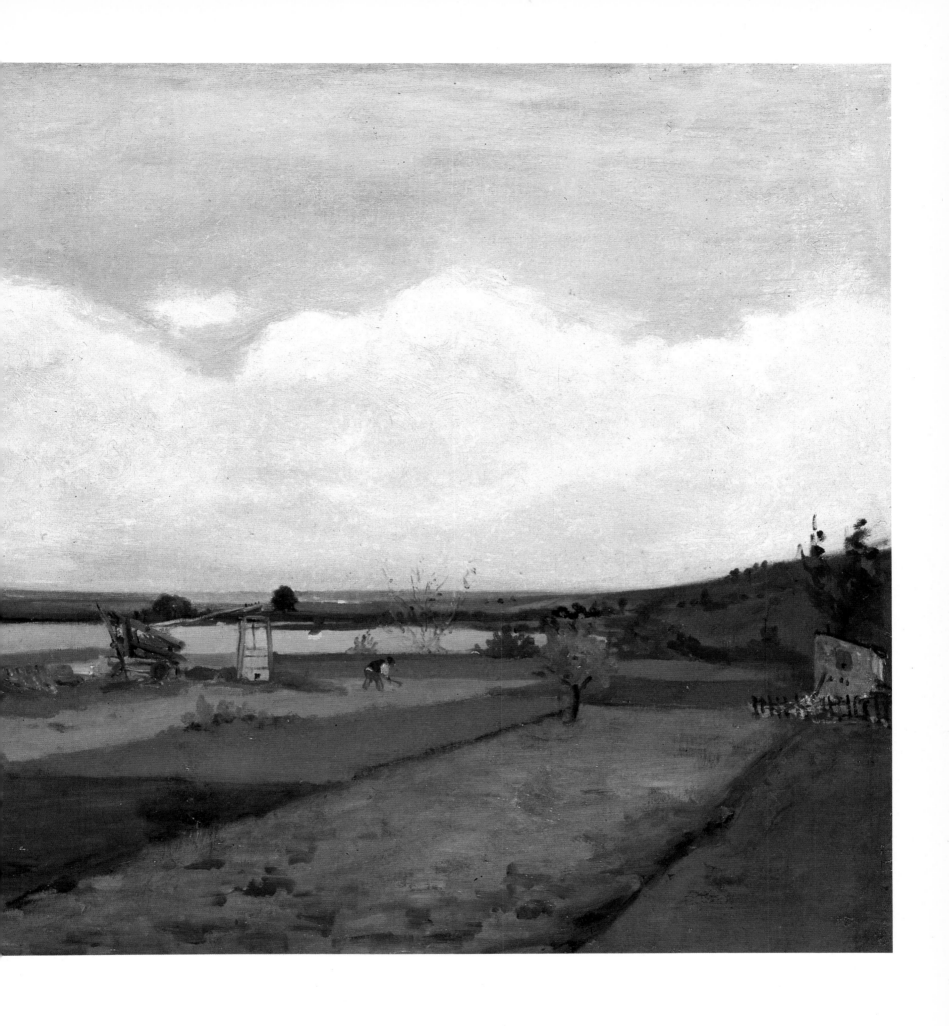

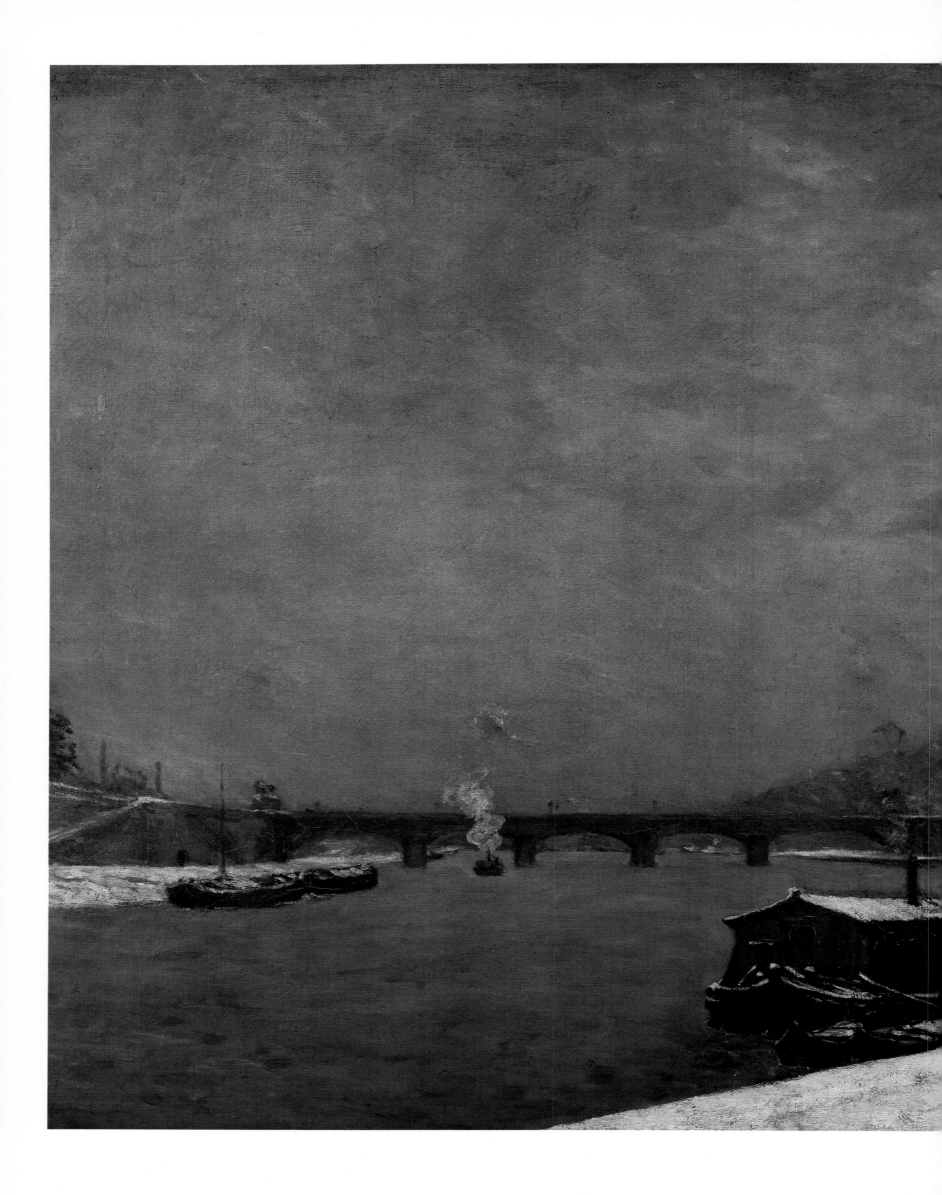

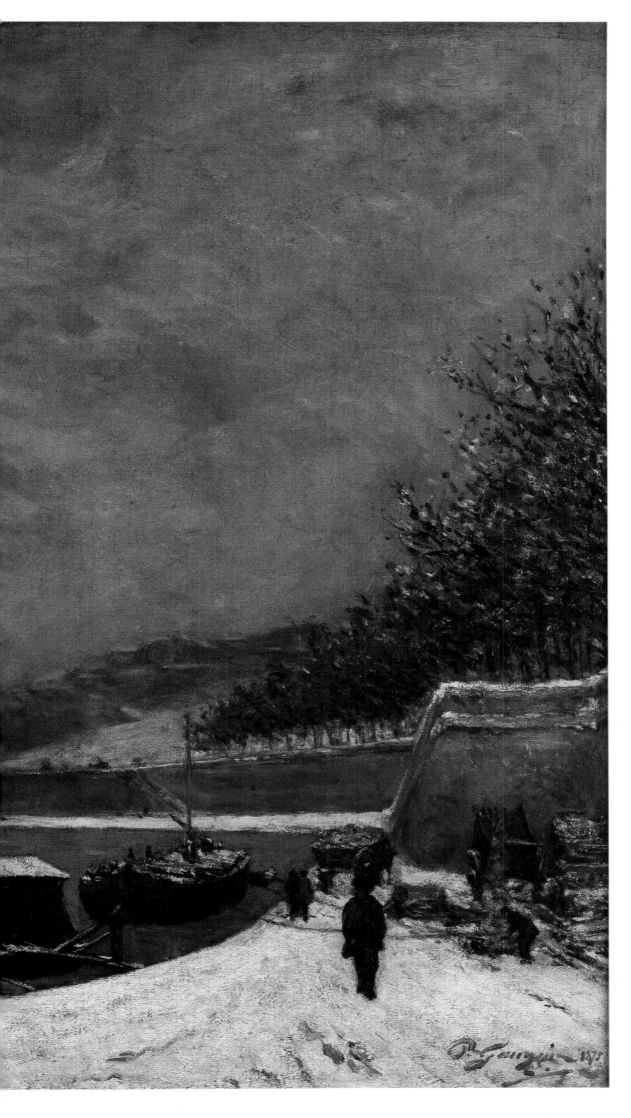

The Seine at the Pont d'Iéna, Snow, 1875

Oil on canvas
25½×36¼ inches (65×92 cm)
Musée d'Orsay, Paris

Painted the year after the first Impressionist show, of which Gauguin must have been aware because of his friendship with Pissarro and Gustave Arosa's interest in art, this painting shows Gauguin's rapid assimilation of new ideas, particularly when compared with the much darker and tighter *Landscape* (page 26). Representations of contemporary Paris were popular with the impressionist circle in the 1860s and early 1870s, when they tended to focus on the effects of industrialization on the capital city. While Gauguin's *Pont d'Iéna* is topographically correct (the hill in the distance is identifiable as Chaillot before the building of the Trocadéro), his city is strangely timeless, with nothing to characterize it as being Paris in the late nineteenth century. This effect is heightened by the snowy landscape, which may have been painted on the spot despite the relatively large size of the canvas. Gauguin has inserted a number of people into the work, and the figure at the right-hand side helps to resolve the broad triangular expanse of snow in the foreground. There is a slight distortion in scale between the different figures, however, and this area is difficult to read. In choosing to depict a snowy environment, Gauguin was probably influenced by the Impressionists' desire to study the effects of color reflexions on a white ground. This work comes very close to a number of canvases by Alfred Sisley painted around this time, in its interest in a snowy landscape and in the large area given over to the sky. Sisley explored the potential of the sky as a means of illuminating the picture and Gauguin may well have taken inspiration from the older artist in this. As well as a very much lighter and brighter palette, the handling in this work also marks a significant development from the 1873 *Landscape*.

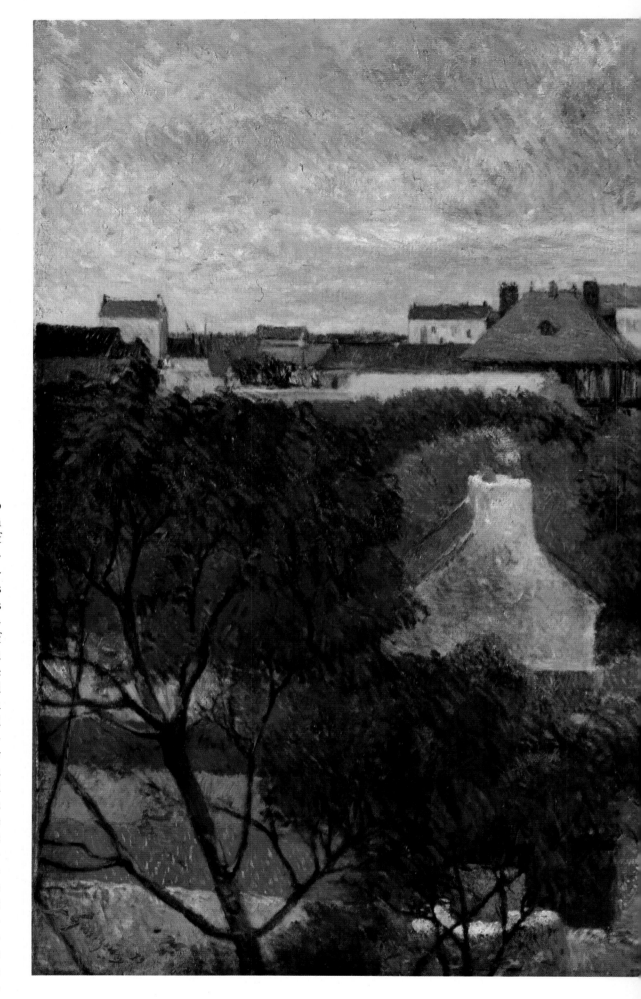

The Market Gardens at Vaugirard, 1879

Oil on canvas
25½×39⅜ inches (65×100 cm)
Smith College Museum of Art,
Northampton, Massachusetts

In 1877 the Gauguin family moved to Vaugirard, which in the nineteenth century was still a village on the south of the Seine, renowned for its market gardens, depicted here. Gauguin has positioned himself at the upper window of his house overlooking the scene, which he has reduced to its bare essentials. The composition is divided into horizontal bands of color and buildings are presented with their gable ends suggested as simple blocks. Even the patches of cultivated ground are almost architectonic in feel. In the alternating areas of architecture and greenery Gauguin comes close to Pissarro's *Côte des Bœufs* (page 12), particularly in the way in which paint is applied in short hatchings. Gauguin has banished earth colors from his palette and relied on pure unmixed tones, particularly the three primaries and their complementaries. The juxtaposed greens and reds mutually influence each other to create a lively coloration. Compared with his earlier landscapes and the *Côte des Bœufs*, however, Gauguin has adopted a dramatically different compositional format, with no road or discernable foreground to lead the viewer's eye back into the picture space. In wishing to exploit the large blocks of color, he has represented the scene from an unusual angle.

This work was probably shown at the Impressionist exhibition of 1880, as a painting of this subject was listed in the catalog. However, the daring composition and the way in which the color has been striped on is perhaps more akin to a slightly later work, after Gauguin and Pissaro had worked with Cézanne at Pontoise in 1881.

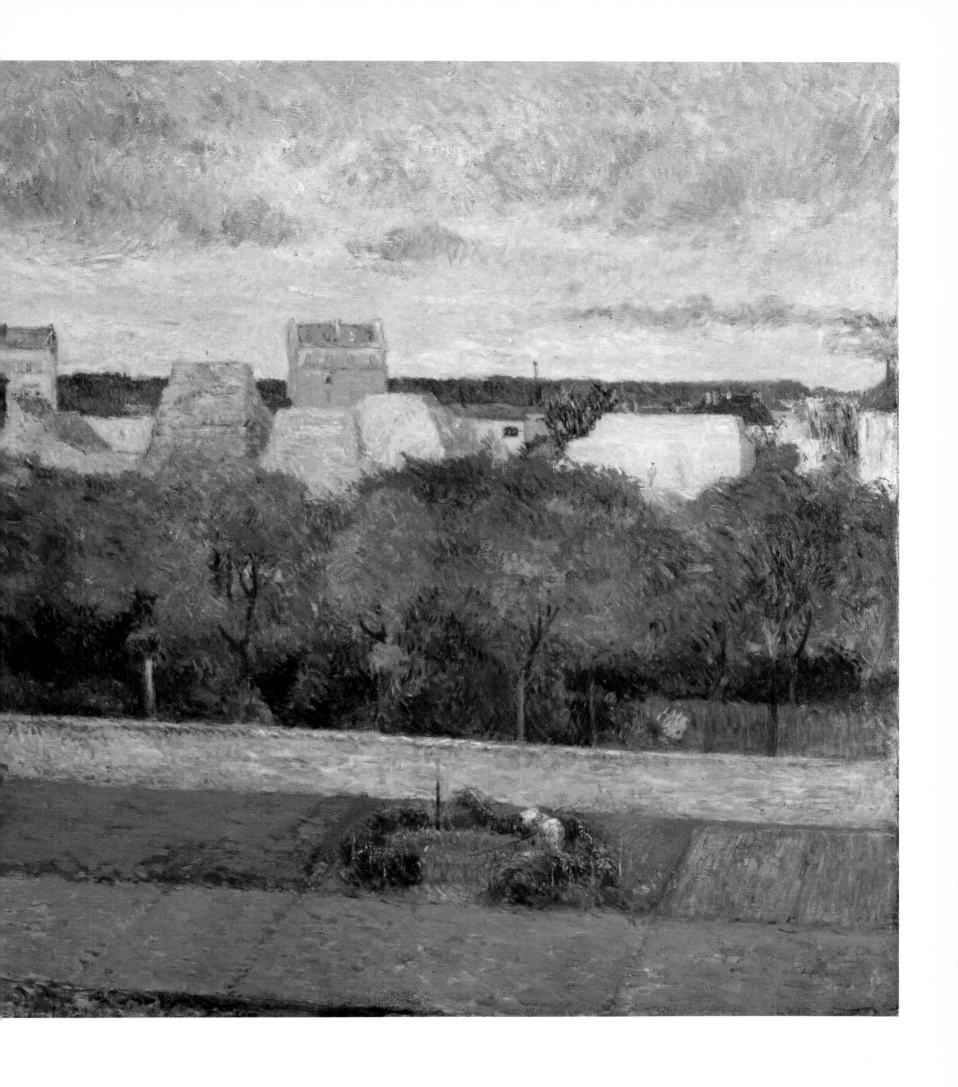

Study of a Nude or Suzanne Sewing, 1880

Oil on canvas
45¼×31½ inches (115×80 cm)
Ny Carlsberg Glyptotek, Copenhagen

When this painting was shown at the sixth Impressionist exhibition in 1881 it earned Gauguin his first unequivocal praise, from the critic J-K Huysmans, who was then a disciple of the Naturalist novelist and art critic Emile Zola. It was in decidedly naturalistic terms that Huysmans viewed this work, praising it above all for its modern quality, both in terms of subject-matter and treatment. He wrote:

She is a contemporary woman, who is not posing for the gallery, who is neither sensual nor simpering, who is quite simply busy mending her old clothes . . . her flesh is . . . no longer the smooth polished skin, without grains, pores, uniformly soaked in a coat of pink and ironed smooth by all the other artists, it is a skin which . . . shudders with nerves, and finally what truth in all the parts of the body, in the rather large stomach falling onto the thighs, in the wrinkles in the slack bosom . . . in the rather bony joined knees . . . M. Gauguin has tried to represent a contemporary woman and . . . he has clearly been successful and he has created a bold and truthful canvas.

Unlike the contemporary Salon nudes which Huysmans implicitly criticizes here, the model has not been made into a sex object but is instead depicted with uncompromising truth. Rather than reclining and presenting herself for the viewer's inspection in an overtly erotic pose, she is sitting huddled in an unflattering position, squashed up against the front of the picture space, and is performing the most mundane of tasks, which further distances her from the languid Salon Venuses.

While the picture is a nude, it is also a genre scene, representing everyday life. And while it is modern in its unflinching approach, loose handling and flattened picture space, it is almost timeless in its traditional subject-matter. The depiction of a woman sewing had been popular with the Dutch school in the seventeenth century and the theme had been taken up by French artists in the eighteenth and early nineteenth centuries. The rustic simplicity of the scene is emphasized by the humble surroundings, and the mandoline and rug hanging on the wall behind the figure.

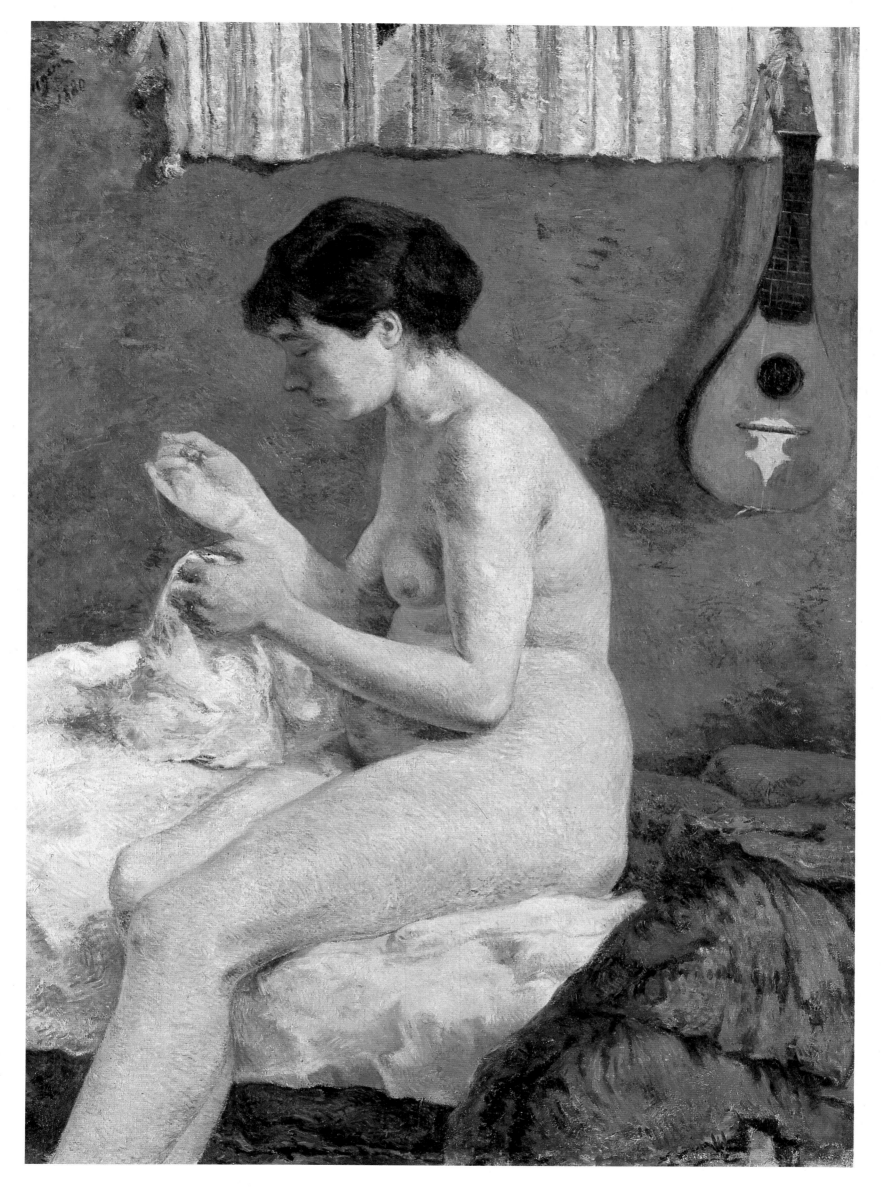

Flowers, Still Life or Interior of the Artist's House, Rue Carcel,

1881
Oil on canvas
51¼×63¾ inches (130×162 cm)
National Gallery, Oslo

One of the largest canvases painted by Gauguin at this time, this painting was most probably included in the seventh Impressionist exhibition which Gauguin helped to organize. Like his other works there, it was displayed in a simple white frame. The work was included in the catalog under the title *Flowers, Still Life* but the alternative title seems more appropriate. Like *Suzanne Sewing*, the subject is an odd hybrid of genres; here Gauguin has combined a traditional still life with a representation of daily life. The vase of flowers occupies the center foreground but the eye is immediately attracted to the two figures in the background. In 1882 Gauguin exhibited a number of canvases in which he used members of his immediate family as models, especially some charming portraits of his young children. Taken together, these works present an image of a financially secure, happy, bourgeois family. The woman seated behind the piano is most probably Mette Gauguin, while the man may represent Gauguin himself as the dutiful husband, or perhaps Emile Schuffenecker, a work colleague and painting companion whose family he was to paint in 1889 (page 94).

After a positive review in 1880, critics were relatively silent about Gauguin's work, but several mentioned that his recent productions were rather dull in comparison with the glowing impressionist paintings on the surrounding walls. The dark background may have been intended to try and resolve the split subject, by throwing the foreground objects on the tabletop into relief.

This work may have occupied a special place in Mette Gauguin's affections, as she kept it until 1917 when the museum in Oslo acquired it from her. Certainly she seems to have looked back with nostalgia on the affluent period of the early 1880s in the rue Carcel, when her husband was still in full-time employment as an insurance broker.

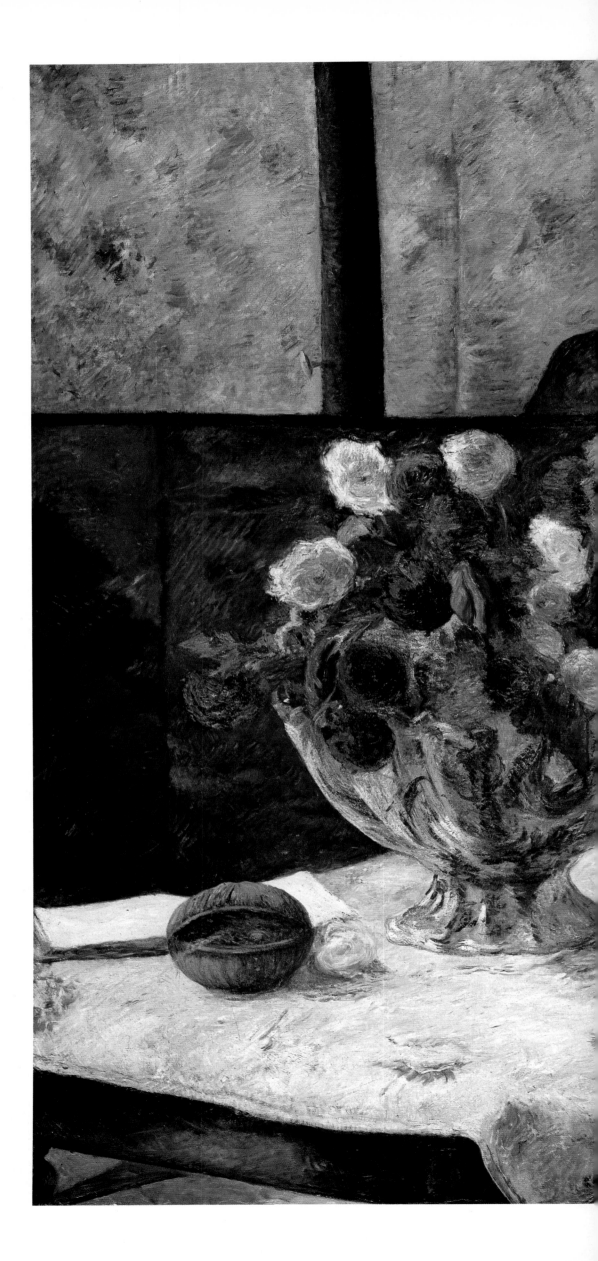

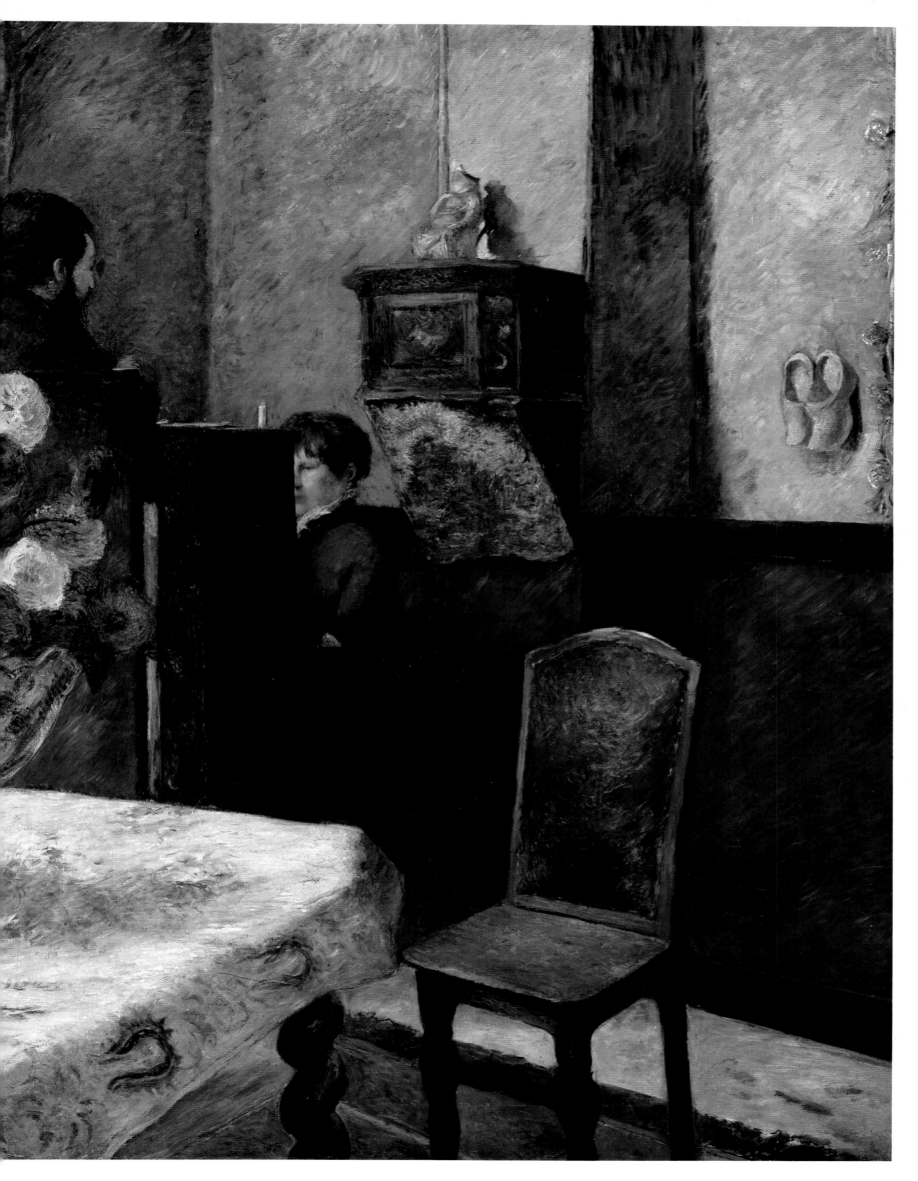

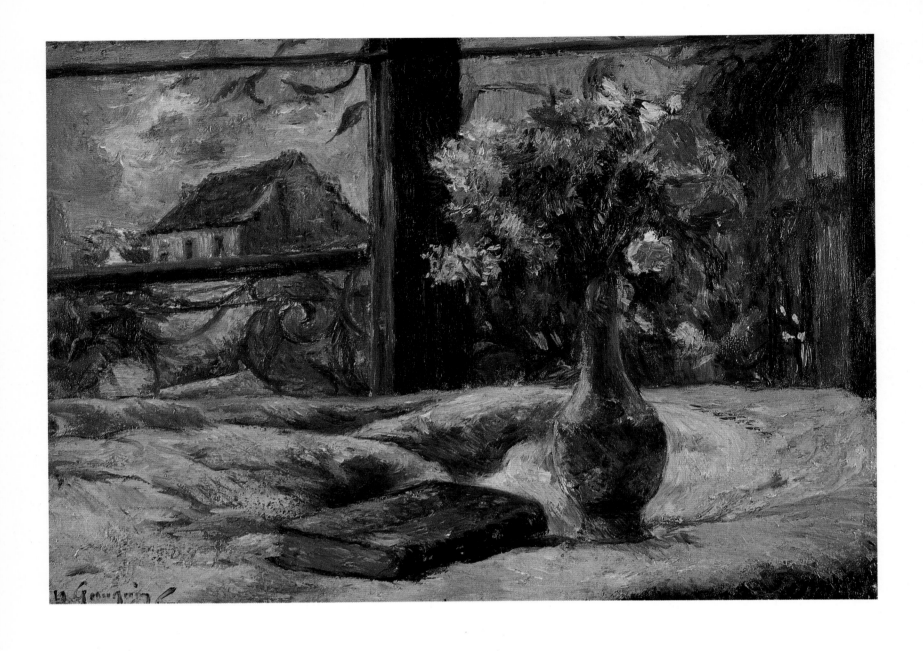

Vase of Flowers, 1881

Oil on canvas
7½×10⅝ inches (19×27 cm)
Musée des Beaux-Arts, Rennes

Like the previous work, this painting was included in the seventh Impressionist exhibition, and it too combined two different genres; in this case a still life and a landscape. Unlike the large canvas used in *Interior of the Artist's House, Rue Carcel*, however, this work is modest in size and therefore quite different in conception. The foreground is given over to a traditional still-life subject, a vase of flowers beside a closed book, with a window in the background looking out onto a landscape. Throughout the handling is loose, with flecks of pure color applied in a fairly free fashion. The critics saw Gauguin's work that year as being very different from the other members of the group, condemning his canvases as 'drab and lifeless'. Henri Rivière wrote that 'Gauguin makes everything dark and his extraordinary execution is dreadfully heavy'.

As with the previous painting, there is a discrepancy between foreground and background elements caused by the odd viewpoint, which effectively eliminates any middle ground. This effect is emphasized by the fact that Gauguin has treated the two areas of the picture in the same way, with very loose brushwork and similar color tones, so that nothing distinguishes the landscape from the foreground still life. However, the experimental nature of this composition is borne out by its tiny size – the *Interior of the Artist's House* is much more definitive simply by virtue of its large scale.

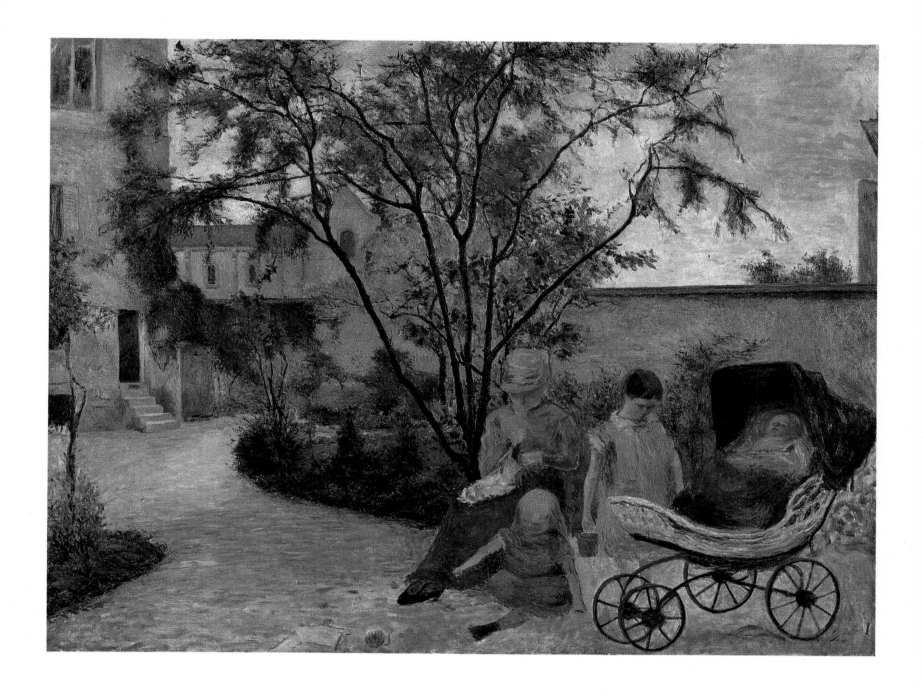

Garden in the Rue Carcel, 1881-2

Oil on canvas
34¼×44⅞ inches (87×114 cm)
Ny Carlsberg Glyptotek, Copenhagen

The Gauguin family moved to the rue Carcel in the summer of 1880 and this work, painted the following summer, shows Mette Gauguin with the baby Jean-René (born in April of that year) accompanied by two of the three older children, either Emil (born August 1874) or three-year-old Aline, and two-year-old Clovis. The identification is difficult because the standing child could either be Gauguin's daughter, whose hair he recommended should be kept short, or could equally well be his eldest son, Emil.

This is one of Gauguin's earliest attempts at representing largescale figures in the open air and he has been beset with the same kind of difficulties which afflicted Pissarro at the same time. In trying to maintain an impressionist technique, with the flickering brushstroke suggesting sunlight and color reflexions on the different surfaces, Gauguin has treated the figures in the same way as the surrounding landscape. While the effect may be successful in the foliage, the figures appear to be beginning to disintegrate. Working at Pontoise that summer with Pissarro and Cézanne, Gauguin was offered a potential solution to this problem in Cézanne's painting, which meant working in a much more premeditated and laborious fashion with the figures better integrated into the landscape.

Once again the picture represents a fairly contented view of his family which was to be disrupted in 1883, when Gauguin lost his job because of the Stock Market crash of 1882 and when he began to experience severe financial difficulties. Oddly enough, despite the availability of his children to model for him, Gauguin used them much less as subjects for his paintings after the early 1880s. The use of children may have been suggested to him by seeing Mary Cassatt's canvases of children at the Impressionist exhibitions, as well as by the obvious convenience of having unpaid models.

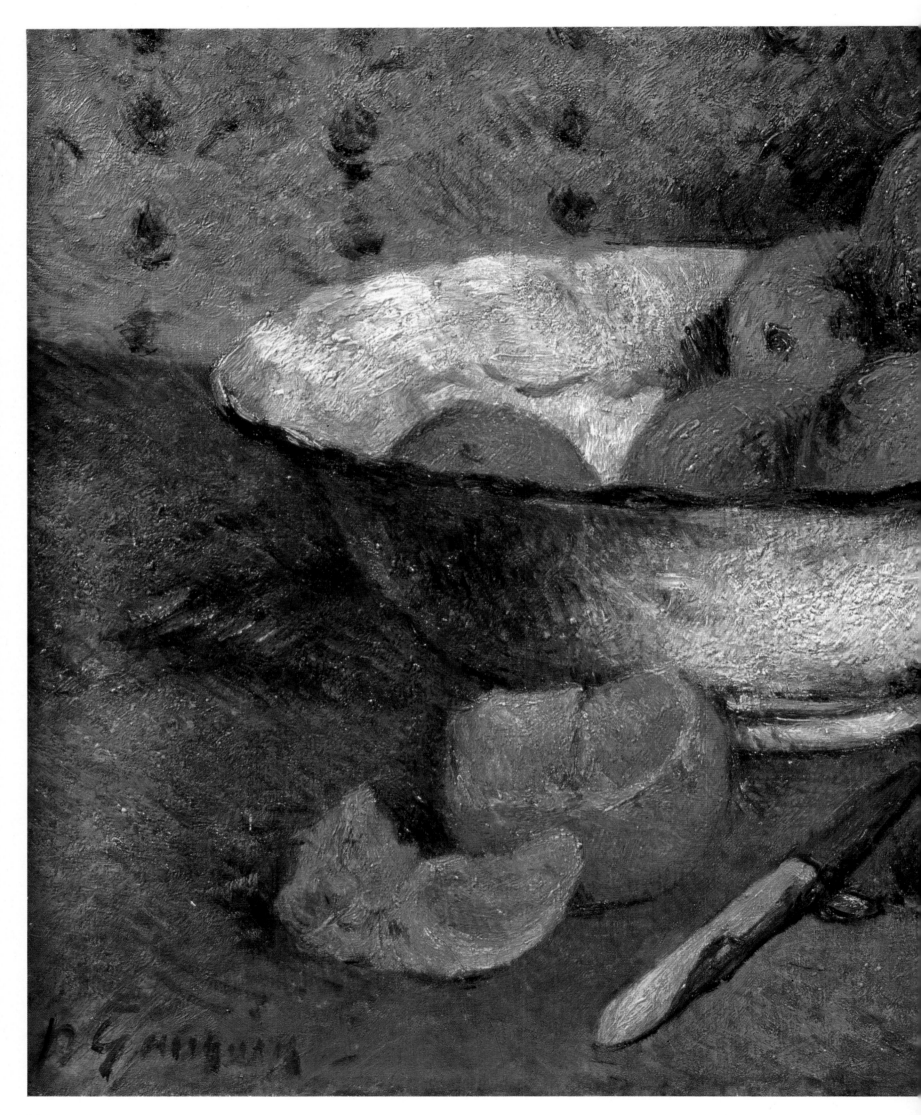

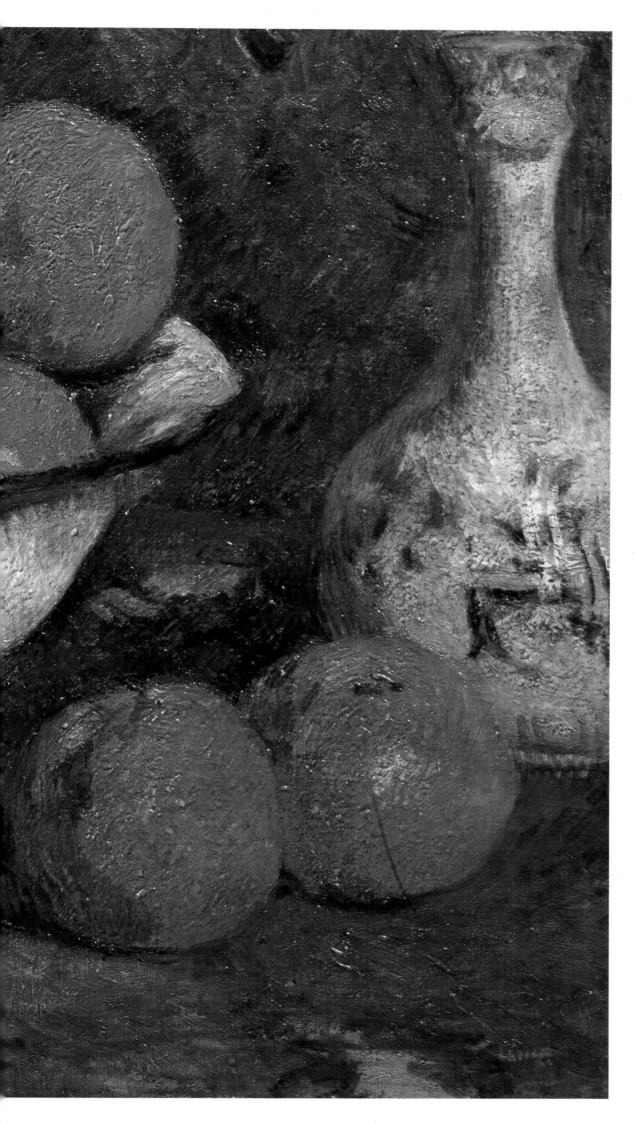

Still Life with Oranges, c. 1881

Oil on canvas
13×18¼ inches (33×46 cm)
Musée des Beaux-Arts, Rennes

Number 26 in the catalog to the seventh Impressionist exhibition in 1882 was a painting by Gauguin entitled *Still Life with Oranges*. As there is no other work by him which corresponds to this title, it is fairly safe to assume that this is the same painting, particularly since the style is similar to that of *Vase of Flowers* (page 36), which was shown at the same exhibition.

In many ways Gauguin has followed the tried and tested formulae of French still-life painting, from Chardin to Cézanne, in this work. The careful positioning of the knife, which points into the picture space, and the judicious balancing of forms demonstrate that he was conversant with the formal language of the traditional still life. He has utilized the wallpaper background which had frequently been used by Cézanne and Pissarro. Moreover, he has introduced a number of odd distortions in this work; the bowl of fruit, which effectively cuts the tabletop in half, prevents the two back edges of the table ever meeting and the ellipses of the rim and base of the bowl are inconsistent. Both of these devices were widely used by Cézanne at this time and Gauguin has adopted them in a fairly undiscriminating way. For Cézanne they were part of his desire to represent the objects as they were experienced by *all* the senses, and this lends a very tactile quality to his still lifes. Gauguin, however, has used the older painter's methods without striving for the same ends. By using the classic impressionist techniques of optical mixing of colors and fragmented brushwork (see detail page 22) to explore the effects of light, Gauguin gives less of a sense of the permanency of the objects in space, and the end result is very different from Cézanne.

The subject-matter of oranges was a rare one in traditional French still-life painting. Gauguin has presumably selected these fruits because they would have allowed him to explore the use of complementary colors. The rich, warm coloration of the oranges is heightened by their juxtaposition with the cool blues which fleck the canvas. The whole work becomes very lively and vivid, not only because the broken brushstroke unites the picture surface but also because of the way in which the orange of the fruit has been carried over into the blue rim of the fruit bowl, so that the two complementaries are mutually enhanced.

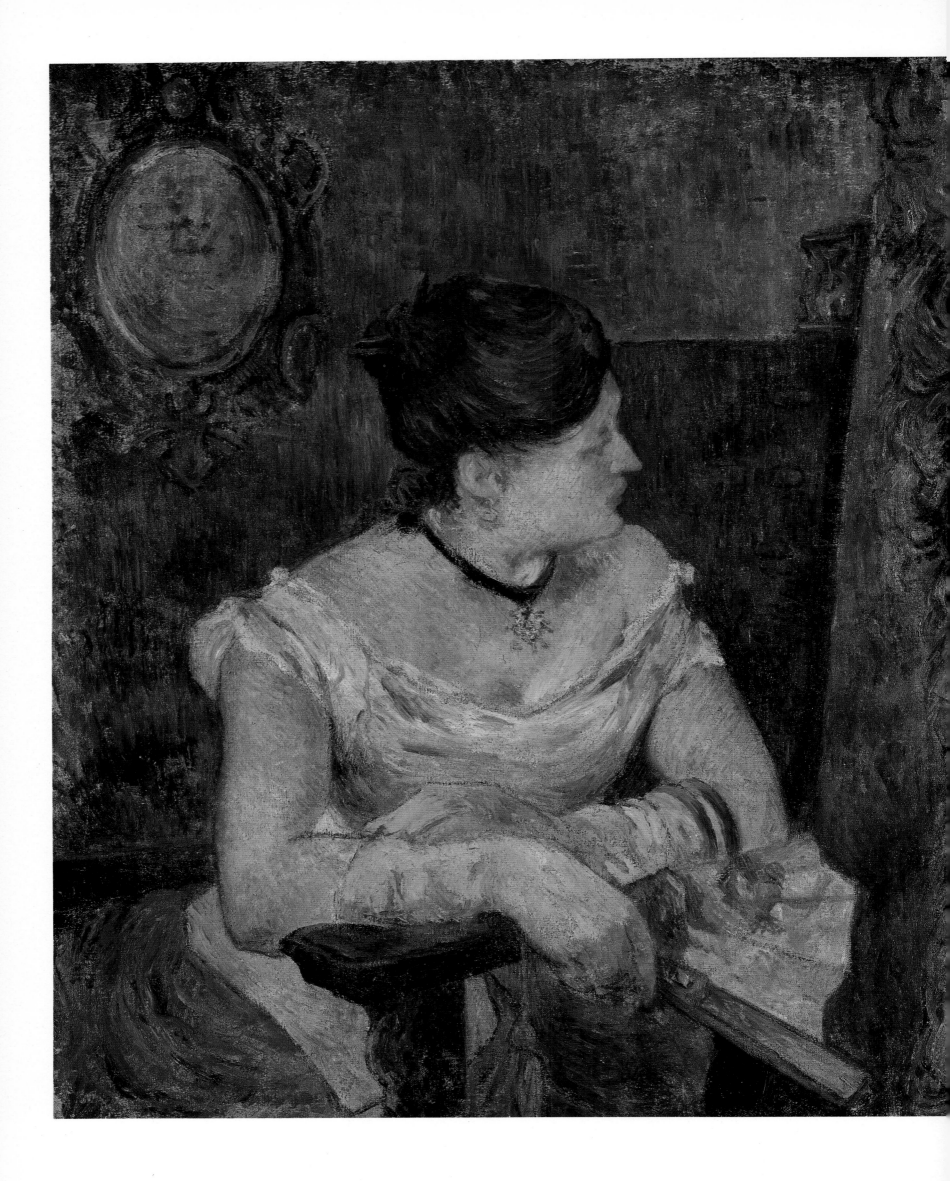

Madame Mette Gauguin, 1884
Oil on canvas
25½×21¼ inches (65×54 cm)
National Gallery, Oslo

Gauguin met his future wife, Mette Sofie Gad, at his guardian's house in the fall of 1872, while she was on vacation. She had been born in Denmark in 1850 and appears not to have had a job, although she later taught French and translated modern novels into Danish. She married Gauguin the following year and they went on to have five children over the next ten years. At first theirs looked like a promising marriage, with Gauguin's career as a stockbroker assuring them a very prosperous life in Paris. It is in this vein that Gauguin has depicted his wife, who is dressed formally and with some taste in a fashionable evening frock. However, once financial cares began to affect them and they went to Denmark at the end of 1884 to live with Mette's family, a rift developed between them. After 1885 they effectively lived apart; Mette kept the children in Copenhagen and Gauguin lived the life of a single man, traveling around the world.

Despite the formal dress of his subject, Gauguin has depicted her in a relaxed fashion, her body twisted round as she sits sideways in her chair. Her face is turned away from the spectator and this introduces a degree of tension into the work. In the informal pose of his middle-class sitter, Gauguin comes close to the work of Degas, whom he greatly admired. In comparison with the smooth marble bust of his wife (page 10), which he had submitted to the Impressionist exhibition of 1880, this portrait offers a much more intimate glimpse of Madame Gauguin. The work remained in her collection and she resisted selling it along with many of her husband's other works.

Blue Roofs (Rouen), 1884

Oil on canvas
29⅛×23⅝ inches (74×60 cm)
Oskar Reinhart Collection 'Am Römerholz', Winterthur

At the beginning of 1884, Gauguin and his family left Paris for Rouen, at Camille Pissarro's suggestion, and he stayed there until November, when he left to join the other members of his family who had gone to Copenhagen in July. 1884 was a remarkably productive year, his first as a full-time painter, and he produced a number of works in and around Rouen.

Here he has used a size 20 canvas (73×60 cm), popular for outdoor landscape painting, but has turned it on its side instead of painting in the normal horizontal format. A number of landscapes from this time are painted on the same size of vertical canvas, and in each he has produced a tightly compressed picture space with a high horizon. This may have been

suggested to him by his study of Cézanne's landscapes, and he has utilized Cézanne's parallel brushstrokes throughout. At the same time, however, he has inserted an odd, anecdotal figure at the bottom left-hand side, perhaps after looking at some of Pissarro's landscapes from this period, which include peasant figures in a landscape. The figure may also have been included in an attempt to resolve the foreground area and to give a sense of scale to the picture.

In this view of Rouen, Gauguin has been remarkably selective – there is no sense of its size or its industries, instead he has presented it within a rural setting, emphasizing the greenery and including few buildings.

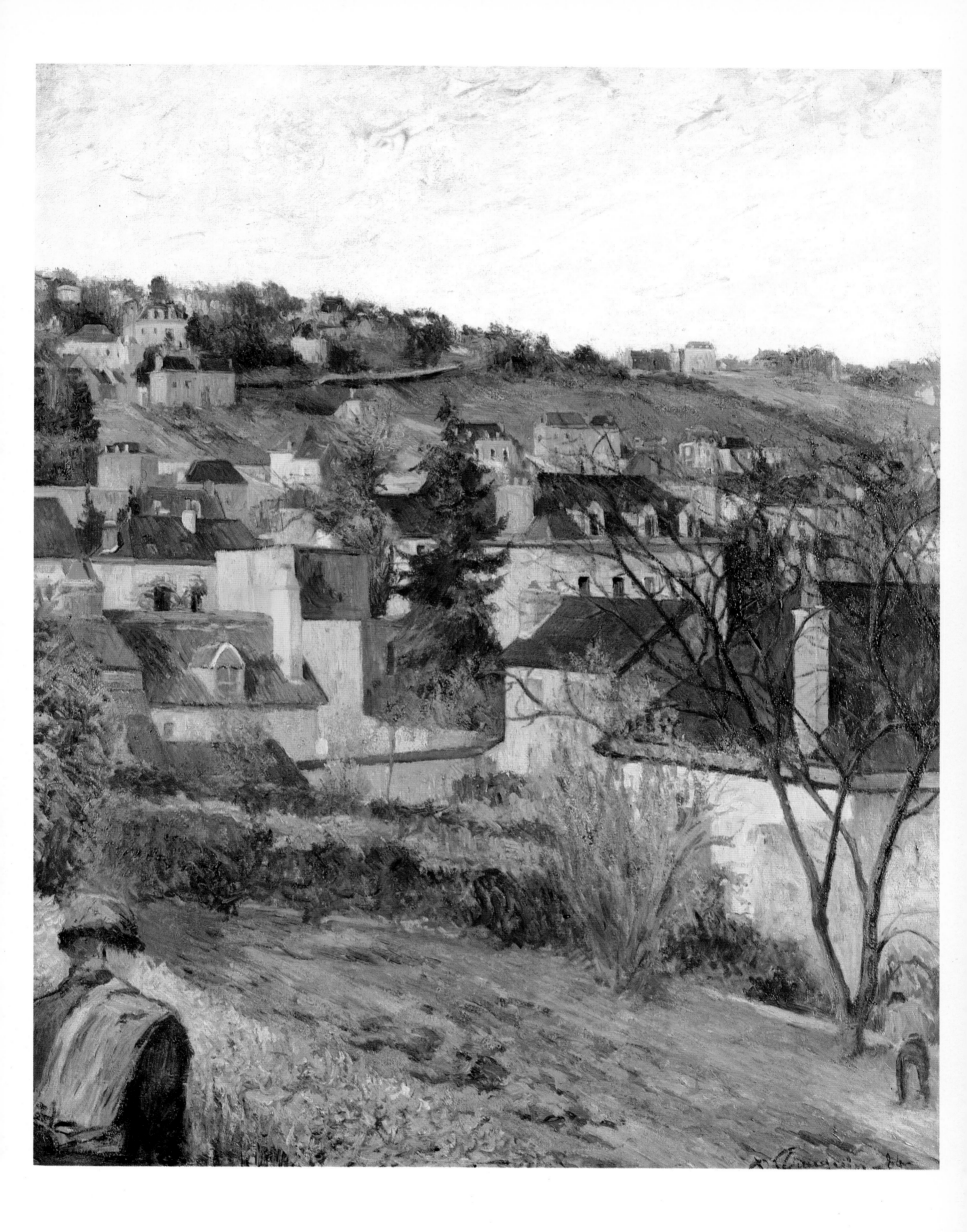

Entrance to a Village, 1884

Oil on canvas
23½×28¾ inches (59.5×73 cm)
Museum of Fine Arts, Boston

Painted after Gauguin had lost his job and had gone to live in Rouen where he was influenced by Pissarro, the canvas shows Gauguin's debt to his older mentor. Pissarro favored a landscape subject in which a solitary figure walks along a road toward a village in the distance, and Gauguin falls back on that traditional theme for this work.

Certain areas of the composition are difficult to read – especially the ocher mass in the foreground, which is only partially resolved by the woman's retreating back, and the buff-colored shape to the left-hand side. This is presumably the roof of a cottage, but placed in isolation like this it takes on an almost abstract quality. To the extreme left-hand side the area of foliage is ambiguous – is it a bush in the foreground or a grass-covered hillside in the middle distance? Added to this, the viewpoint is misleading. The artist appears to have painted the work looking down a hill and into a valley, but the high horizon seems to suggest that he is simultaneously looking up and across at the distant hills. This manipulation of the picture space, which deviates from the normal one-point perspective used in landscape painting, was perhaps suggested to Gauguin by looking at Cézanne's paintings. Pissarro too began to adopt high horizons in his landscapes at the same time. The work is markedly different from the *Landscape* (page 26) of 11 years previously, where the low horizon gave the artist an opportunity to represent an atmospheric sky. By the time he painted the *Entrance to a Village*, Gauguin was no longer concerned with depicting the effects of light and weather conditions; indeed, it is difficult to ascertain the time of day in this work. The brushwork is similar to Pissarro's at this time, and makes the picture space appear rather cluttered and unresolved.

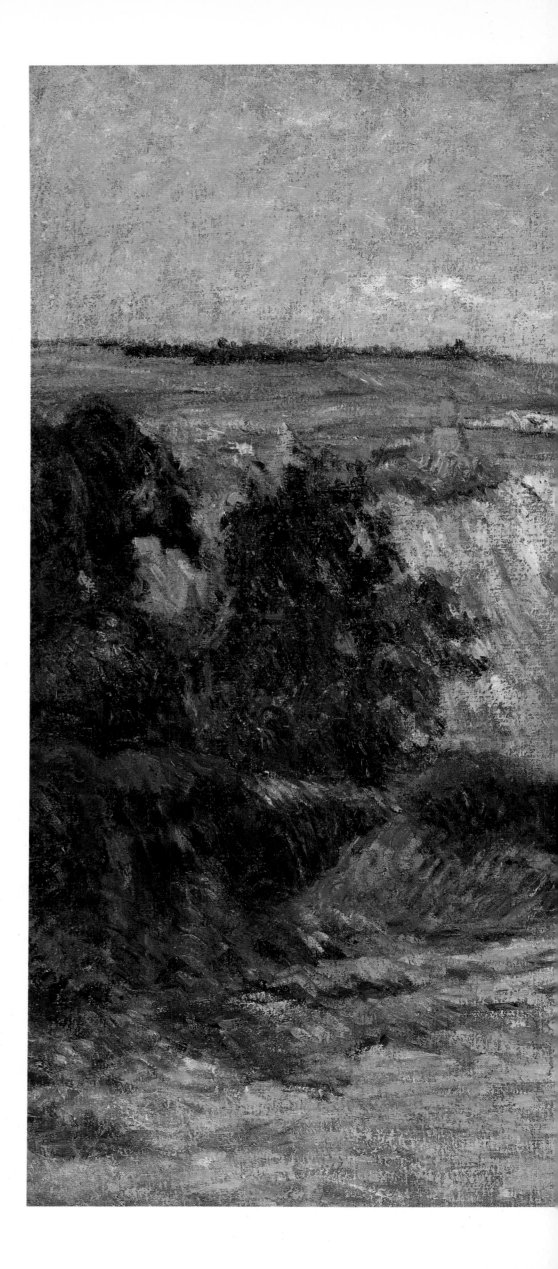

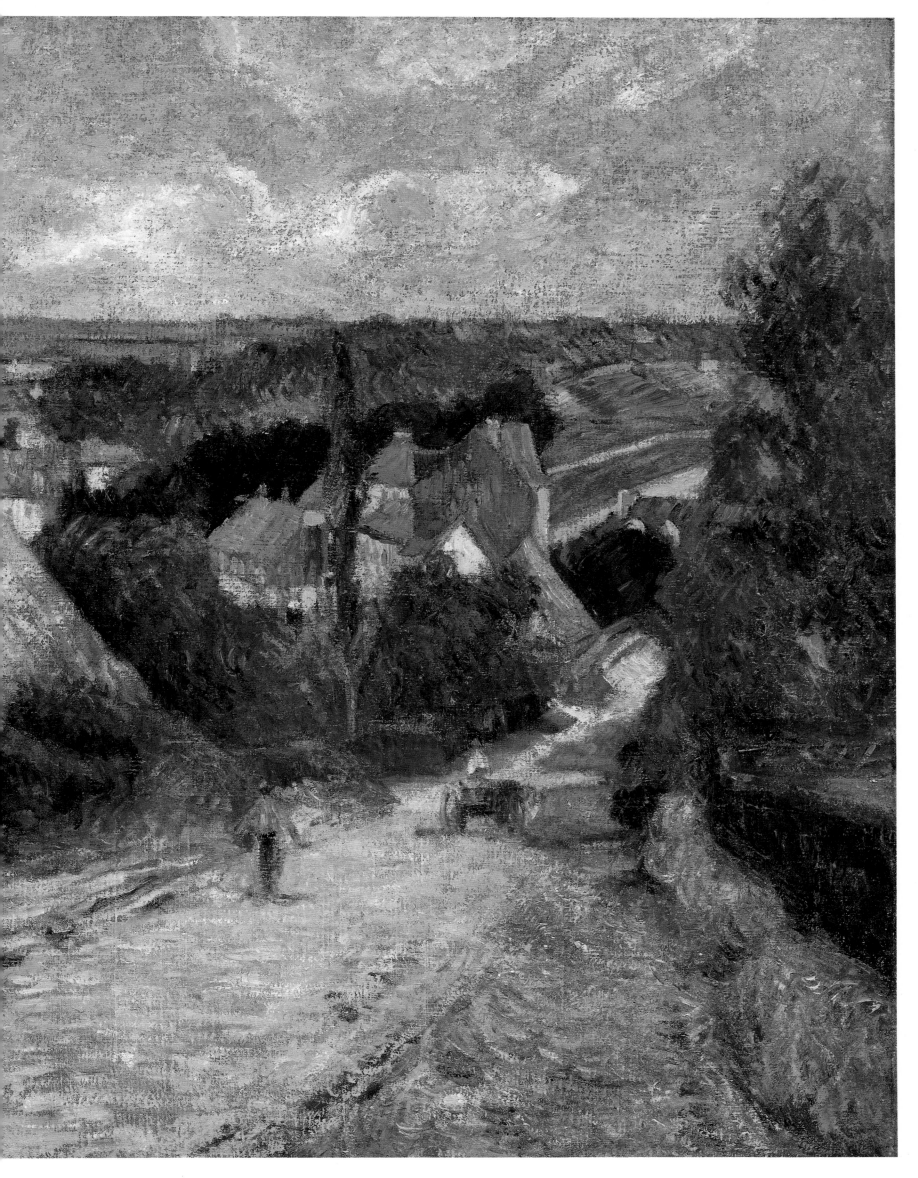

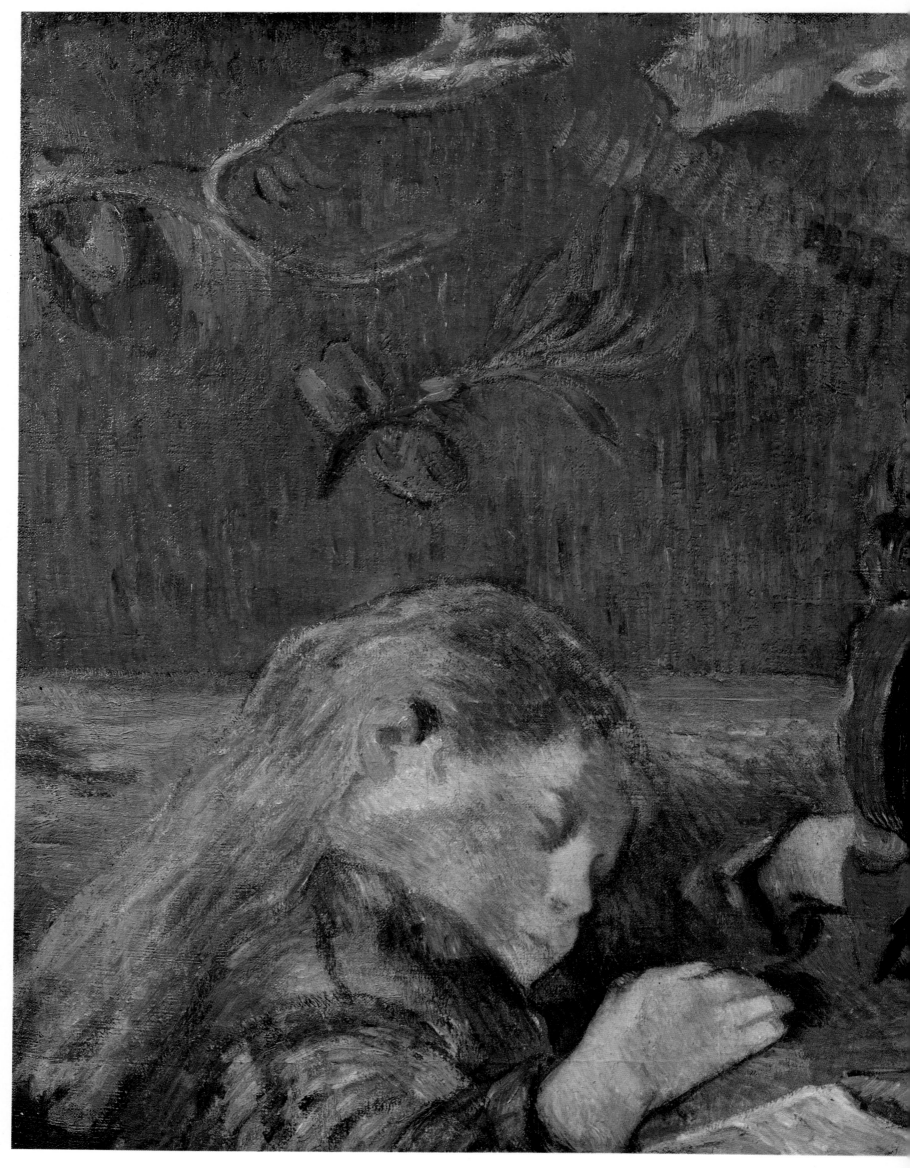

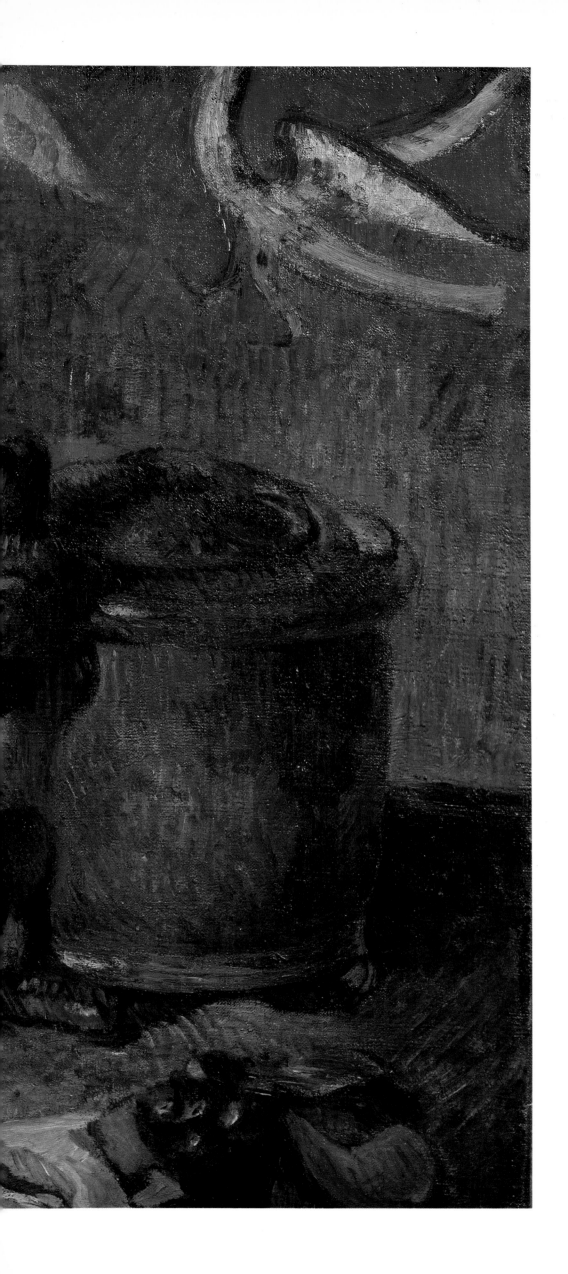

Sleeping Child, 1884

Oil on canvas
18⅛×21⅞ inches (46×55.5 cm)
Josefowitz collection

Like the portrait of *Madame Mette Gauguin* (page 40), Gauguin has used one of the members of his family for this sensitive depiction of a sleeping child, painted while they were living in Rouen. The child's identity is not clear; it is not his daughter Aline, who had short dark hair, but perhaps either his son Jean-Réné (born 1881) or Clovis (born 1879), who is shown with long golden curls in a contemporary photograph. The work is not strictly a portrait but rather a generalized study of a sleeping child. The dark blue wallpaper with its swirling shapes, which occupies a large part of the picture space, suggests the world of dreams. Gauguin went on to develop the use of colored papers to suggest internal emotions, most notably in his striking *Self-Portrait (Les Misérables)* (page 74).

Gauguin possibly borrowed the formal device of a boldly patterned wallpaper in the background of his painting from his study of Cézanne's still lifes. The *Sleeping Child* is composed like a traditional still-life painting, with the objects, including the sleeping child, arranged on the table-top. The odd discrepancy in scale between the Norwegian tankard and the child's head encourages the viewer to regard the objects as having equal weight within the picture space, and the traditional hierarchy between people and inanimate objects is broken down.

The rich coloring of the painting, which contributes to its moody atmosphere, is achieved by the juxtaposition of ruddy oranges and cool blues. Like other members of the Impressionist group, Gauguin was well-acquainted with contemporary research into color theory and this is one of the best examples of its use in his work.

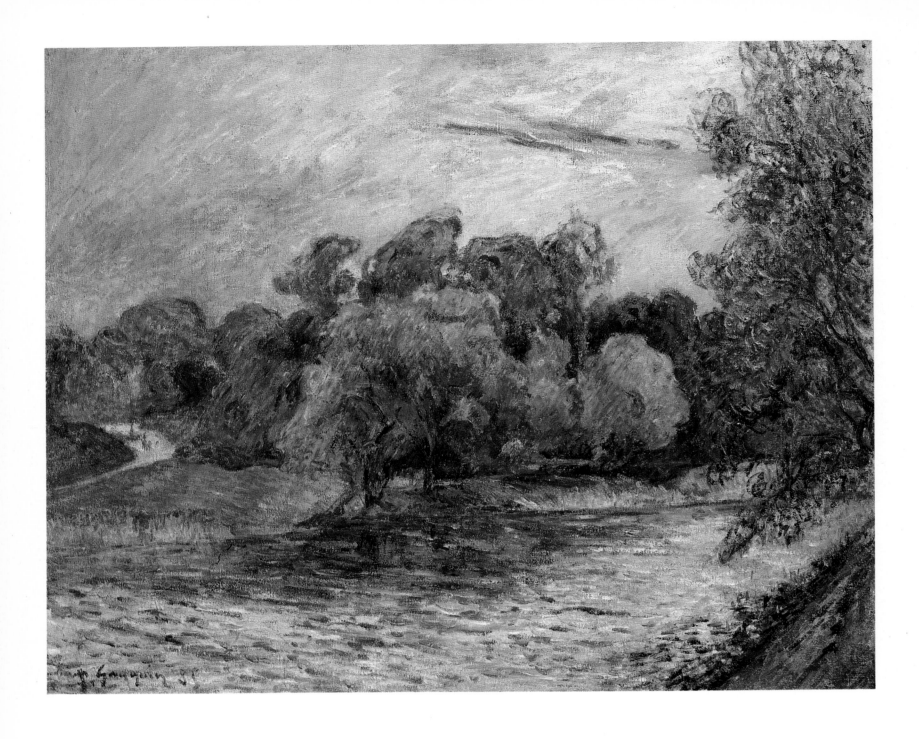

Oestervold Park, Copenhagen,
1885
Oil on canvas
23¼×28¾ inches (59×73 cm)
Glasgow Art Gallery and Museum

This landscape was painted toward the end of Gauguin's eight-month stay in Copenhagen, after which he took his son Clovis and returned to a precarious existence in Paris. He disliked living in the Danish capital, because of its provincialism in comparison with Paris, what he regarded as the coldness of the Danes, and his mistrust of his in-laws whom he felt exercised too strong a control over his wife.

Copenhagen offered fewer opportunities for painting in the open because of its longer and colder winters, but Gauguin most probably painted this work out of doors. It is a pure landscape, without any anecdotal figures. The artist positioned his easel on one riverbank, which is glimpsed in the foreground and from which the right-hand tree springs, and looked across to a copse of trees on the opposite bank. The composition with its foreground river is similar to Cézanne's *Castle at Médan* (page 10), which Gauguin had with him in

Copenhagen along with his other Impressionist works. The directional brushstroke which Cézanne employed also recurs in Gauguin's landscape. The river is painted with horizontal dabs of color, while the trees are built up with a diagonal stroke exactly like that used by Cézanne in his foliage. Despite having worked alongside Cézanne in 1881, it is only in the mid-1880s that the younger artist started employing in any systematic way his methods of building up the picture space. This would suggest that Cézanne's influence was at one stage removed – Gauguin learned more from studying the canvases than he did from the man. Perhaps this was because he had to fall back on his collection of paintings in the relative cultural isolation of Denmark. The work may have been shown at the final Impressionist exhibition, where Gauguin was represented by a number of recent landscapes painted in Rouen and Copenhagen.

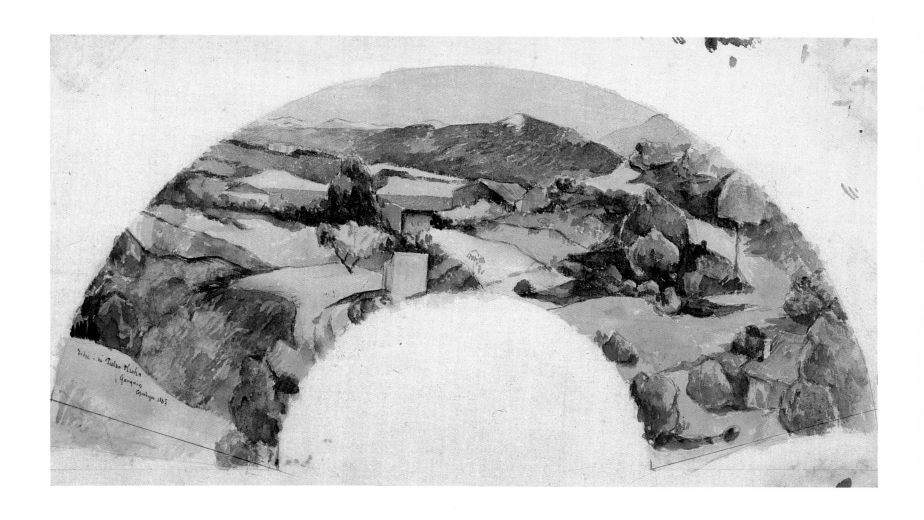

Provençal Landscape (after Cézanne), 1885

Gouache on fan
11×21⅝ inches (28×55 cm)
Ny Carlsberg Glyptotek, Copenhagen

Gauguin may have been introduced to the idea of painting fans by Pissarro, who produced a number of them. Certainly they were popular items at the time (Mette Gauguin holds one in her portrait). Once again Gauguin looked for inspiration to his collection of paintings and it was to Cézanne that he turned, drawing on his *Mountains at l'Estaque* (page 10). The fan is painted in opaque watercolor and is a relatively free transcription of the Cézanne – Gauguin has not hesitated to add areas to the left- and right-hand sides of his model in order to fill the fan. He wrote to Schuffenecker from Copenhagen:

Look at Cézanne, the misunderstood, an essentially mystic Eastern nature . . . In his methods, he affects a mystery and the heavy tranquillity of a dreamer; his colors are grave . . . his horizons are lofty, his blues most intense, and with him red has an amazing vibration.

Cézanne's work was not widely known in Paris at the time and, because he worked in virtual isolation in the south of France, he acquired almost mythical status with a number of younger artists. Gauguin seems to have read into Cézanne's painting characteristics which were almost wishfulfilling: Cézanne would presumably not have agreed with the assessment of him as an Eastern mystic or a dreamer. Unlike Gauguin, his method was rigorous in its constant reference to the model, although in quite a different way to the spontaneous approach of the impressionist style as evolved by Monet and Renoir in the late 1860s and early 1870s. While in *Oestervold Park* (page 48) Gauguin studied Cézanne's brushwork, here what has interested him is his color and the way in which he built up the picture space by alternating warm and cool tones and by emphasizing the architectonic aspects of the landscape.

The work is signed, dated and inscribed 'Copenhagen 1885' and dedicated to Pietro Krohn, an artist whom Gauguin had first met in Paris in 1878. The painting was never folded and used, but remained in the Krohn family until 1935.

49

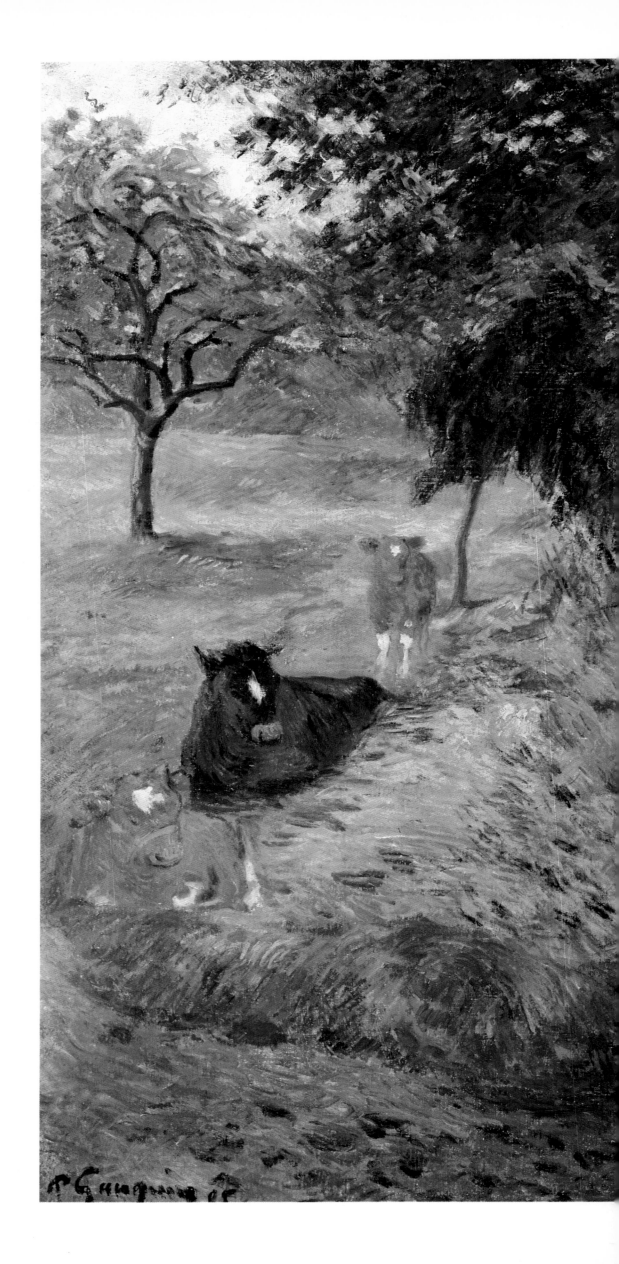

Cows in a Landscape, 1885

Oil on canvas
25¼×31½ inches (64×80 cm)
Museum Boymans van Beuningen,
Rotterdam

A painting entitled *Cows Resting* appeared in the catalog of the final Impressionist exhibition, and is most probably this work. The critic Gustave Geffroy wrote in his review of the exhibition:

There are some still lifes among the 19 canvases Gauguin exhibits, but mainly they are landscapes. He has searched out willows, ponds, farmyards and roads. . . . There is firmness in most of these studies . . .

A number of the landscapes were painted during Gauguin's time in Rouen and are more rural than anything he had done previously; at this stage they include reddish-brown cattle but no people. They tend to be fairly claustrophobic in atmosphere, with the sky almost hidden by a thick screen of trees.

In this work Cézanne's 'constructive stroke' is used to build up the picture space and unite the cows with the landscape, lending the work a rather cluttered appearance. Writers were critical of Gauguin's apparent lack of care in rendering perspective. Henry Fèvre wrote:

Frequent shortcomings weaken Gauguin's painting. It is tossed off in a haphazard fashion with confused perspective and rather smothered colors.

It was perhaps to this work that he was referring when he mentioned the perspectival difficulties – there is a marked imbalance between the central standing cow and the very much smaller cattle to the left-hand side of the picture, and the effect is almost one of a dual perspective.

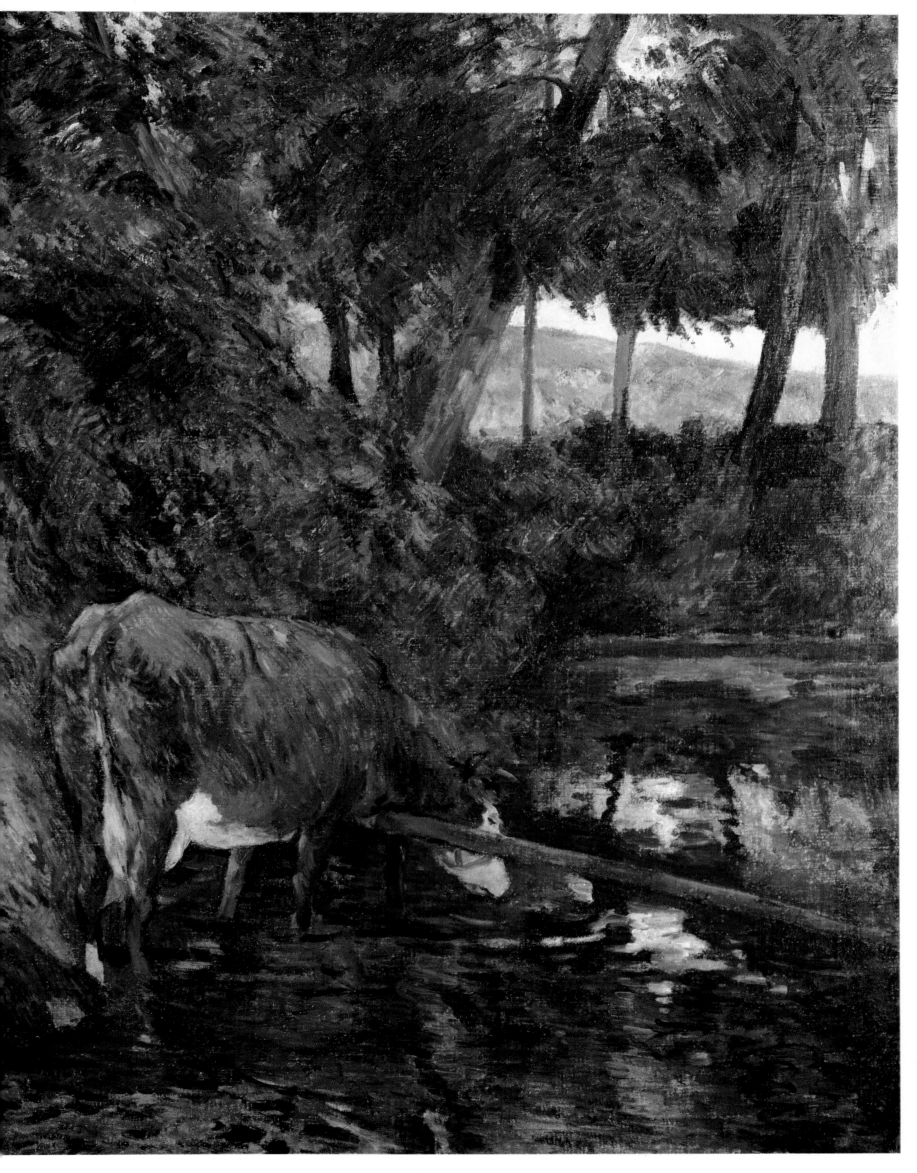

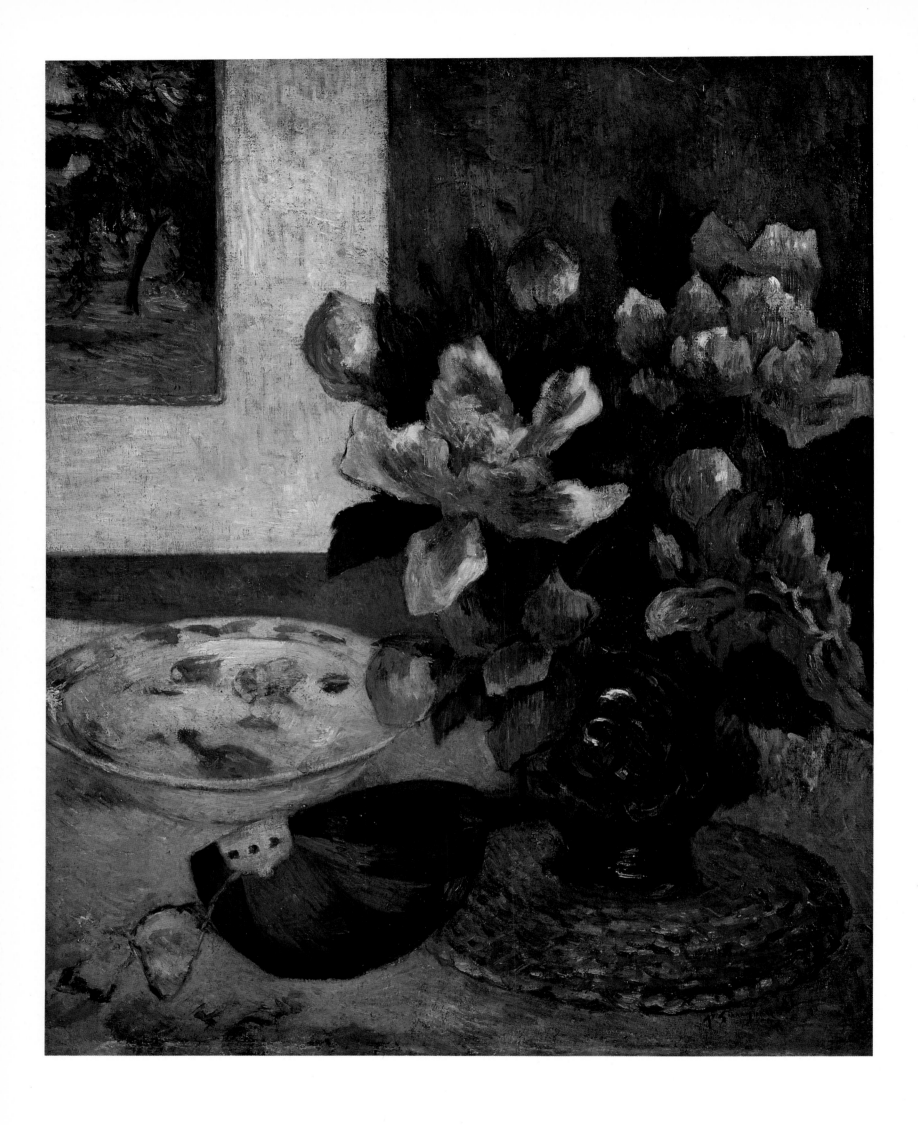

Still Life with Mandoline, 1885

Oil on canvas
24×20 inches (61×51 cm)
Musée d'Orsay, Paris

Gauguin has reworked the traditional still life and brought it up to date. He has retained a number of conventional ingredients – the vase of flowers on a tabletop, the china dish and the mandoline. Unlike earlier still lifes, however, he has not studied the different textures of the objects – the peonies are as solid as the wood of the instrument or the plate. Nor do these objects appear to have been chosen for their allegorical connotations – the flowers are not a timely reminder of death, simply because they appear so strong; the mandoline does not serve as a reminder of the brevity of pleasure. If anything their symbolism is personal; the vase is very similar to those Gauguin was to start making in the winter of 1886, and the mandoline accompanied him on all his trips (it

also hangs behind *Suzanne*, page 32). The picture on the wall behind the tabletop arrangement belonged to Gauguin's collection and is by the artist Guillaumin, who exhibited with the Impressionists and who painted in company with Cézanne, Pissarro and Gauguin in the summer of 1881 at Pontoise.

While this is demonstrably a still life, it differs from the earlier examples (page 34 and 38) in its inclusion of a landscape painting on the background wall, an effect very similar to a view glimpsed out of a window, as in *Vase of Flowers* (page 36). This opens up the background of the composition and helps make the upper half more understandable; without it the background would appear to be on the same plane as the foreground objects.

Women Bathing, 1885

Oil on canvas
15×18¼ inches (38.1×46.2 cm)
National Museum of Western Art, Tokyo

Painted in Dieppe in the summer of 1885, this work was exhibited at the final Impressionist exhibition the following year. In marked contrast to the Rouen landscapes at the same show, figures have begun to dominate the artist's view of nature. He has treated the theme of women in the waves, to which he is to return on several occasions, for the first time. Gradually the subject became more overtly symbolic, as the waves assume a metaphor for sexual union (for example *Ondine,* page 106). At this stage, however, Gauguin seems more interested in exploiting the decorative potential of the four female figures, so much so that the pattern of their bodies makes them appear to be engaged in some ritualistic dance. The women's bodies are echoed by the sailing ships on the high horizon, while the decorative aspect of the work is heightened by the strangely disembodied head of the man behind them. The witty character of this figure makes him appear as if plucked from a Manet or Degas.

Gauguin has deliberately limited his palette to a few colors, with the emphasis on blues and greens enlivened by the odd touch of red. Coupled with the simplified shapes of the women, the lack of any modeling in their flesh and the use of a blue outline around the figures which both flattens and unites them, this is an indication that many of his more mature characteristics are already present in this work.

When Gauguin met the Van Gogh brothers towards the end of 1887, this was one of the paintings which Theo purchased from him for 300 francs on 26 December. He sold it two days later for 450 francs.

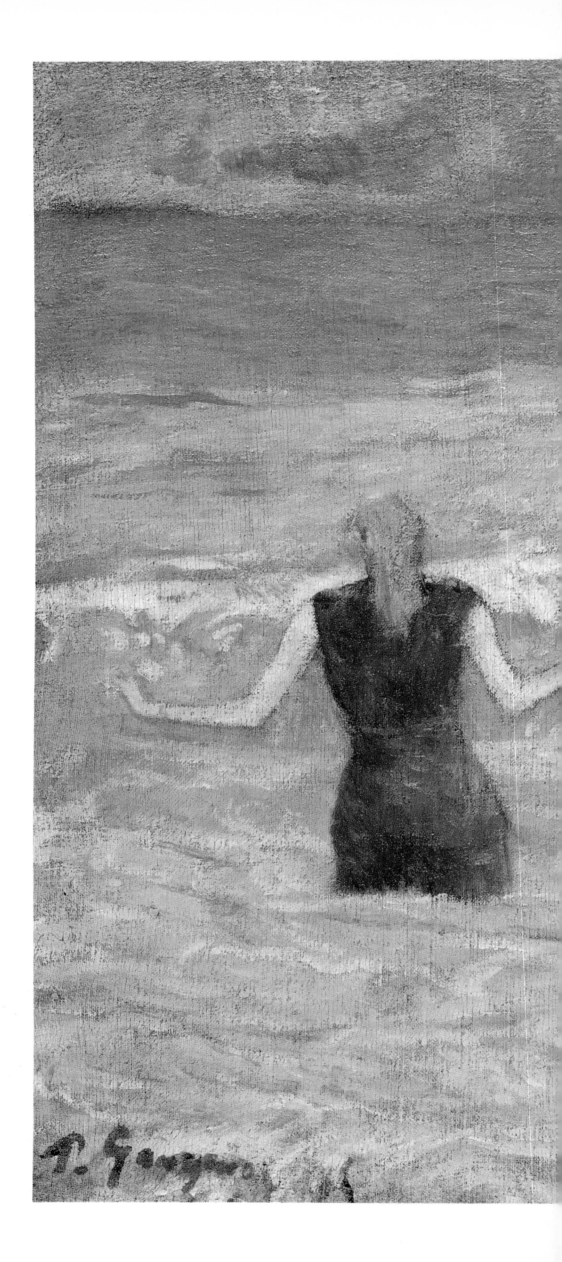

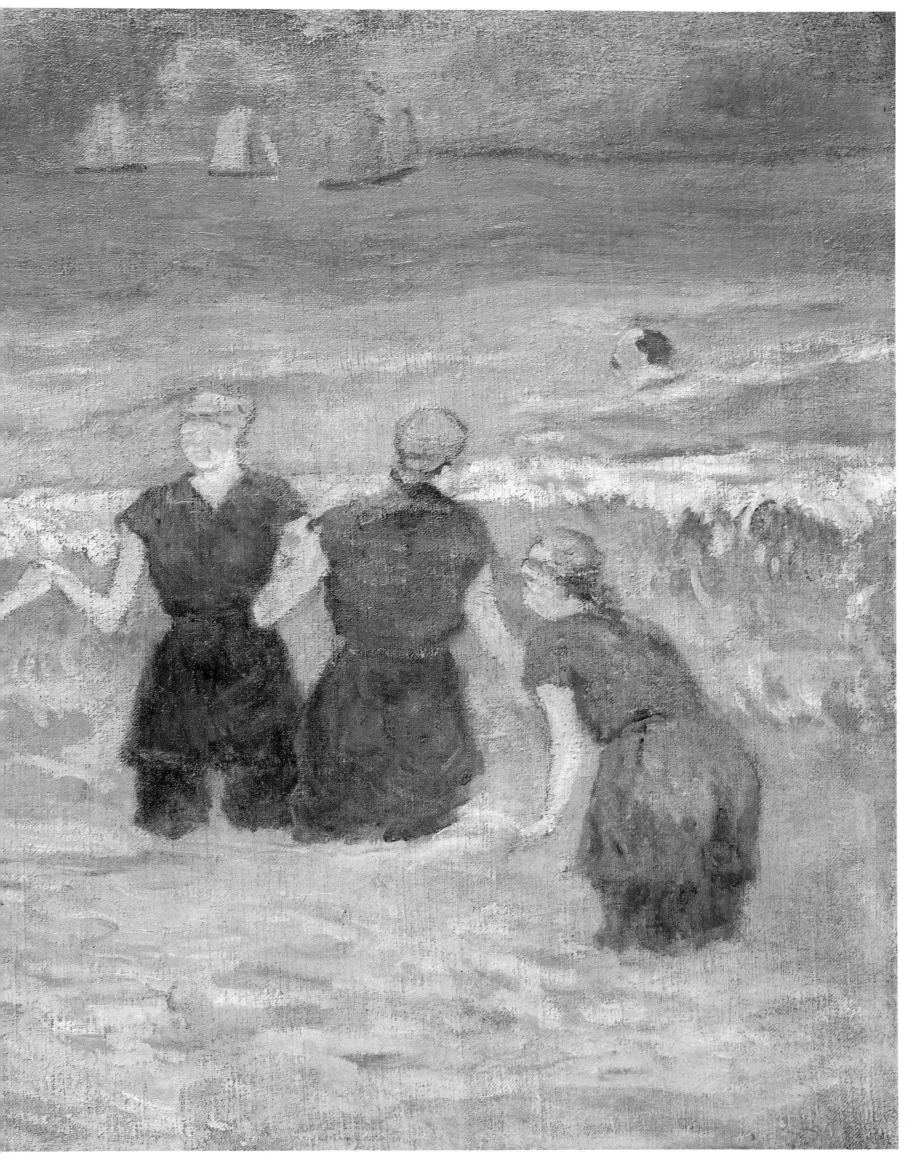

The Breton Shepherdess, 1886

Oil on canvas
24×28 inches (61×73.5 cm)
Laing Art Gallery, Newcastle-upon-Tyne

This is one of the earliest works Gauguin painted after arriving at Pont-Aven in 1886, in which he dealt with the impressionist theme of the figure in a landscape. The work was not painted on the spot in the traditional impressionist fashion, however, but has been built up after the event from a number of studies, including one of the little shepherdess, and from sketches of the animals and the blue-smocked peasant. In the finished work Gauguin has simplified the landscape, ignored certain aspects of the scene, and shown no concern for a legible representation of space. The shepherdess sits on a hillock, overlooking a plateau on which the animals graze, but the effect is of a flattened space in which the figure and the sheep are on the same plane.

The idea of the peasant theme had perhaps been suggested to Gauguin by Pissarro, for whom the subject assumed great importance in the 1880s as he became more interested in anarchist politics, and it was an obvious opportunity for him to explore the relationship between man and nature. The subject of the peasant was a common one in French art from the middle of the nineteenth century, so much so that by the 1880s it tended to be hackneyed sentimental Salon fare, such as Dagnan-Bouveret's *Pardon in Brittany* (page 14), and had lost the impact of its original social comment. Gauguin's motivation was quite different from Pissarro's, however – no one ever seems to work in his peasant pictures and the sense of rural bliss is all-pervasive. The subject of girl and sheep, which was not only picturesque and decorative but also lent itself to bold simplifications, appears on a number of his ceramics.

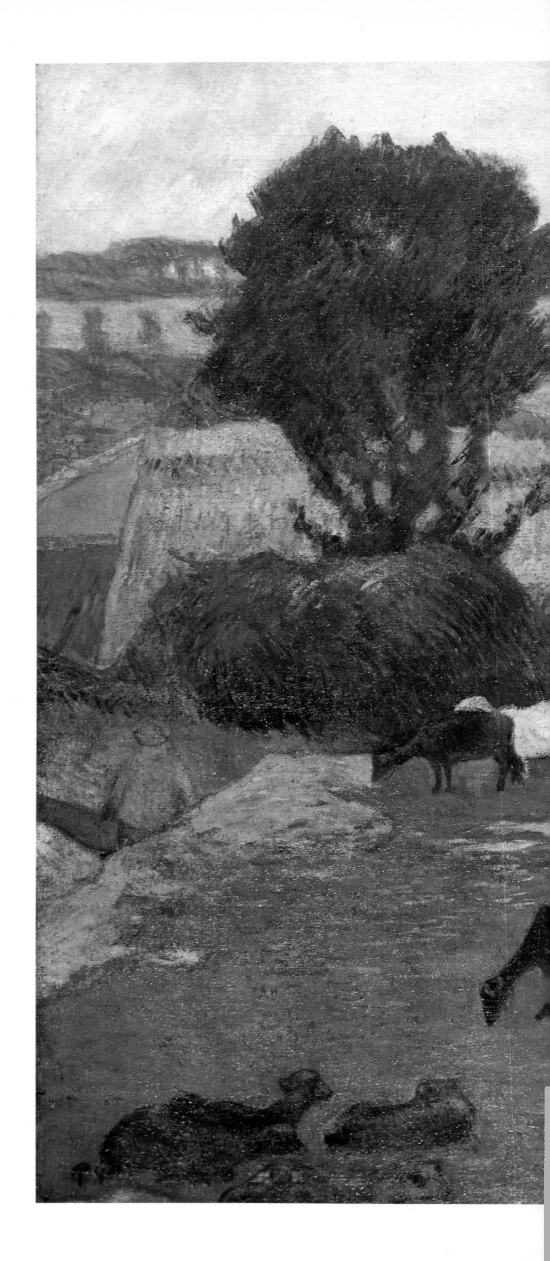

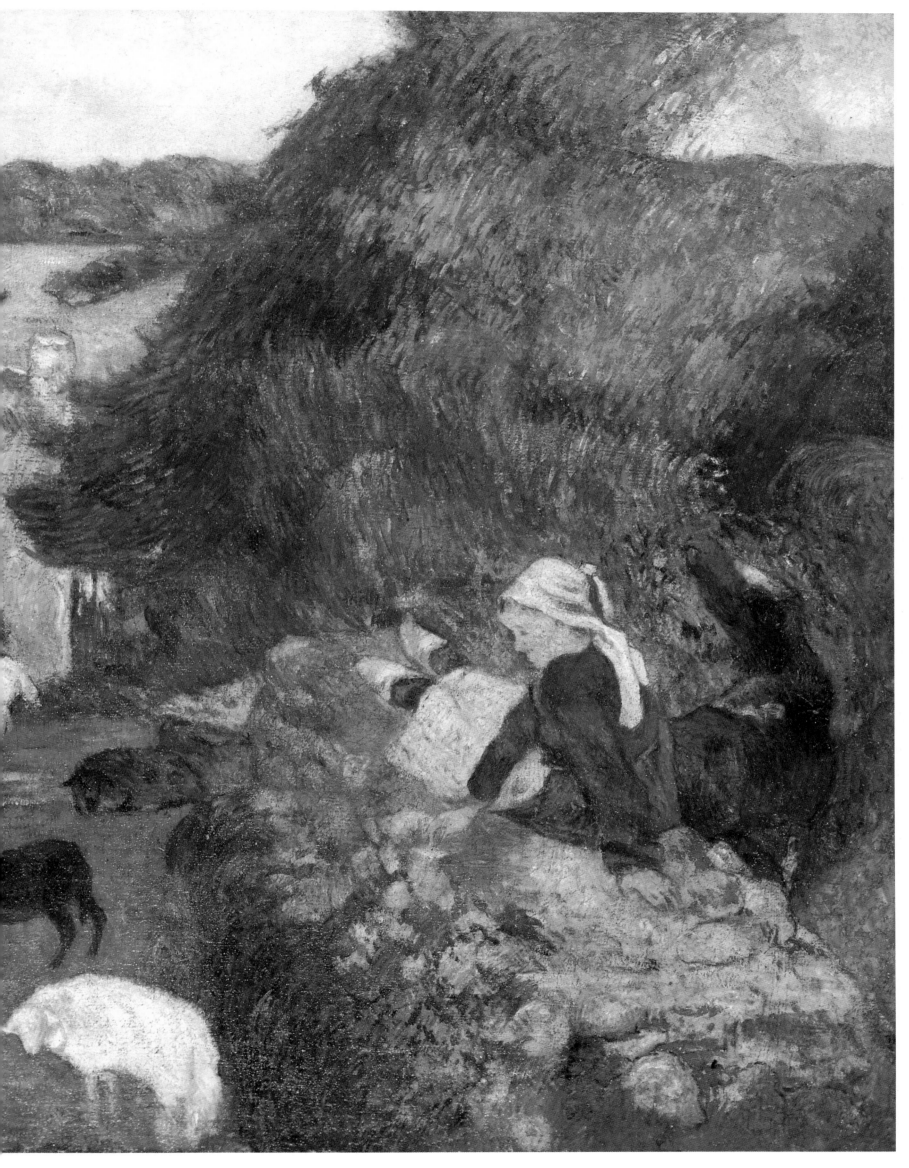

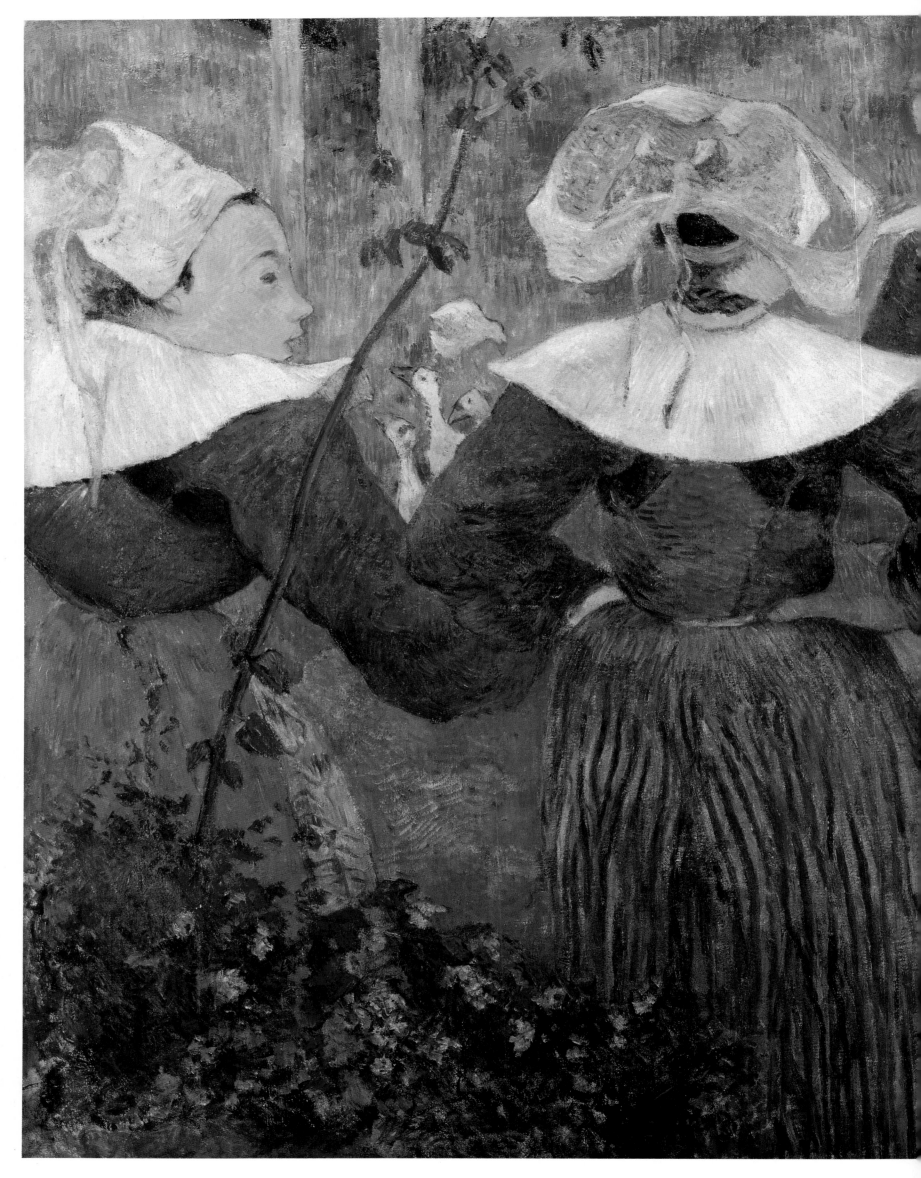

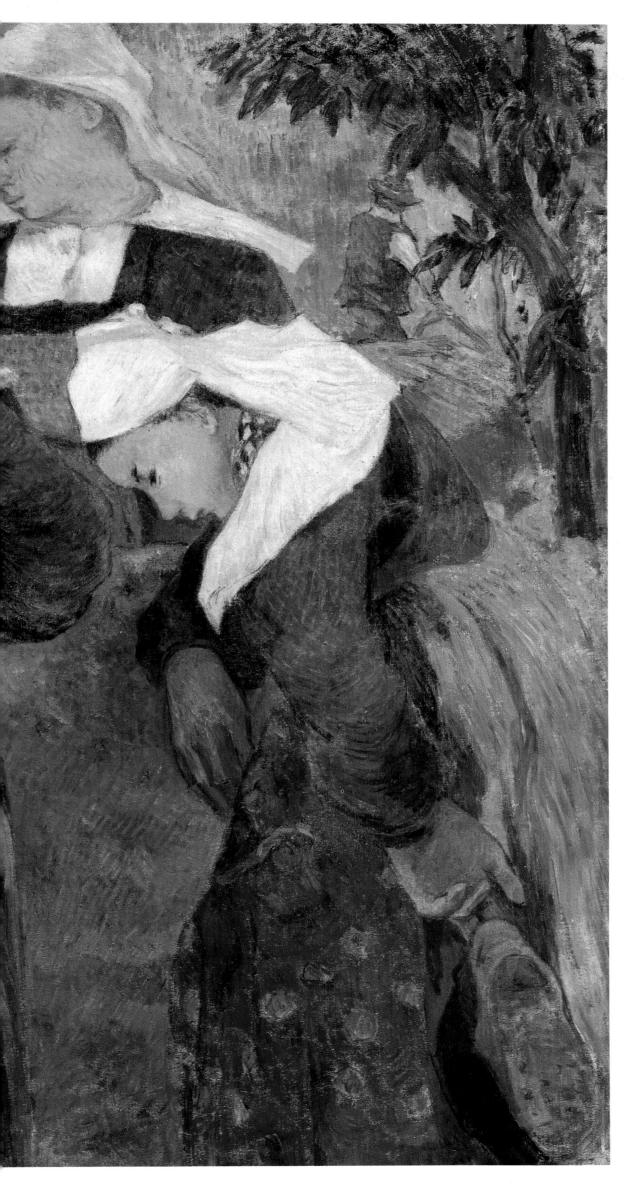

Four Breton Women, 1886

Oil on canvas
28⅜×35⅜ inches (72×90 cm)
Bayerischen Staatsgemäldesammlungen,
Munich

Despite depicting a Breton scene, this work
was probably painted in the studio in Paris
in the winter of 1886, from a number of
studies Gauguin had made during the
summer in Pont-Aven (page 24). In this he
was abandoning traditional impressionist
practice and trying to achieve a much more
synthetic effect, relying on simplified
forms and colors, where his memory and
imagination began to play an important
role in his production. The picture space
has been deliberately flattened – there is no
suggestion of a horizon and the figures
have been compressed into a shallow area
in the foreground. Gauguin has concen-
trated on the flowing rhythmical line between the figures, which is so marked that
the work has sometimes been identified as
depicting a dance. However, a wall separ-
ates the three foreground women from the
fourth figure. The detail of the right-hand
figure who adjusts her clog is reminiscent
of a Degas ballerina.

While the formal arrangement of the
work is innovative, the subject-matter is
highly conventional. Gauguin has adhered
to the popular view of the 'otherness' of
peasant women, which was popular in nos-
talgic depictions of Brittany at the Salon
(for example in Dagnan-Bouveret's *Pardon
in Brittany*, page 14, painted the following
year). Gauguin has depicted the women in
their traditional dress of skirt, bodice and
elaborate *coiffe*. It was perhaps this picturesque quality that appealed to Theo Van
Gogh, who bought the painting from Gauguin – he clearly recognized its marketable
subject-matter.

Still Life with Profile of Laval,

1886

Oil on canvas

18⅛×15 inches (46×38 cm)

Josefowitz collection

In this work Gauguin returns to and re-works the traditional genre of still life, as he had done in earlier works (pages 38 and 52). The composition of the still-life elements is conventional enough – apples and a ceramic pot set upon a white linen cloth on a tabletop – but Gauguin has upset the norms of still-life painting by introducing the comic profile of his pupil Charles Laval (1862-94) on the right-hand side of the painting. The two artists had met at Pont-Aven in the summer of 1886 and were to travel together to Panama and Martinique the following year. This work is sometimes thought to have been painted shortly after their meeting, but the inclusion of one of Gauguin's pots suggests that it was in fact painted in Paris in the winter, after he had started working in ceramics.

The painting is a homage to Gauguin's mentors Cézanne and Degas. The apples at the center of the composition are treated with the small directional brushstroke and the glowing colors found in the work of Cézanne, such as *Still Life with Compotier* which Gauguin represented in the background of *Portrait of a Woman with a Still Life by Cézanne* (page 118). The device of the abruptly cut-off head derives from Degas, and the effect here is to give a sense of immediacy to the otherwise rather generalized still life. At the same time as acknowledging his debt to Cézanne and Degas, Gauguin is drawing a parallel with what he perceives as his own role as a teacher by introducing Laval's studious examination of his ceramic pot. Thus the work is much more than a simple still life with the portrait of a friend, and becomes a hybrid of different artistic styles and a complex commentary on the nature of artistic originality.

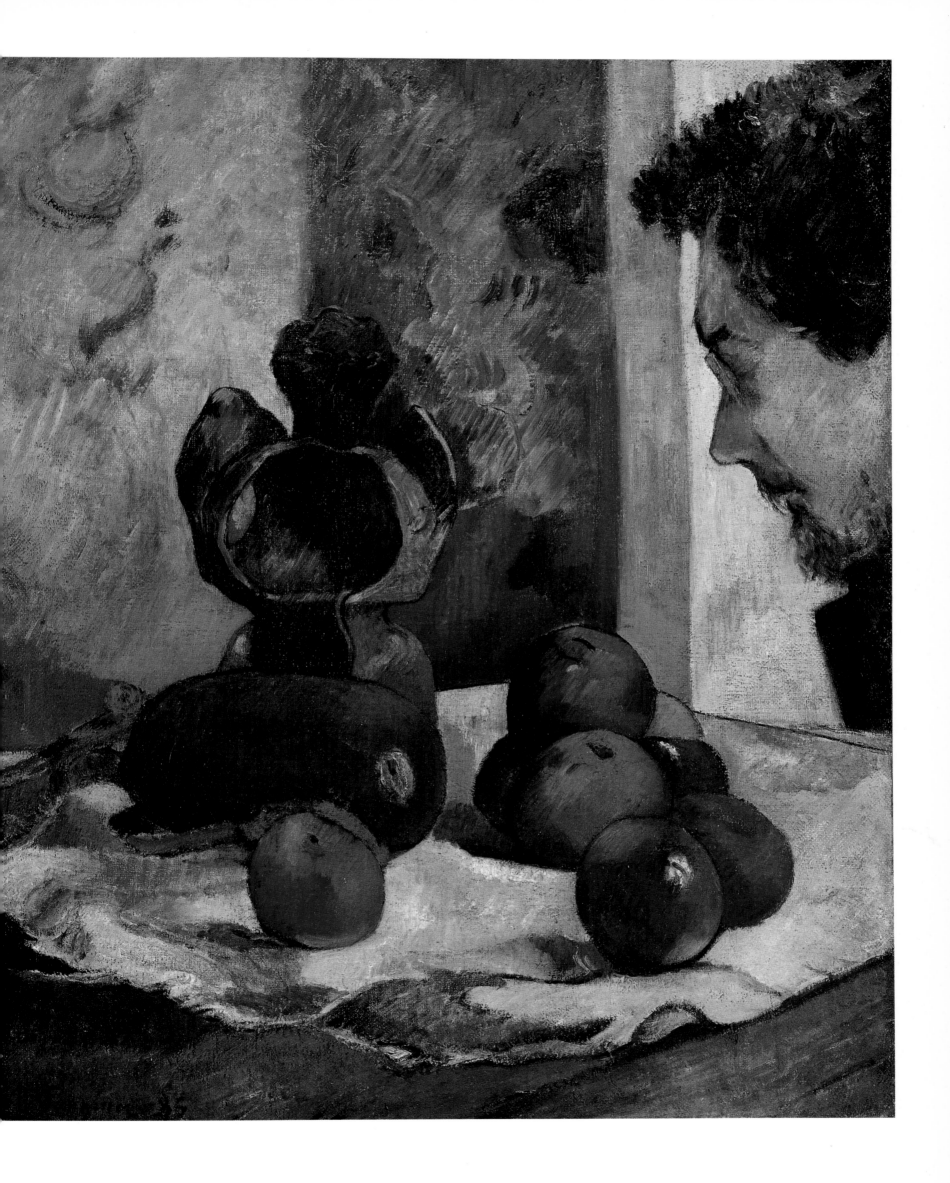

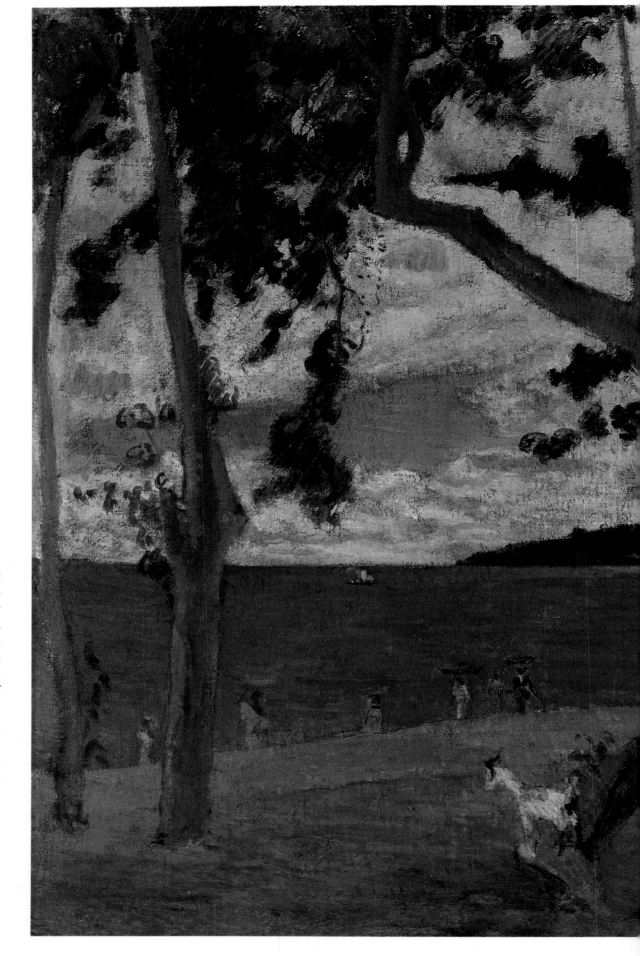

By the Sea, Martinique, 1887

Oil on canvas
21¼×35½ inches (54×90 cm)
Ny Carlsberg Glyptotek, Copenhagen

Gauguin went to Martinique toward the end of May 1887, after an abortive trip to Panama when he was forced to earn money by helping construct the canal. He was accompanied by the artist Charles Laval and for a time they lived in a native hut near Saint-Pierre, where Gauguin painted a number of similar landscapes, most of them including larger figures and all employing rich, glowing colors and with the picture space built up in a much more monumental way. Shortly after settling in Martinique, Gauguin fell ill with malaria and dysentery and made urgent requests to his friends back in Paris to send him money; eventually he managed to return to France by working his passage aboard a ship. Although the trip to Martinique was fraught with difficulties, he clearly benefited from it artistically and it generated in him a taste for the exoticism of the tropics which was to lead ultimately to his move to Tahiti in 1891.

Gauguin has provided a vision of life in Martinique quite different from that in Brittany, with the emphasis placed on the harmony between people and landscape. The decorative aspects of the trees are stressed; they are much more linear and rhythmic than his previous dense shrubs. Behind their interlocking shapes the landscape is divided into broad horizontal bands. It was perhaps a work such as this that Theo and Vincent Van Gogh admired in Portier's gallery in December 1887.

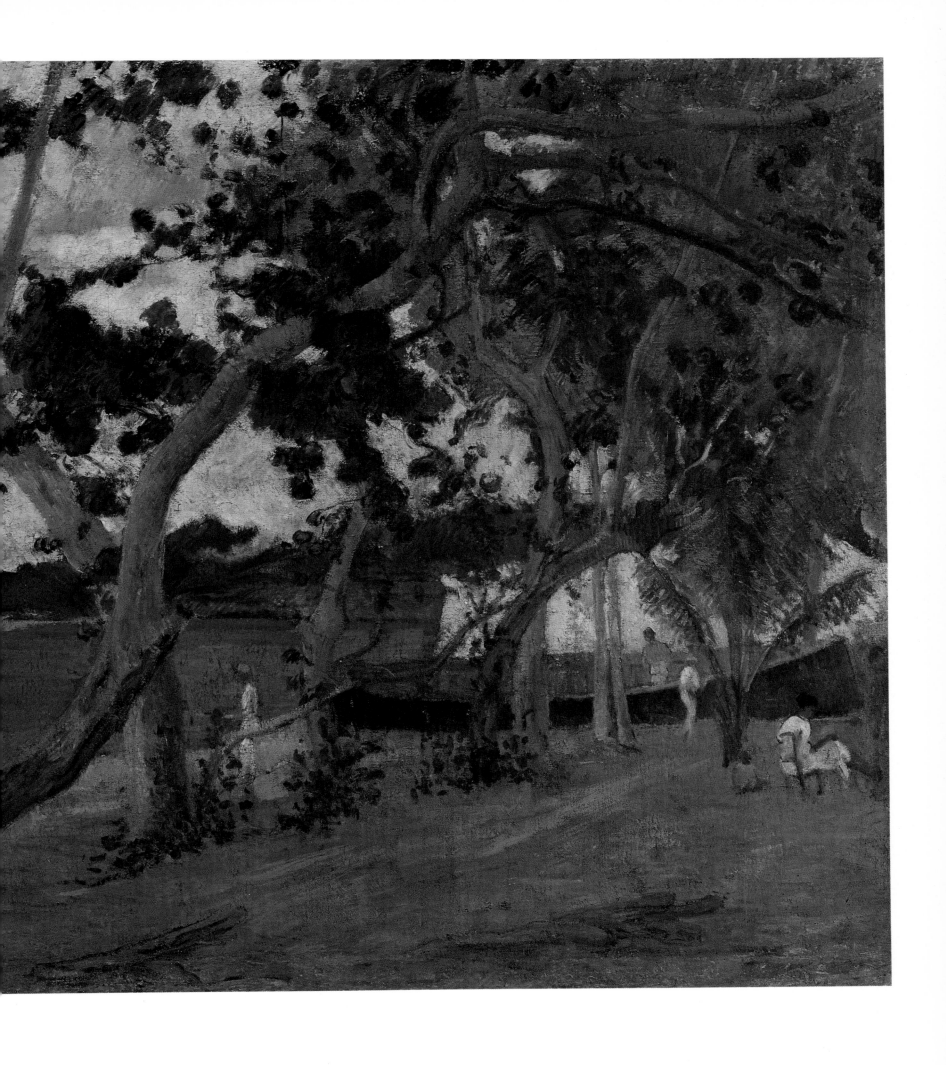

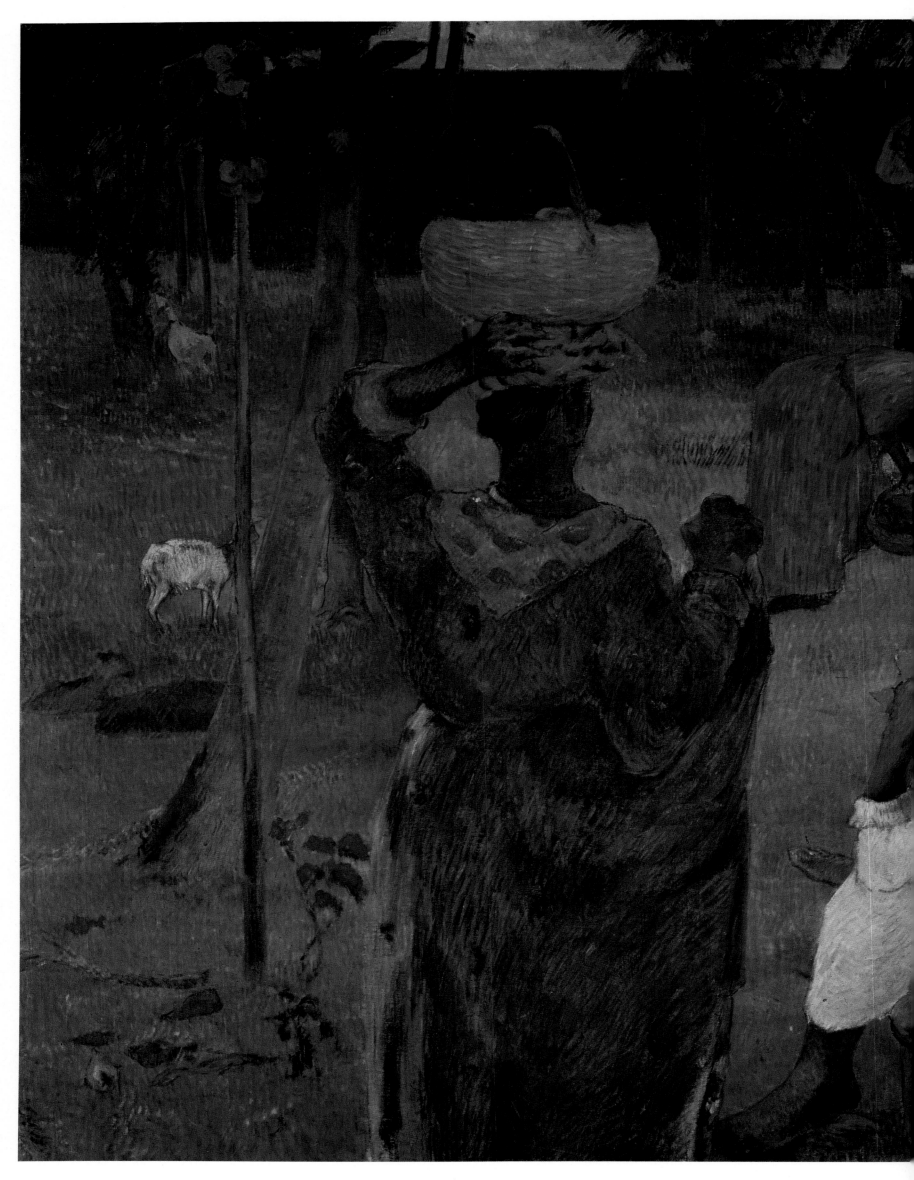

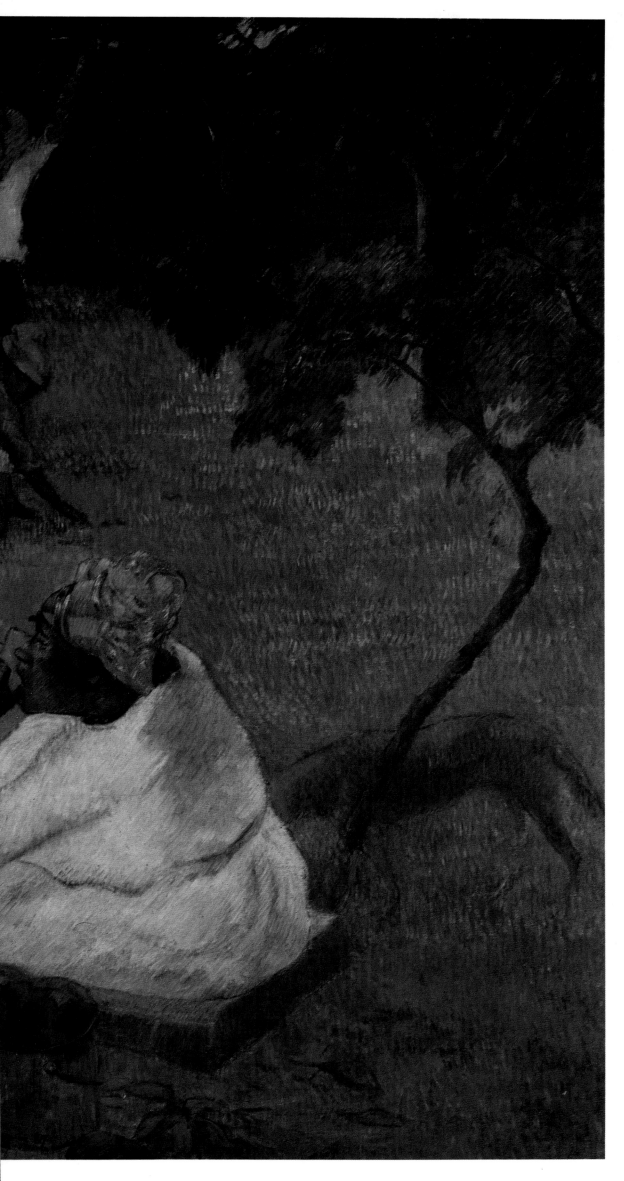

Mango Pickers, Martinique, 1887

Oil on canvas
35×45¾ inches (89×116 cm)
National Museum Vincent Van Gogh,
Amsterdam

Painted in the studio, this work was built up from sketches which Gauguin made on the spot of the woman with the basket on her head and the seated figure. Only the merest strip of sky suggests the very high horizon – Gauguin has again presented the viewer with a picture space which is difficult to resolve. We appear to look down on the seated woman from a high vantage point and then up towards the distant sea. The curving arabesques of the trees which he had used in *By the Sea, Martinique* (page 62) are used again to echo the curves of the women. Gauguin wrote to Schuffenecker shortly after his arrival in Saint-Pierre:

The shapes and forms of the people are most appealing to me, and every day there are constant comings and goings of negresses in cheap finery, whose movements are infinitely graceful and varied; for the time being I have restricted myself to making sketch after sketch of them, so as to penetrate their true character, after which I shall have them pose for me. They gossip constantly even when they have heavy loads on their heads. Their gestures are very unusual and their hands play an important role in harmony with their swaying hips.

As an insight into Gauguin's working methods this letter is especially revealing; it is clear that he has left the impressionist method far behind him and is working in a selective manner in which he tries to distil the essence of his subject into a clear statement, relying on memory and imagination. This was only to receive its full exposition after Gauguin came into contact with Symbolist aesthetics, but letters and paintings such as this indicate that he was already working in a synthetic manner by this time.

This work was sold to Theo Van Gogh for 400 francs and remained in his collection until his death.

65

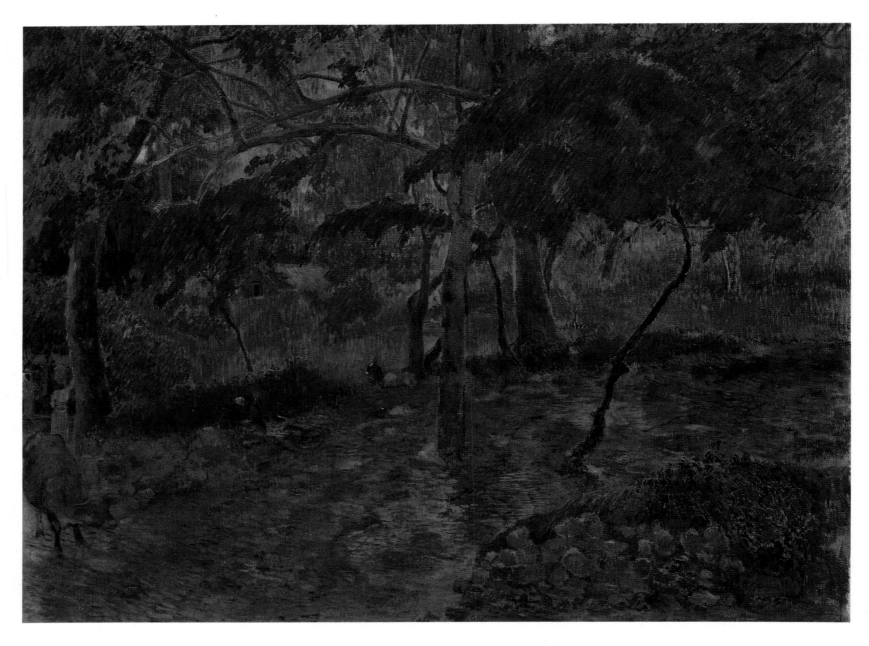

Tropical Landscape on Martinique, 1887

Oil on canvas
35½×45¾ inches (90×116 cm)
Bayerische Staatsgemäldesammlungen,
Munich

Tropical Landscape was painted in Martinique, though perhaps more akin to some French works by Pissarro such as the *Côte des Boeufs* (page 12), in which the effect is one of a dense thicket with slim foreground trees creating a linear pattern across the background vegetation. In this painting, as in other Martinique works, Gauguin has utilized Cézanne's directional brushstroke as a means of constructing the picture space and holding together what might otherwise have been a work lacking in focus. The parallel strokes on the trees run diagonally while those on the

ground are applied horizontally, much as Gauguin had observed in Cézanne's *Castle at Médan* (page 10), which remained with his wife in Copenhagen and the loss of which he was to continue to lament.

Yet *Tropical Landscape on Martinique* has not been painted on the spot, but worked up away from the motif. In this, Gauguin's practice was quite different from that of both Pissarro and Cézanne. The right-hand tree is exactly the same as that on the right-hand side of *Mango Pickers, Martinique* (page 64), suggesting that Gauguin kept a repertoire of sketches of trees and bushes as well as figures on which to draw for his paintings. The work is the same size as *Mango Pickers* and *Martinique Landscape* (page 67), a standard size 50 canvas such as was sold already stretched by color merchants and which was recommended in artists' manuals for figure painting.

Martinique Landscape, 1887

Oil on canvas
45¾×35 inches (115.5×89 cm)
National Gallery of Scotland, Edinburgh

Once again, as in a number of his other Martinique landscapes, Gauguin has used a size 50 canvas (116×90 cm). This time, however, instead of the traditional horizontal format of the landscape painting, he has turned the canvas on its side, and the vertical shape has allowed him to exploit the perpendiculars in his work to decorative effect. The two upright branches of the tree run parallel to the edge of the canvas.

The picture represents a scene close to where Gauguin and Charles Laval were staying in Martinique, with a view across the bay of Saint-Pierre towards the volcanic Mont Pelée in the background. The distant objects are depicted with as much clarity as the closer foreground elements; Gauguin was not concerned with suggesting the effects of atmosphere or the haziness of the view across the bay. Instead he has assembled the various components with as much regard for the surface pattern of the work as for a faithful interpretation of the scene. The interlocking shapes and the restricted palette contribute to an effect

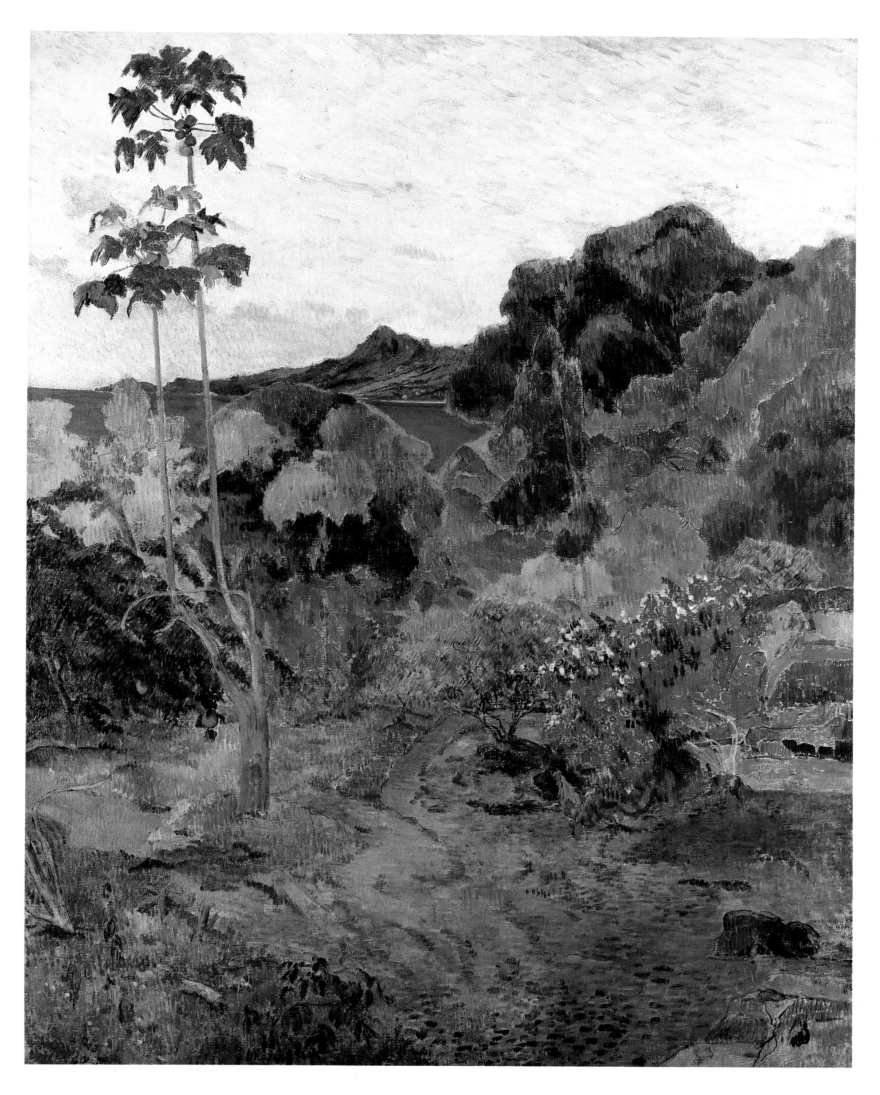

which is concerned predominantly with pattern-making. The colors are limited to greens and blues offset with little saturated patches of vermilion, particularly in the bright red of the cockerel beside the bush.

Again the brushwork owes much to Cézanne's influence. Its consistent use across the canvas, together with color as saturated in the background as in the foreground, contributes to the flattening of the

picture. The diagonal brushstroke ties the different planes together, with the result that the bushes in the middle distance appear to merge easily into the hills along the bay.

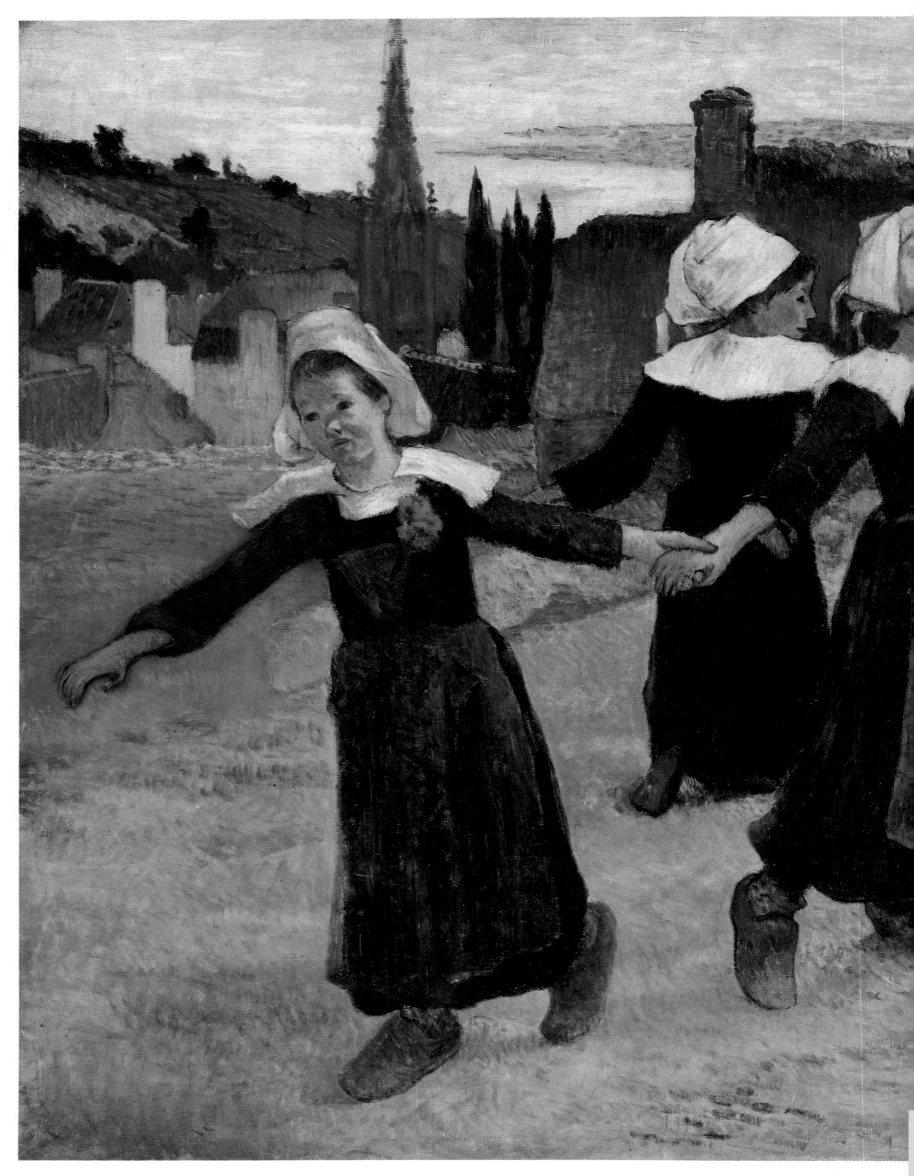

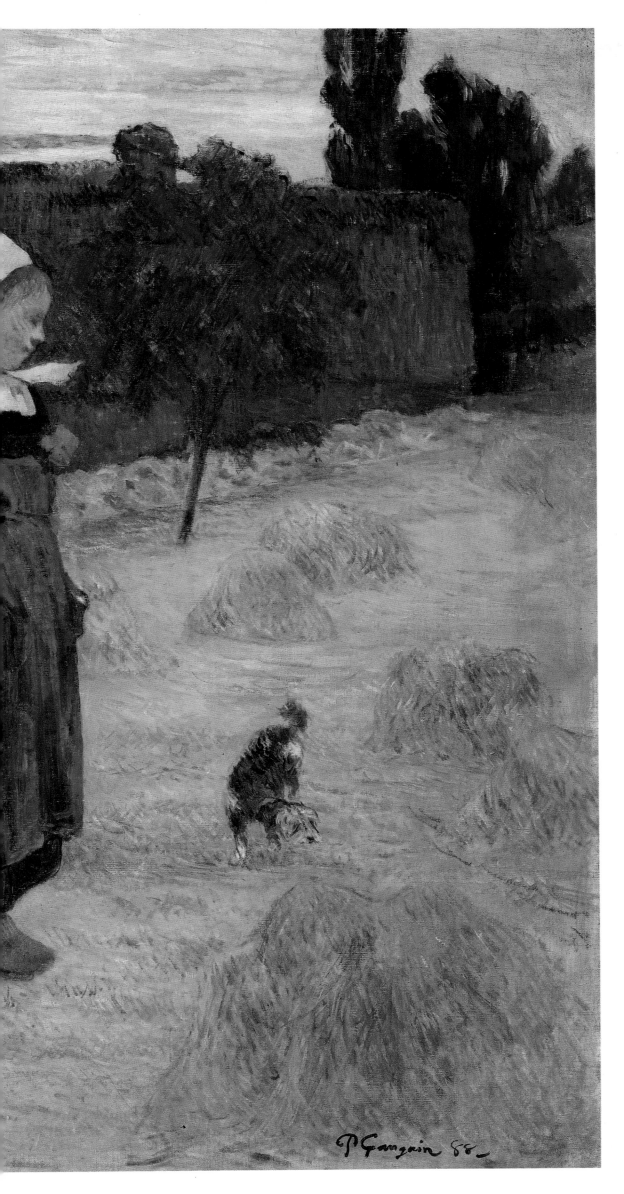

Breton Girls Dancing, Pont-Aven, 1888

Oil on canvas
28¾×36½ inches (73×92.7 cm)
National Gallery of Art, Washington

After Gauguin had gone to Arles to join Vincent Van Gogh, Theo sent him this work, which he had been exhibiting in his gallery in Paris, accompanied by an apologetic note.

I could have sold The Dance of the little Bretonnes but it needed a small retouch. The hand of the little girl, which comes up to the edge of the canvas, assumes an importance which it doesn't appear to have when one sees only the canvas (without the frame) . . .

A collector had expressed an interest and was willing to pay 500 francs for it if Gauguin would amend the offending hand. Gauguin complied with the request, although the work was not finally sold until a year later. This incident demonstrates that even unconventional artists like Gauguin were not above making their work acceptable to potential buyers. The subject-matter itself would have appealed to collectors, the theme of Breton peasants and their rituals having been popular at the Salon for some time. Gauguin has exploited the picturesque ingredients in the work, choosing to depict a traditional haymaking dance and concentrating on the headdresses, heavy clogs and collars of the little girls.

The work was included at the Volpini exhibition of 1889, where the majority of Gauguin's paintings were recent Breton works. The relatively somber colors, applied with a brushstroke which retains some of the vestiges of Cézannesque touch, are relieved by two brilliant flashes of scarlet.

Young Bretons Bathing, 1888

Oil on canvas
36¼×28¾ inches (92×73 cm)
Kunsthalle, Hamburg

Perhaps painted as a companion to *Breton Girls Dancing, Pont Aven* (page 68), this work is in a sense its male equivalent. In both the Breton characters are engaged in a picturesque ritualistic display; in this case the bathing may be part of the traditional Breton pastime of wrestling, an important part of the religious ceremonies which were preserved and encouraged by the tourist trade by the 1880s. The composition is similar, with the figures in each compressed into the bottom left-hand corner, leaving a large area of empty ocher ground. A similar pair of youths occurs in *Boys Wrestling* (page 72), painted in the same year, which represents the previous stage in the ritual when the boys are locked in combat. Both works are unusual in that they depict male models. In Brittany and elsewhere Gauguin favored female models, partly because of the greater decorative possibilities offered by their clothing. In this work, the contorted poses of the nudes and their averted faces are reminiscent of the work of Degas, to whom Gauguin continued to owe an important debt in his figure painting.

The painting is an odd composite of styles and in this sense represents a transitional stage in his development. The stripey brushmarks within the landscape and the flesh remain but this is coupled with a firm use of outline, particularly around the two figures, bringing them into sharp relief against the landscape backdrop.

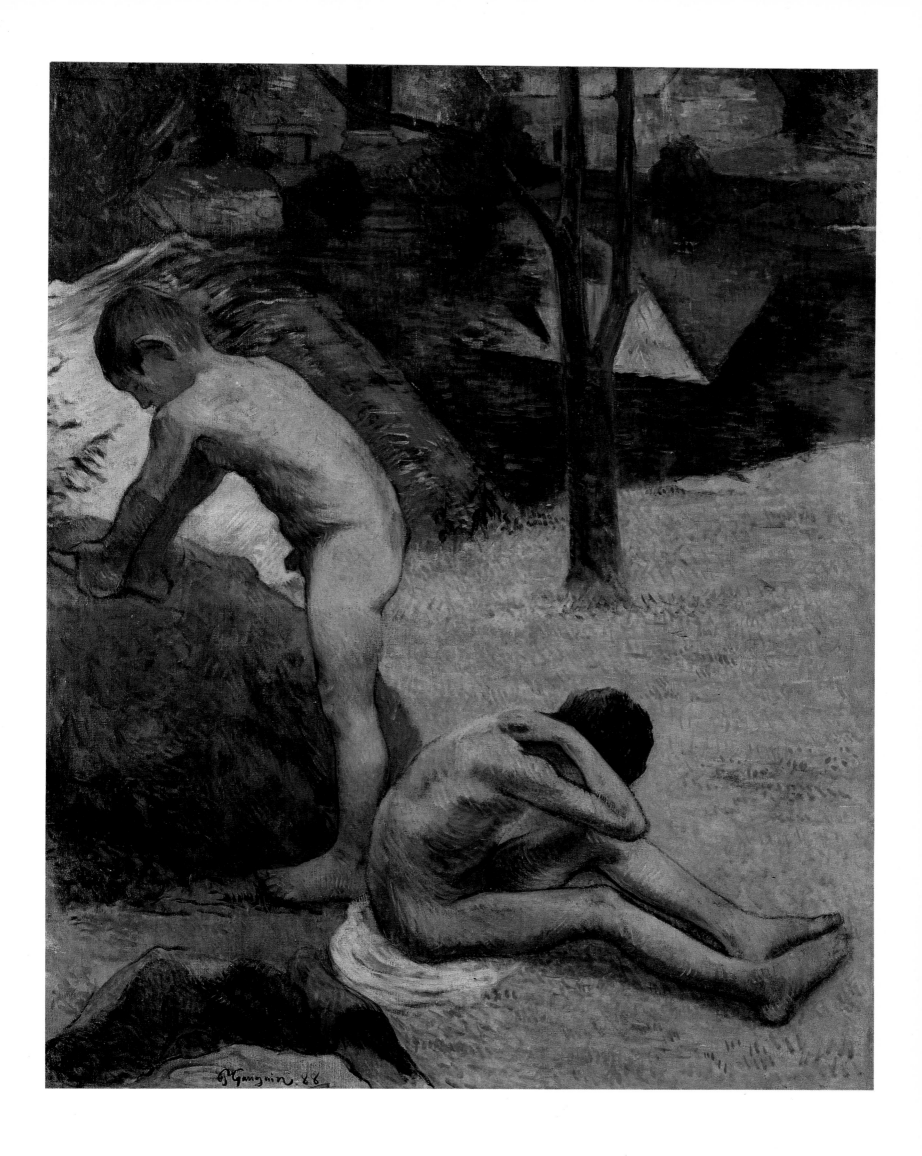

Boys Wrestling, 1888

Oil on canvas
36⅝×28¾ inches (93×73 cm)
Josefowitz collection

On 24 or 25 July 1888 Gauguin wrote to Vincent Van Gogh in Arles including a schematic sketch of this painting and describing it:

. . . I've just finished a Breton wrestling scene which I'm sure you'll like. Two boys, one wearing blue shorts, the other vermilion. Above right, a boy coming out of the water – pure Veronese green, shading off into chrome yellow: the surface unrefined, as in Japanese *crépons*. Also above, a waterfall in pinkish white, with a rainbow on the edge of the canvas just beside the frame. Below, a white patch, a black hat, and a blue smock.

The work was conceived of as a companion to *Young Bretons Bathing* (page 70) and Gauguin painted both of them on a size 30 canvas. Both deal with the relatively unusual subject of nude adolescent males, here engaged in a wrestling ritual which formed an important part of the religious pardons. Like the *Breton Girls Dancing* (page 68) the young Bretons are represented as being gauche and unsophisticated, with grossly enlarged feet and odd anatomical distortions. They are locked together in a contrived pose which has little to do with physical combat. They appear ill at ease within the landscape and seem rather to have been posed in the studio, to conform to Gauguin's pre-existing notions of the 'savage' subject-matter. The manipulation of the natural setting, with its high horizon, oblique angle and flattening, resembling, as Gauguin implied in his description of the painting to Van Gogh, the depiction of space in Japanese prints, heightens the sense of an artist trying to distance himself from western conventions.

The still-life elements of the discarded clothing in the foreground play an important part in the composition, breaking up the unrelieved expanse of green as they had done in *Young Bretons Bathing*. In both paintings the white linen holds Gauguin's signature and highlights it for the viewer. Throughout the work Gauguin has balanced colors and juxtaposed complementaries, particularly on the figure of the boy in blue, who has a bright patch of red under his left arm, contrasting with the green of the grass.

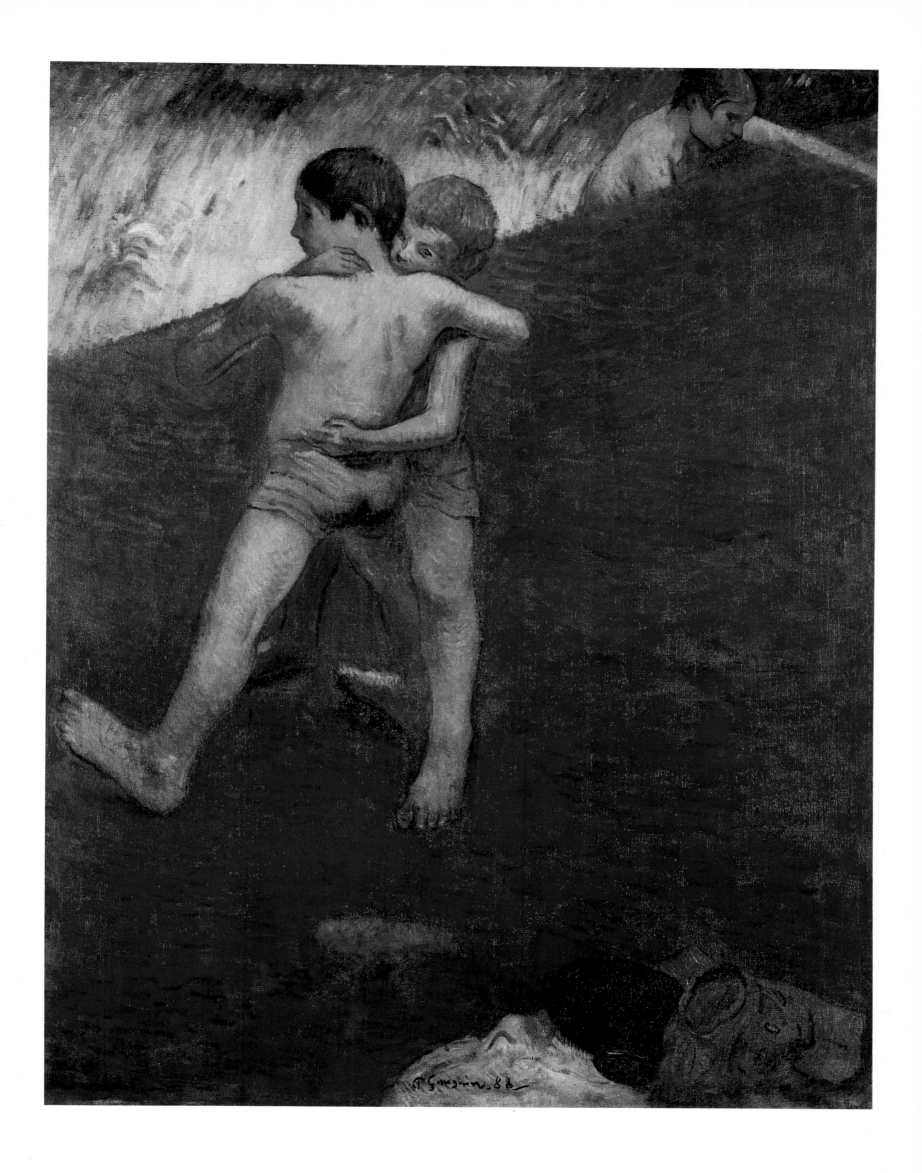

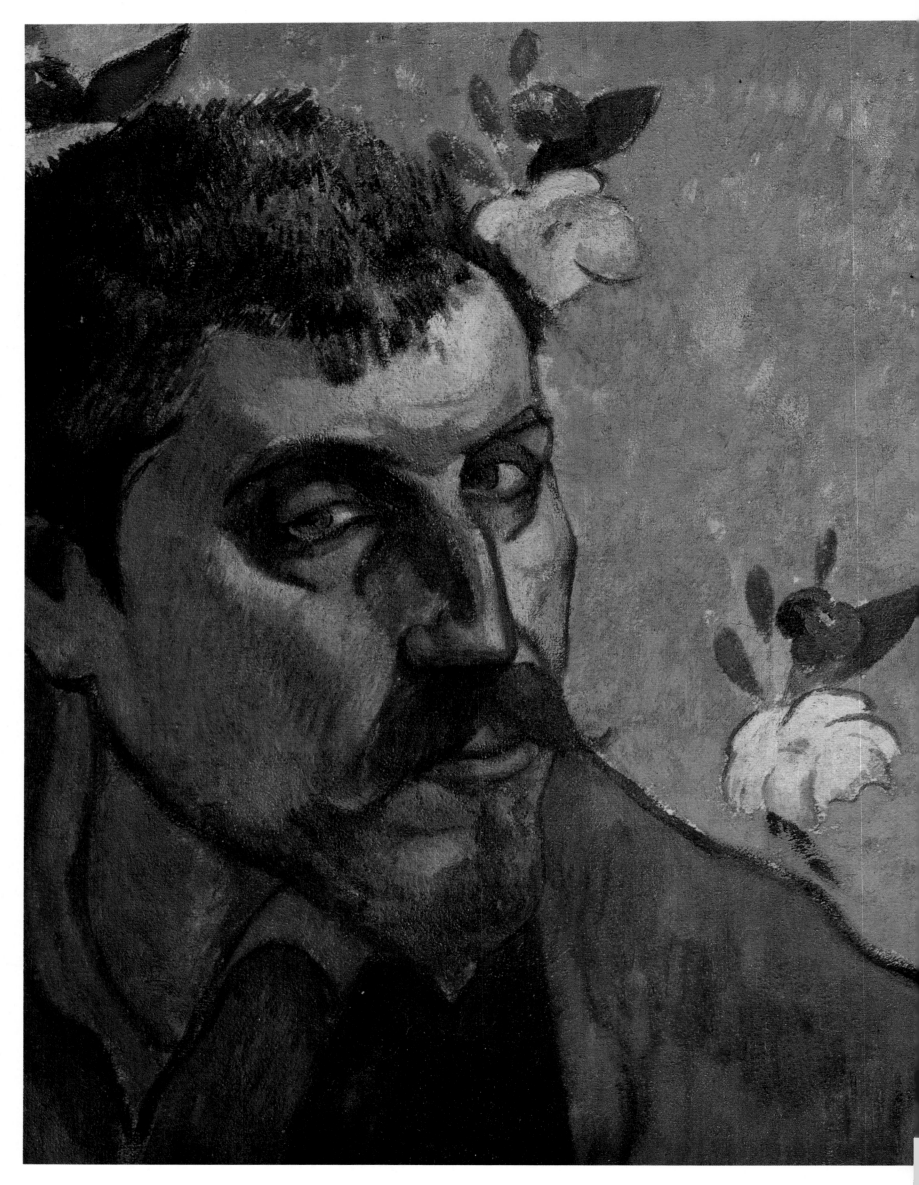

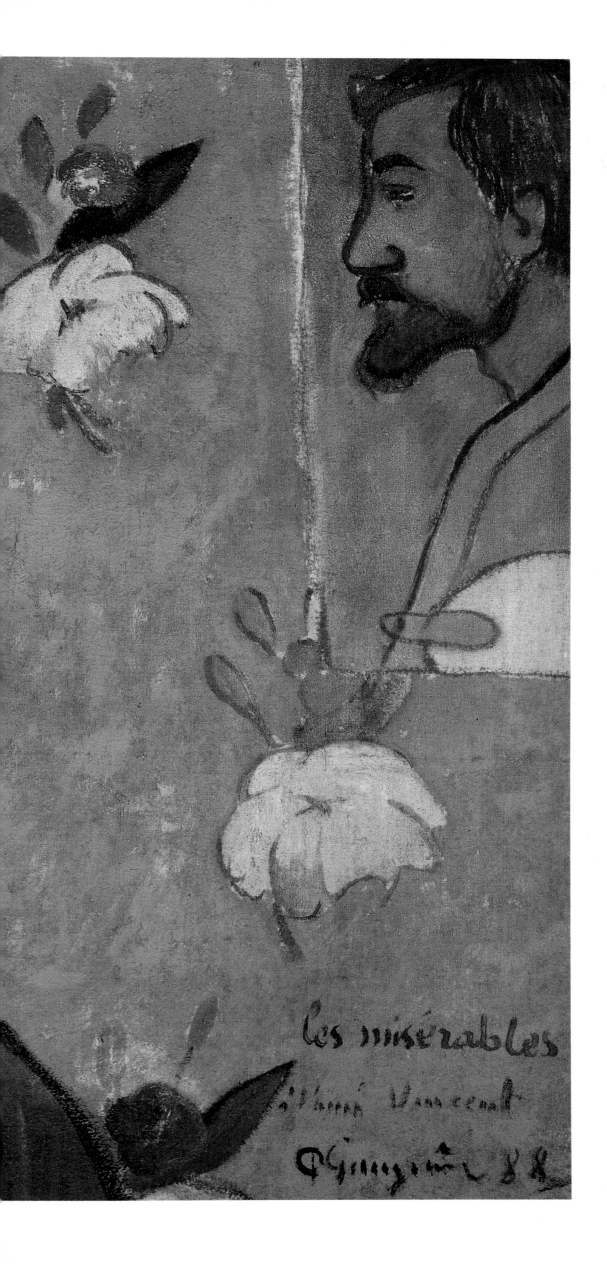

Self-Portrait (Les Misérables),
1888

Oil on canvas
17¾×21⅝ inches (15×55 cm)
National Museum Vincent Van Gogh,
Amsterdam

In September 1888 Vincent Van Gogh
wrote from Arles to Emile Bernard and
Paul Gauguin in Pont-Aven, suggesting
that they should exchange portraits. In a
letter to Schuffenecker Gauguin described
the work that resulted:

I've done a self portrait for Vincent who had
asked me. I believe it is one of my best things:
absolutely incomprehensible (for example) it is
so abstract. Head of a bandit in the foreground,
a Jean Valjean (from Victor Hugo's *Les
Misérables*), also personifying a disreputable
impressionist painter who is always chained to
the world. The drawing is particularly special, a
complete abstraction. The eyes, mouth, and
nose are like the flowers of a Persian carpet also
revealing the symbolic aspect. The color is one
far from nature; imagine a vague memory of
pottery twisted in a high heat. All the reds, violets, striped by bursts of fire like a furnace ema-
nating from the eyes, center of the struggles of
this painter's thoughts. All this on a chrome
yellow background strewn with childish bou-
quets. Bedroom of a young maiden. The Impressionist is still pure, not yet sullied by the
putrid kiss of the Beaux-Arts (academic style).

The work was the first of a number of
self-portraits which Gauguin painted
during 1888 and 1889, by far his most productive years when he began to make use
of the theories of Symbolism in his painting and writing. And in *Les Misérables* it is
a very literary Symbolism which is
employed, but at the same time he has
attempted to suggest certain emotions and
feelings by the use of color and form. He
has established a dialogue between innocence or purity, symbolized by the flowers
on the wallpaper like a halo behind his
head, which appears to be illuminated by
it, in contrast to the world-weary bandit.
The small window on the upper right-hand
side includes a profile of Emile Bernard,
who sent his own portrait to Van Gogh at
the same time (page 22).

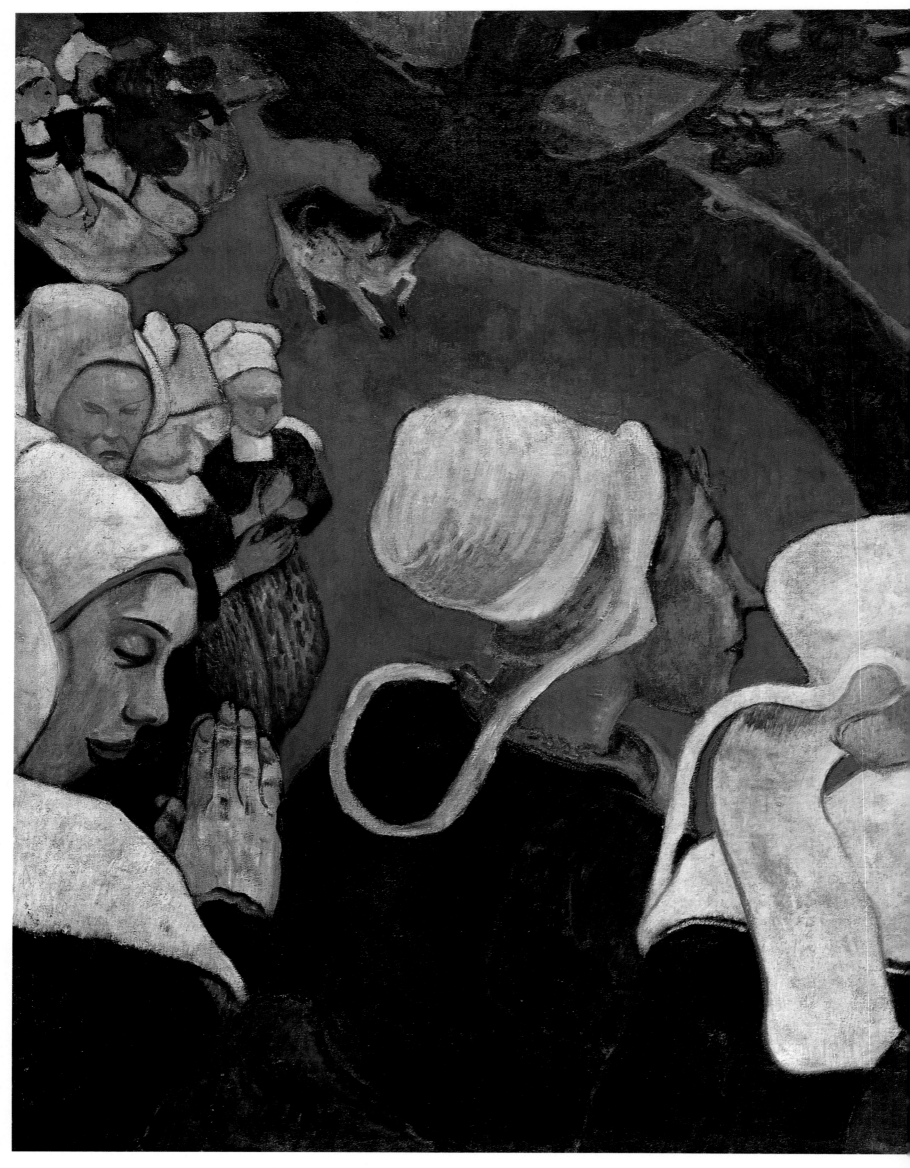

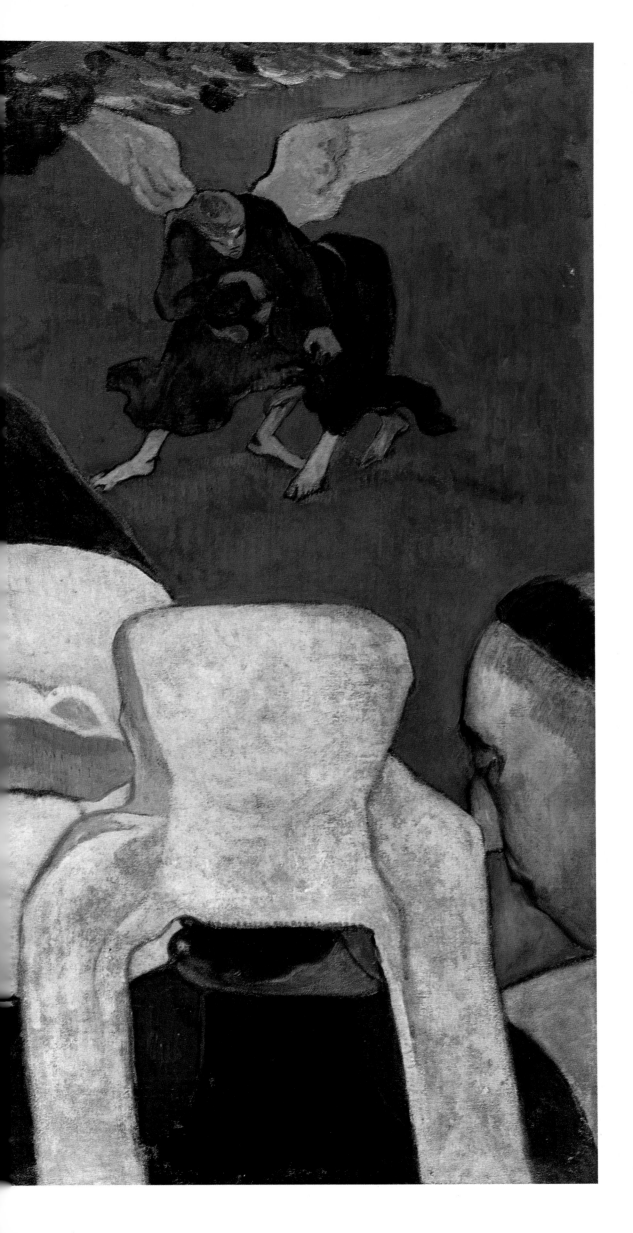

Vision after the Sermon or Jacob Wrestling with the Angel, 1888

Oil on canvas
28¾×36¼ inches (73×92 cm)
National Gallery of Scotland

From 1891 and the appearance of Albert Aurier's article 'Symbolism in Painting: Paul Gauguin', this work has been regarded as the turning point in Gauguin's art; the moment when he finally abandoned impressionism for a style which no longer had any pretence to naturalism and was truly modern in asserting the two-dimensionality of the picture space, rather than creating an illusionistic equivalent for the external world. Many of these characteristics were already apparent in Gauguin's art before this date, however, and to stress these purely formal innovations is to fail to appreciate the different layers of meaning in the work.

The flattening of space which had been apparent in paintings from the first period in Pont-Aven and from Martinique is taken to further extremes here. It would appear that Gauguin has referred to non-western artistic conventions such as those of Japanese prints in his denial of conventional perspective. Here the effect is to remove any middle ground in the work, emphasizing the split between the women and the scene which they are witnessing, and thus contributing to the narrative. The tree effectively cuts them off, in their innocence, from full knowledge of what is happening in the distance. The color is applied in flat washes, which contrasts with the brushwork to be found in works as late as 1887, when Cézanne still exercised a potent influence. This is coupled with the use of firm outline (most notable in the headdresses).

In a letter to Vincent Van Gogh which accompanied a sketch after the painting, Gauguin wrote:

. . . I think I have achieved great simplicity in the figures, very rustic, very superstitious, the overall effect is very severe . . . the landscape and the fight exist only in the imagination of the people praying after the sermon, which is why there is a contrast between the people who are natural, and the struggle going on in the landscape which is unnatural and out of proportion.

Originally painted for a church in Brittany but refused by the priest, the work has the quality of a devotional icon and is the first of a number of religious works which Gauguin produced in Pont-Aven.

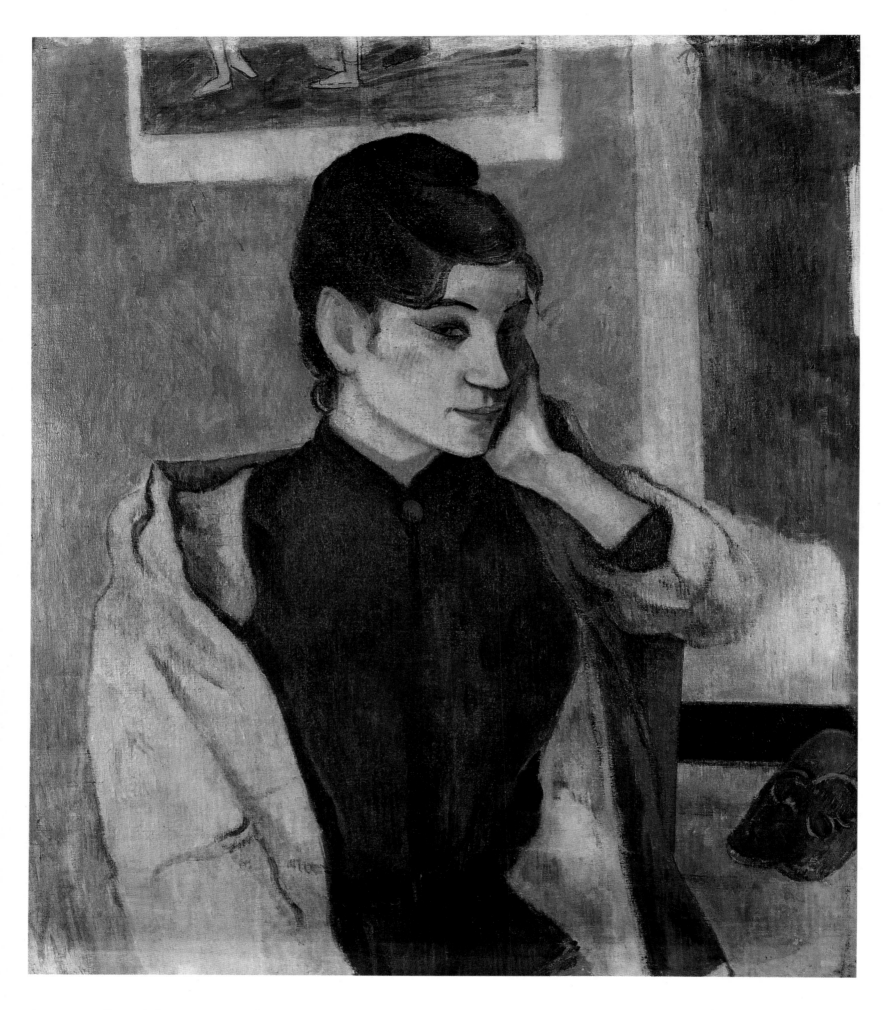

Portrait of Madeleine Bernard,

1888

Oil on canvas
28⅜×22¾ inches (72×58 cm)
Musée de Grenoble

When Emile Bernard went to Pont-Aven in the summer of 1888, he was accompanied by his mother and his younger sister Madeleine (1871-95) with whom Gauguin fell in love, apparently without his affection being reciprocated. Madeleine was a willing model for both artists; Bernard painted two portraits of her in a landscape setting (page 18), although in his memoirs he wrote '. . . of course, neither Gauguin nor I

managed more than a caricature of my sister . . .' The kind of distortion evident in both paintings creates a portrait which is full of character, transcending the apparently innocent nature of the 17-year-old girl and making her appear seductive, with her sideways glance and disheveled garment.

On the wall behind Madeleine, Gauguin has provided us with another clue to the

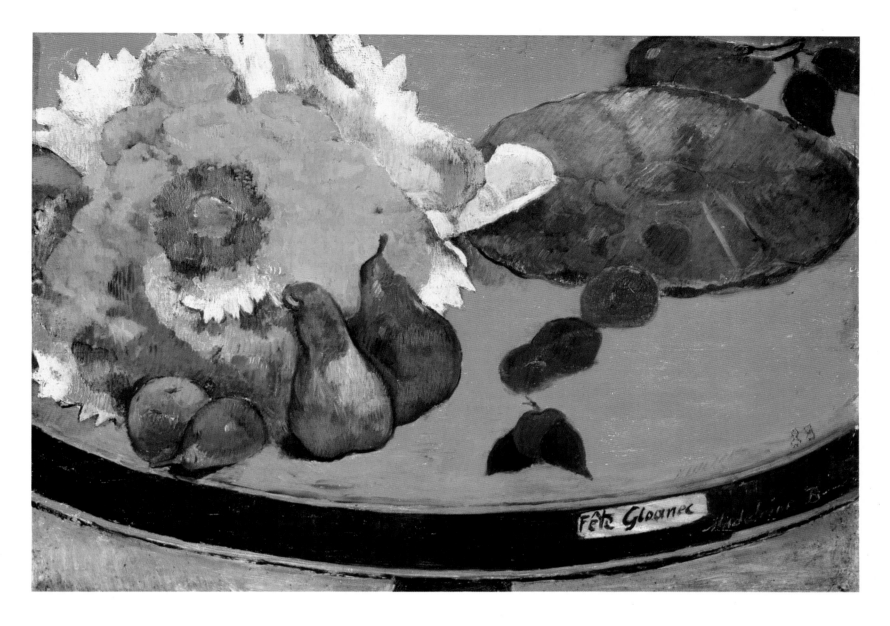

sitter's personality, much as he provided the image of Bernard in the background of *Les Misérables* (page 74). The cropped picture on the wall resembles a Degas ballerina but is in fact part of an engraving by one of his followers, the artist Jean Louis Forain (1852-1931), which had appeared in a newspaper earlier that year. The legs of the ballet dancers may be a reference to what Gauguin regarded as a hidden aspect of Madeleine's virtuous personality. As in *Les Misérables* a juxtaposition is set up between two apparently contradictory aspects of the sitter's character. This ambivalent view of women, which was common enough in the nineteenth century, was to be stated much more explicitly in Gauguin's later works.

After painting the work, Gauguin presented it to Emile Bernard. On the reverse of the portrait is a landscape painting, since he had been forced to reuse an old canvas which by that time he reckoned to be superseded by his later style.

Still Life Fête Gloanec, 1888
Oil on wood
15×20⅞ inches (38×53 cm)
Musée des Beaux-Arts, Orleans

This small work, painted on wood, is inscribed '*Fête Gloanec*' and signed 'Madeleine B.', on the edge of a round table. Maurice Denis later related the story of this strange caption. Apparently the guests at her *pension* would present Marie-Jeanne Gloanec with a suitable gift on her *fête* day (probably her saint's day rather than her birthday) and Gauguin had wished to give her this work, to be hung with other paintings in the dining-room. The more conservative artists at the inn objected to his daring style, however, and he therefore adopted the ruse of signing it with Madeleine's name, rightly calculating that they would not object to a work which appeared to be by the young woman. Naturally no one was duped by Gauguin's strategy, and the work therefore takes on a wider meaning, as a private homage to the 17-year-old with whom he had fallen in love. He produced other works for her, including a pot, and painted her portrait, but her father forbade her to communicate with the middle-aged, married Gauguin.

In this work, the objects are placed on a bright red ground very similar to that in *The Vision after the Sermon* (page 76). They are painted in isolation from one another rather than grouped in a pleasing, harmonious group, as was common practice in more traditional still lifes. This effect is heightened by the dark outlines around the fruit. The round shapes of the objects on the table are echoed in the curve of the table's edge.

Still Life with Three Puppies, 1888

Oil on wood
36⅛×24⅝ inches (92×63 cm)
Museum of Modern Art, New York

In November 1888 Gauguin wrote to Emile Bernard from Arles:

Look at the Japanese, who are certainly excellent draftsmen, and you will see life depicted in the open air and in the sunshine without shadows, color only being used as a combination of tones, various harmonies, giving the impression of warmth etc . . . I would avoid as much as possible that which gives the illusion of a thing, as shadow is the *trompe l'oeil* of the sun, I am constrained to suppress it. If shadows come into your composition as a necessary formula, that is quite another matter . . . So then, my dear Bernard, put in shadows if you consider them useful; or keep them out, it comes to

the same thing, provided you refuse to be at the mercy of shadows.

In this painting Gauguin has used shadows to contribute to the overall design, that under the drinking dish being most marked, while there are only touches of blue paint under the fruit, none under the glasses, and the blue under the puppies is in fact the floral motif on the tablecloth. The effect of pattern-making is enhanced by the artist's grouping of objects into threes. Once again the separate items in a still life stand isolated against the background cloth, rather than united in traditional fashion into a harmonious composition.

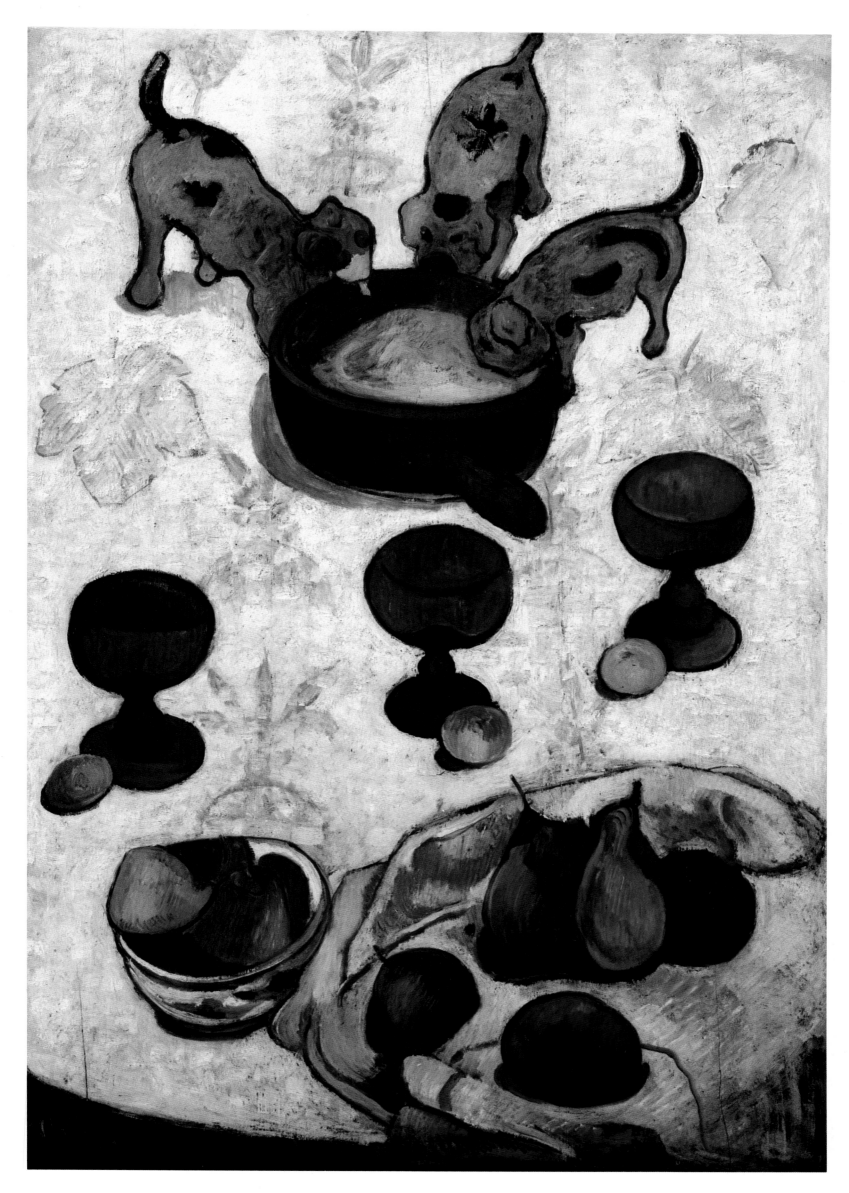

Van Gogh Painting Sunflowers,

1888
Oil on canvas
28¾×36¼ inches (73×92 cm)
National Museum Vincent Van Gogh,
Amsterdam

Gauguin arrived in Arles on 23 October
1888 to stay with Vincent Van Gogh, who
had been proposing since May of that year
that they work together. Theo was paying
Gauguin a monthly allowance of 150 francs
in return for one work and on the understanding that Gauguin would provide
companionship for Vincent, who had set
about decorating the Yellow House in
Arles in anticipation of his friend's arrival.
In November Vincent wrote to Theo that
Gauguin had bought various household
items for his new home and 20 metres of
strong canvas, which he has clearly used in
this work. The effect of the coarse canvas is
to give a much broader, grainy effect.

Painted inside the house at Arles, in a
fairly cramped space, the picture gives the
effect of Gauguin standing above his
friend, with any sense of distance completely suppressed; the easel, for example,
is reduced to a couple of lines. Unlike Gauguin, Van Gogh clearly still worked with
reference to the model as he painted his
sunflowers, despite Gauguin's urging him
to paint more from memory.

The decorative background is painted in
the *cloissoné* style used by both Bernard
and Gauguin in Brittany, so called because
of its resemblance to the technique used in
enamelling in which metal fillets are used
to separate one area of bright color from
another. The intense colors of the boldly
simplified background planes are divided
from each other by use of contours. In its
simplifications and intense colors, this picture also resembles the popular prints
which Gauguin referred to at this time, and
which presented him with alternative conventions for the representation of space in
his work.

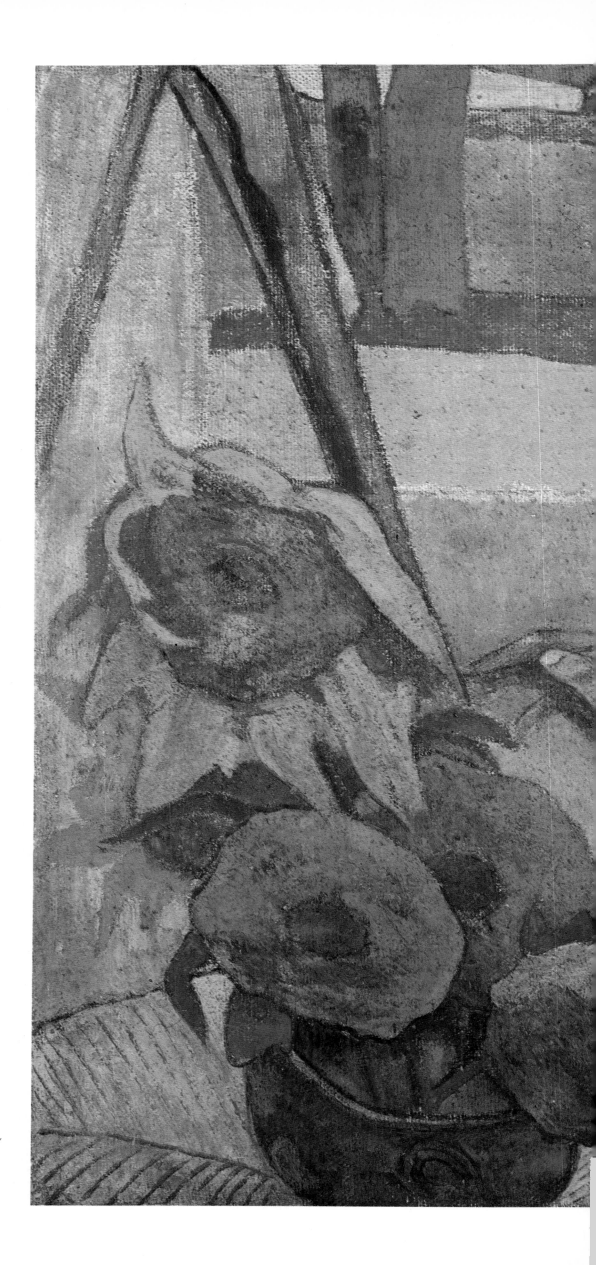

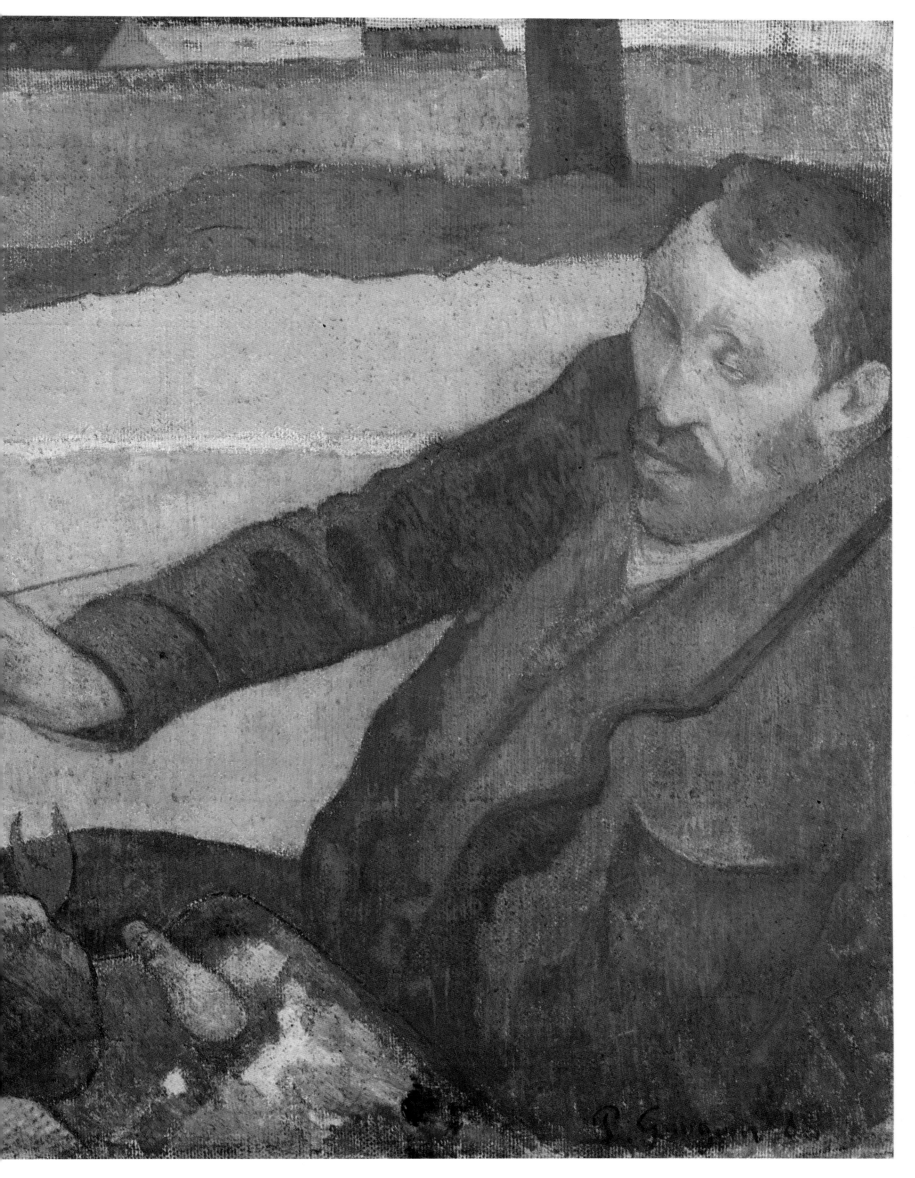

Night Café at Arles (Madame Ginoux), 1888

Oil on canvas
28¾×36¼ inches (73×92 cm)
Pushkin Museum, Moscow

Early in November 1888 Vincent Van Gogh mentioned in a letter to Theo that Gauguin was tackling a painting of the same night café he had already painted in a major canvas (page 17). Gauguin himself wrote to Bernard:

I've done the café which Vincent likes very much and I like rather less. Basically it isn't my thing, and the coarse local color doesn't suit me. I like it well enough in other people's work, but I'm always apprehensive . . . At the top, red wallpaper and three prostitutes. One with hair bristling with hair curlers, the second seen from behind, in a green shawl. The third in a vermilion shawl. At left, a man asleep. A billiard table. In the foreground, a fairly well-finished figure of an Arlésienne with a black shawl and white [indecipherable] in front. Marble table. The picture is crossed by a band of blue smoke, but the figure in front is much too proper. So much for that.

The picture is signed in two places, on the marble-topped table in the foreground and on the billiard table, suggesting that Gauguin reworked the canvas, and from a sketch after the painting, which Gauguin sent Bernard, it is clear that the work was changed at a later date. The picture originally included only the four background figures, the slumped man to the left-hand side and the three prostitutes. The two men who were added later were friends of Van Gogh's, whom he had also portrayed. Perhaps by adding these identifiable figures Gauguin was trying to suggest their relationship to the prostitutes, whom he had apparently seen in the local brothel.

The composition is based on a system of horizontals and verticals, with recession suggested by the horizontal planes of the picture space. The white of Madame Ginoux's bodice and the vermilion of the prostitute's shawl are echoed by the billiard balls.

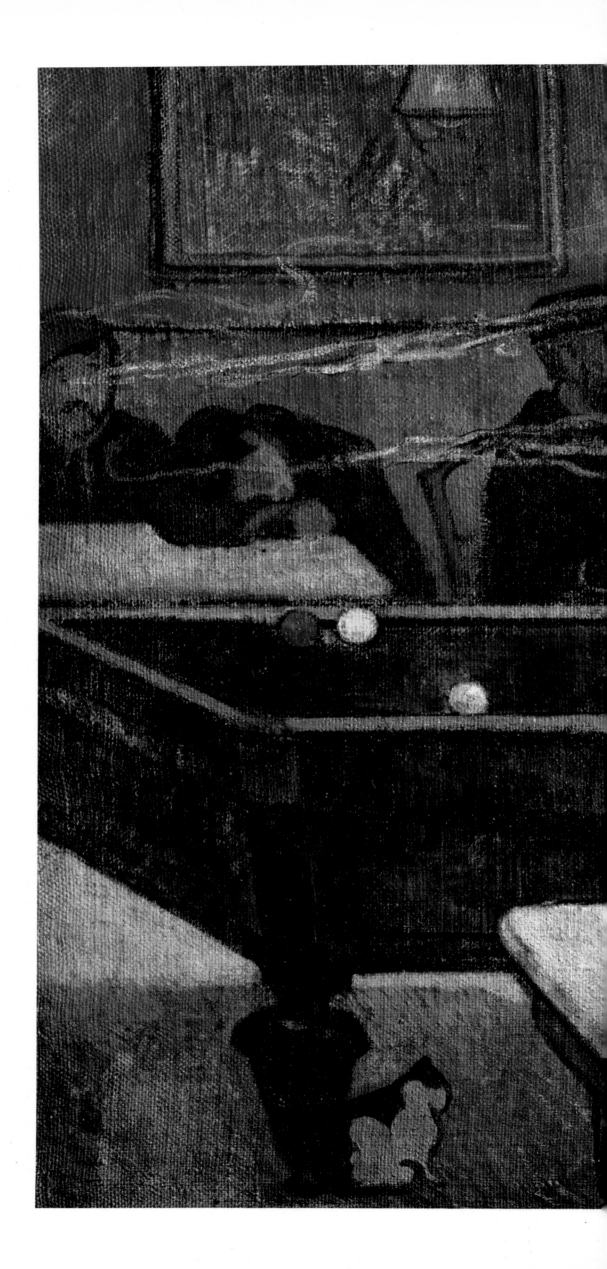

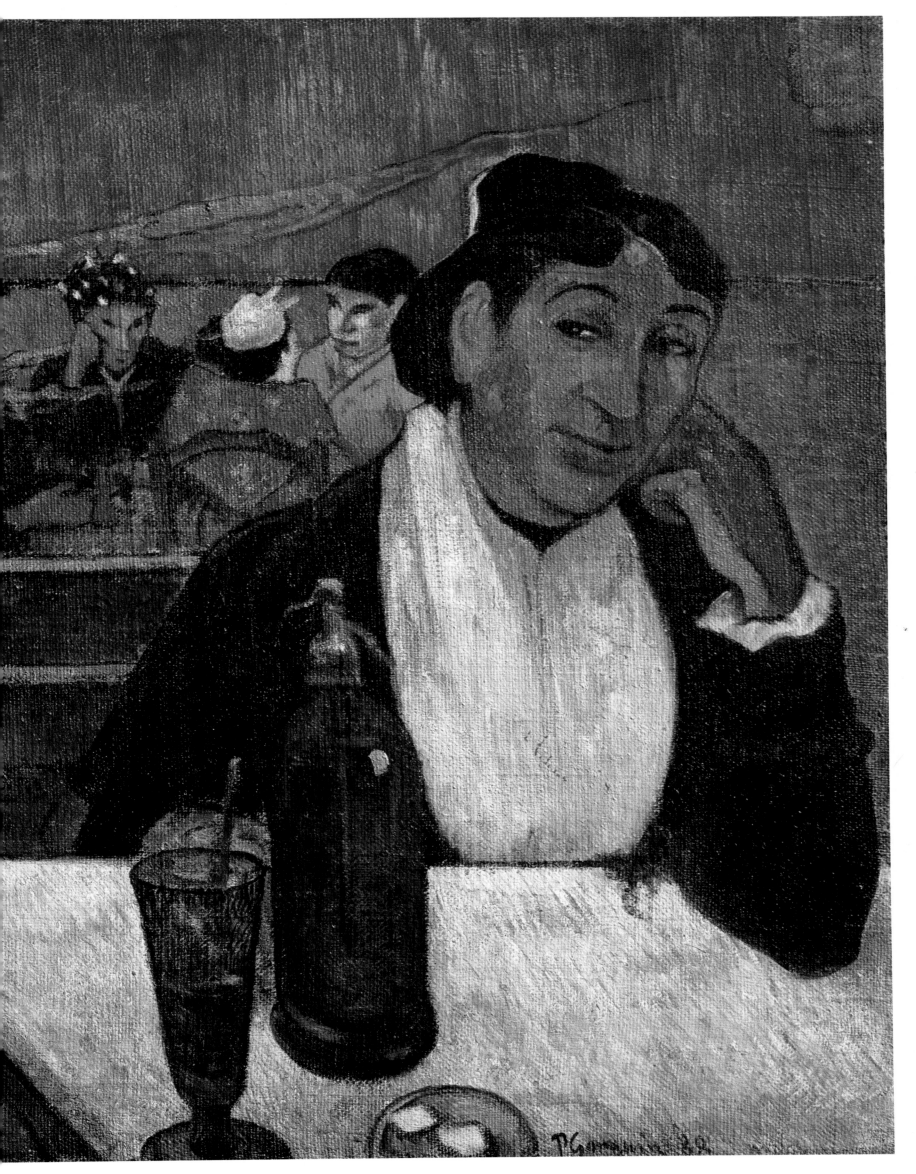

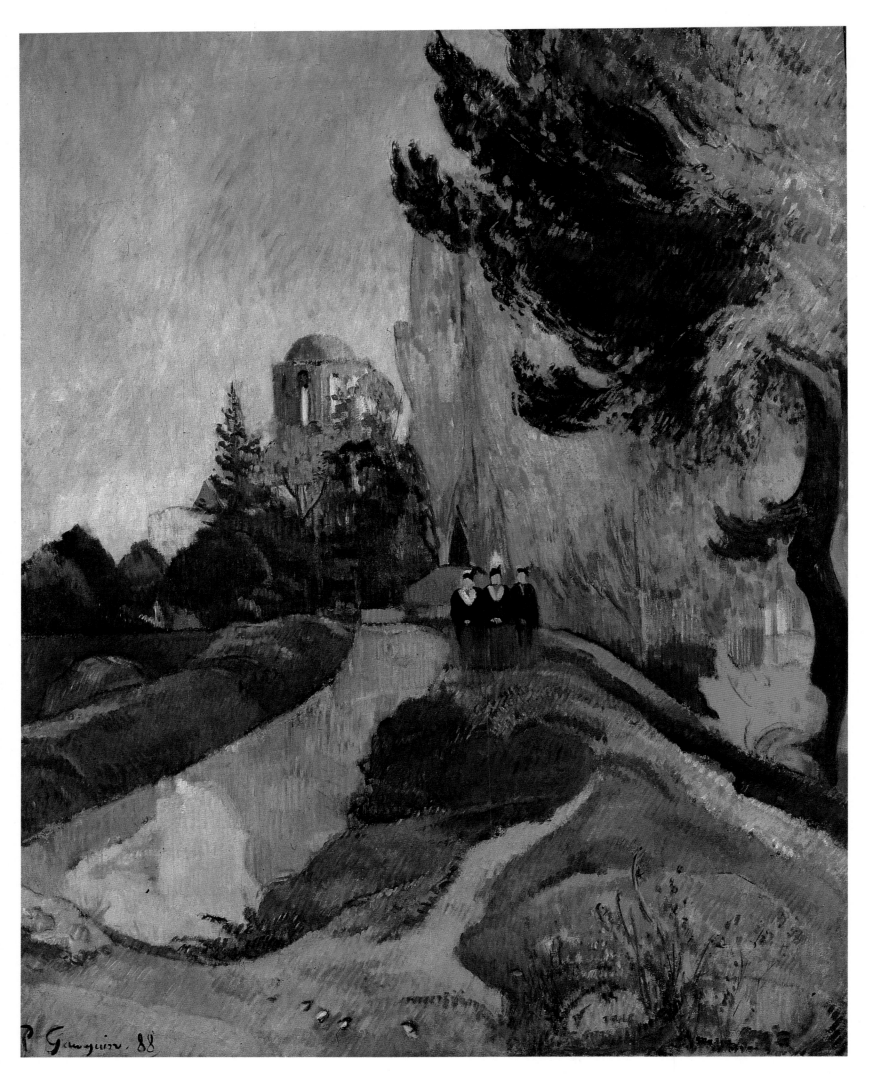

The Alyscamps, 1888

Oil on canvas
36¼×28¾ inches (92×73 cm)
Musée d'Orsay, Paris

In the fall of 1888, shortly after Gauguin arrived in Arles, Vincent Van Gogh wrote to his brother Theo that he was working on a canvas of the Alyscamps. This was an ancient Roman burial ground, with marble tombs lining an avenue punctuated by cypresses. At the end of the road, and in the background of Gauguin's painting, is the partially-ruined twelfth-century church of Saint-Honorat. Van Gogh wrote:

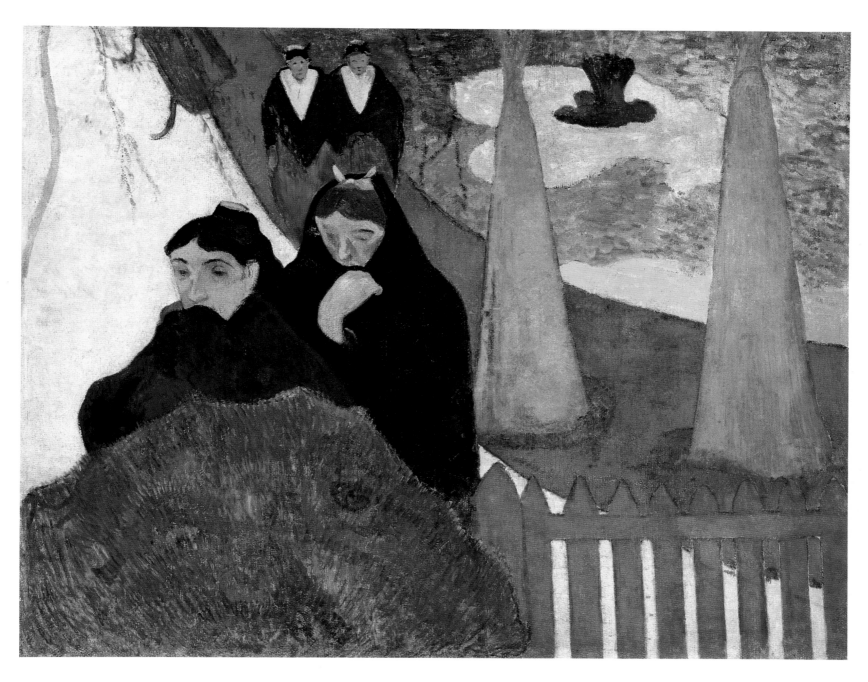

The trees are lined like pillars along an avenue where to right and left there are rows of old Roman tombs of a blue lilac. And then the soil is covered, as with a carpet, by a thick layer of yellow and orange fallen leaves. And they are still falling like flakes of snow . . . And in the avenue little black figures of lovers.

Between them, Van Gogh and Gauguin painted a number of views of this atmospheric and picturesque site. In this work, Gauguin has not exploited the vista offered along the straight, tree-lined avenue, but has focused on the rich coloration of the autumnal landscape, mentioned in his friend's letter. The intense red and deep yellow and the simplified vegetation is reminiscent of Sérusier's *The Talisman* (page 17), painted in September in Brittany under Gauguin's direction.

The lovers whom Van Gogh mentioned in his letter, and who peopled his views of the public gardens in Arles, do not occur in Gauguin's work, but when he sent this canvas to Theo Van Gogh in Paris he jokingly entitled it *The Three Graces at the Temple of Venus*, an ironic reference to the bell-tower of Saint-Honorat in the background and the three Arlésiennes.

Old Women at Arles, 1888

Oil on canvas
28¾×36¼ inches (73×92 cm)
Art Institute of Chicago

Theo Van Gogh bought this canvas from Gauguin for 300 francs, under the title of *Arlésiennes, Mistral*, and the effect is of a cold winter day. The women are huddled up against the wind and the strange conical shapes in the middle distance are possibly young trees swathed in straw as protection against the frost and the mistral.

The painting was probably executed in response to a number of works by Van Gogh depicting public spaces in Arles but he sees the gardens as idyllic places, peopled with lovers. Gauguin, however, has made them a hostile environment, with the pairing of the two sets of figures and the cones imparting a degree of menace. A sense of alienation is suggested by the anonymous faces and the shrub and gate, which effectively separate the figures from the viewer. The foreground woman is probably Madame Ginoux, whose portrait both Van Gogh and Gauguin (page 84) painted; this quotation from another work

confirms that the painting was executed away from the motif.

The paint is applied in large areas of flat wash, apart from the speckled pond in the background and, most notably, the bush in the foreground which is painted with short brushstrokes. It is sometimes suggested that this shrub contains an enigmatic self-portrait; certainly the image of his own face was a constant source of inspiration to Gauguin at this time, and he represented himself in a number of guises, not all of which are immediately identifiable.

Landscape near Arles, 1888

Oil on canvas
36×28½ inches (91×72 cm)
Museum of Art, Indianapolis

Previously thought to represent a Breton scene, this work was painted in Arles in the fall of 1888, despite the fact that hay-making takes place in June in the south of France. The anachronism in this work was not unusual, as Gauguin often painted works in the studio from memory or imagination; this is one such scene which he could never have witnessed. The solid Provençal *mas* in the background allows us to identify this as a southern landscape, but the temptation to assign it to a slightly earlier period is perhaps due to the re-appearance of Cézannesque parallel hatchings in the brushwork and the fluid paint, seen in such earlier works as Oestervold Park, Copenhagen (page 48). Presumably it was to Cézanne that Gauguin looked, in his first confrontation with the Provençal landscape, the solidly constructed land-scapes which Cézanne painted in his native south being very different from the spontaneous impressionist works painted in and around the Ile de France.

At the same time Van Gogh's influence is also apparent in the work, not only in the choice of subject-matter – he used the same theme in a number of his canvases – but also in the pairing of intense blue with a medley of yellows. Once again the two artists have suggested motifs to each other, and Gauguin has attempted a subject which he might otherwise have ignored. He has treated the landscape in a personal way, however, simplifying the elements to geometric shapes, rearranging nature to suit a preconceived idea, grouping to-gether different shapes of haystack to build up the picture space.

Gauguin's haystack is radically different from Monet's famous series of *Haystacks* from three years later. There the stack is merely an opportunity for the artist to ex-plore the effects of light, changing climatic conditions and time of day on the natural elements, and the final effect is one of im-permanence and change, in contrast to the substantial objects depicted by Gauguin.

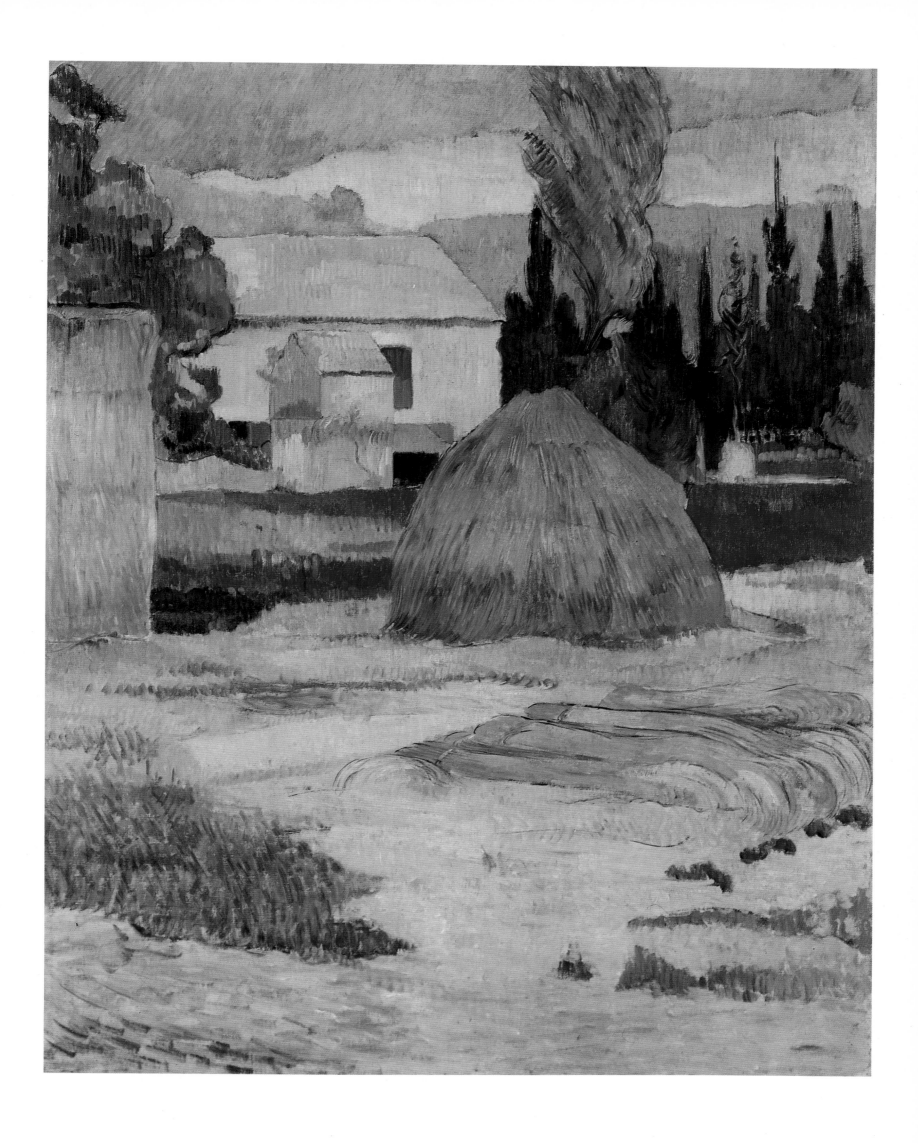

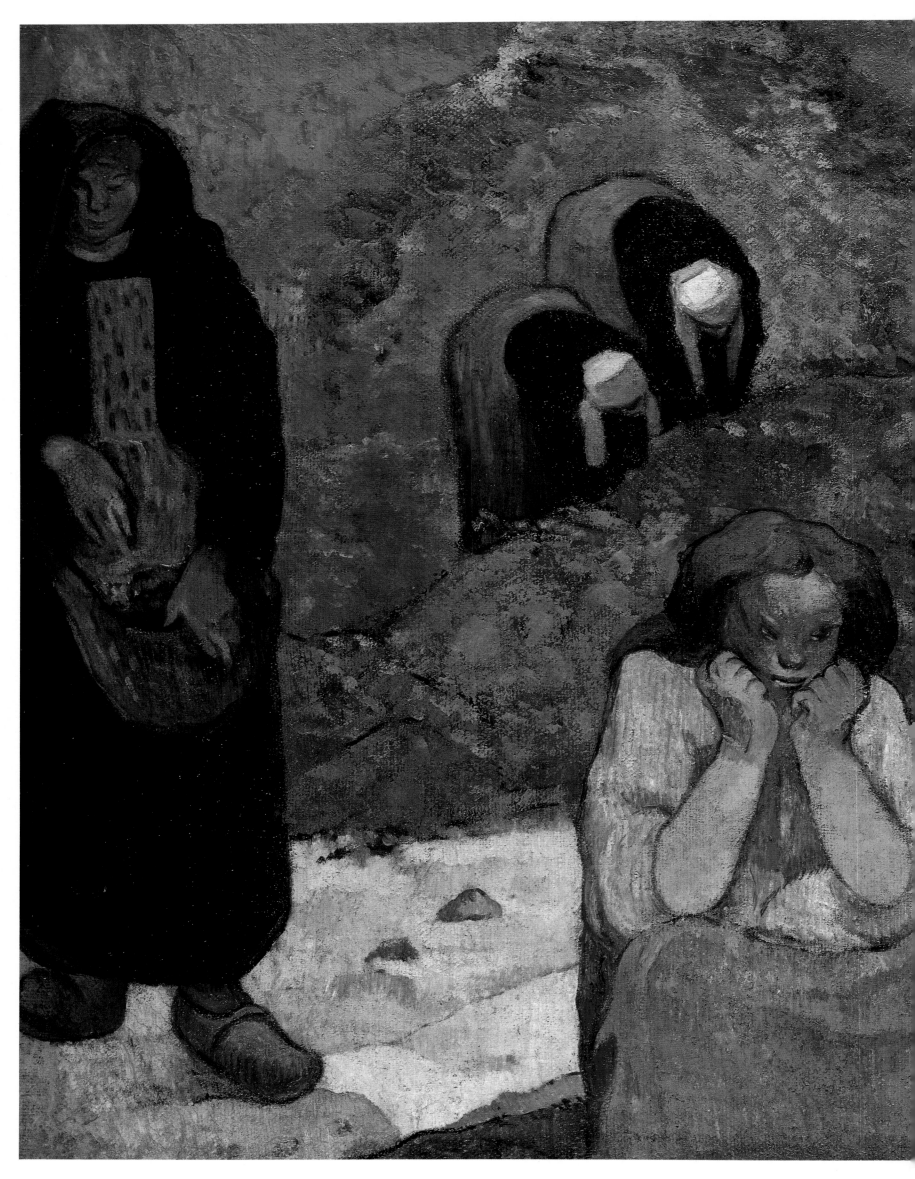

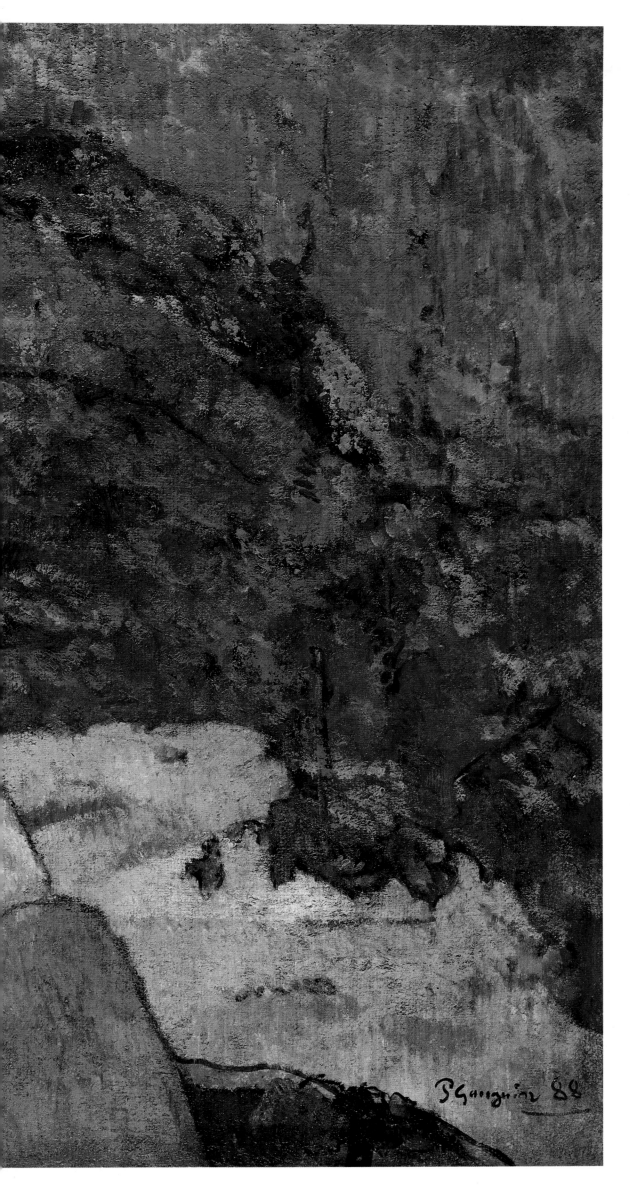

Grape Harvest at Arles, Human Anguish, 1888
Oil on canvas
28¾×36¼ inches (73×92 cm)
Ordrupgaard Collection, Copenhagen

At the beginning of November 1888 Vincent wrote to his brother in Paris:

Just now [Gauguin] has in hand some women in a vineyard, altogether from memory, but if he does not spoil it or leave it unfinished it will be very fine and very unusual.

Gauguin himself described it to Bernard as follows:

. . . purple vines form a triangle on top of chrome yellow. To the left, a Breton woman from Le Pouldu in black with a gray apron. Two bending Breton women wearing blue-green dresses with black bodice. In the foreground, a pink ground and a poor woman with orange hair, a white blouse and a skirt in *terre verte* mixed with white. It is all painted broadly . . . with the palette knife, very thickly on a coarse sackcloth. It is an impression of vines which I saw at Arles. I've placed Breton women there, so much for accuracy. It's the best canvas of this year, and as soon as it's dry I shall send it to Paris.

The work was originally called *Grape Harvest at Arles* but Gauguin renamed it *Human Anguish*, shifting the emphasis from the landscape to the women within it. This new title seems to suggest a symbolic interpretation; the three Breton figures are very similar to those in *Old Women at Arles* (page 87) and the woman with the black shawl over her head looks like a traditional figure of mourning. The central seated figure may also be transposed from Brittany but her lack of headdress makes her difficult to place. She recurs in a number of later works (for example page 110) and is also a direct quotation from a Peruvian mummy which Gauguin had seen in the ethnographic museum in Paris (page 7). She is hunched in a pose which suggests grief and guilt, in particular sexual guilt; perhaps her lack of headdress and her loosened hair is intended to imply a post-coital scene. The harvest behind her suggests fecundity and we may be meant to regard this as a metaphor for human reproduction or, conversely, it may be an ironic comment on her lack of fertility. Certainly the woman expresses great sadness. Gauguin was to continue to explore the subject of female sexuality and guilt, using a number of variations on the theme of Eve and the Fall of Man.

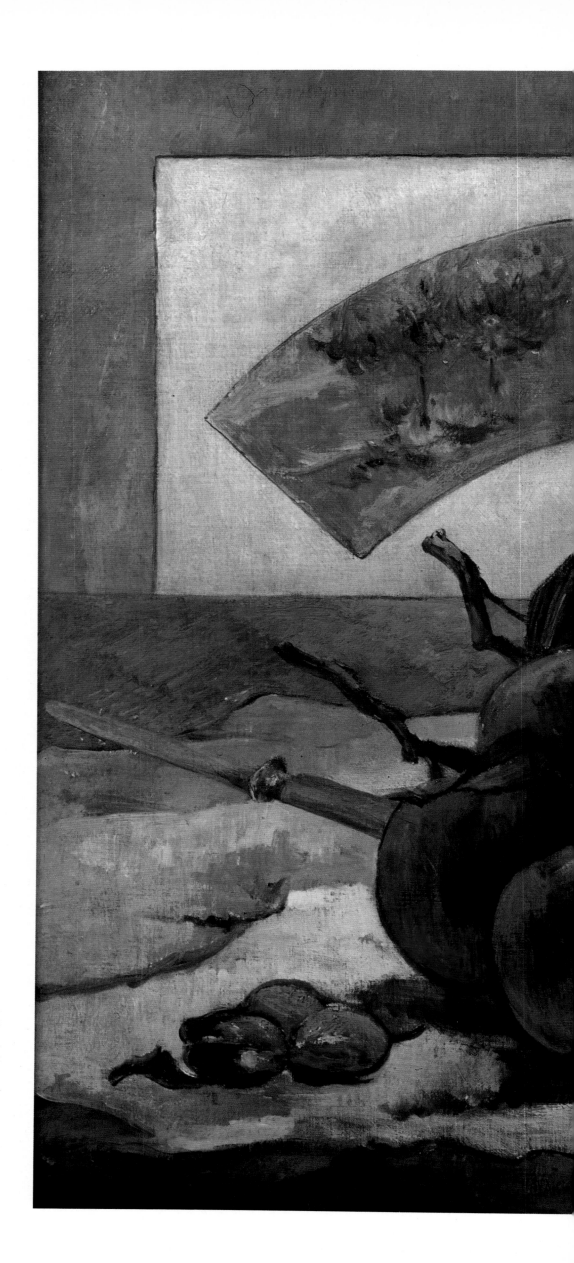

Still Life with Fan, c. 1889

Oil on canvas
19¾×24 inches (50×61 cm)
Musée d'Orsay, Paris

Compared with other still lifes from around this time (pages 79 and 80), in which Gauguin chose a deliberately high angle from which to represent the objects, this work is almost conventional in its depiction of space and in the way in which the elements have been grouped within the painting. The viewer is presented with a clearly discernable tabletop and looks towards a wall in the background, to which the fan is pinned. Even the various objects are similar to those found in traditional still lifes: the white napkin on which the fruits are represented; a plate of fruit which is cut in half by the picture space; and the knife projecting back into the picture space, a traditional device for creating a convincing illusion of recession. The separate elements are held together by the rhythmical line of the napkin. However, Gauguin was not interested in exploring the different textures of the objects represented; the kind of *trompe l'oeil* illusionism of Chardin's still lifes, where the viewer is duped into imagining the fruit is edible, so convincing is it in its realism, did not interest him. The odd horned object in the background is difficult to read, not only because of its unusual shape but also because no clues are given about its tactile qualities. There is nothing to distinguish the flesh of the fruit from the linen of the cloth.

The strange object to the right-hand side is in fact one of Gauguin's ceramics, made in the winter of 1887/8, which he sketched and Van Gogh mentioned in a letter. The fan was probably one of his own works.

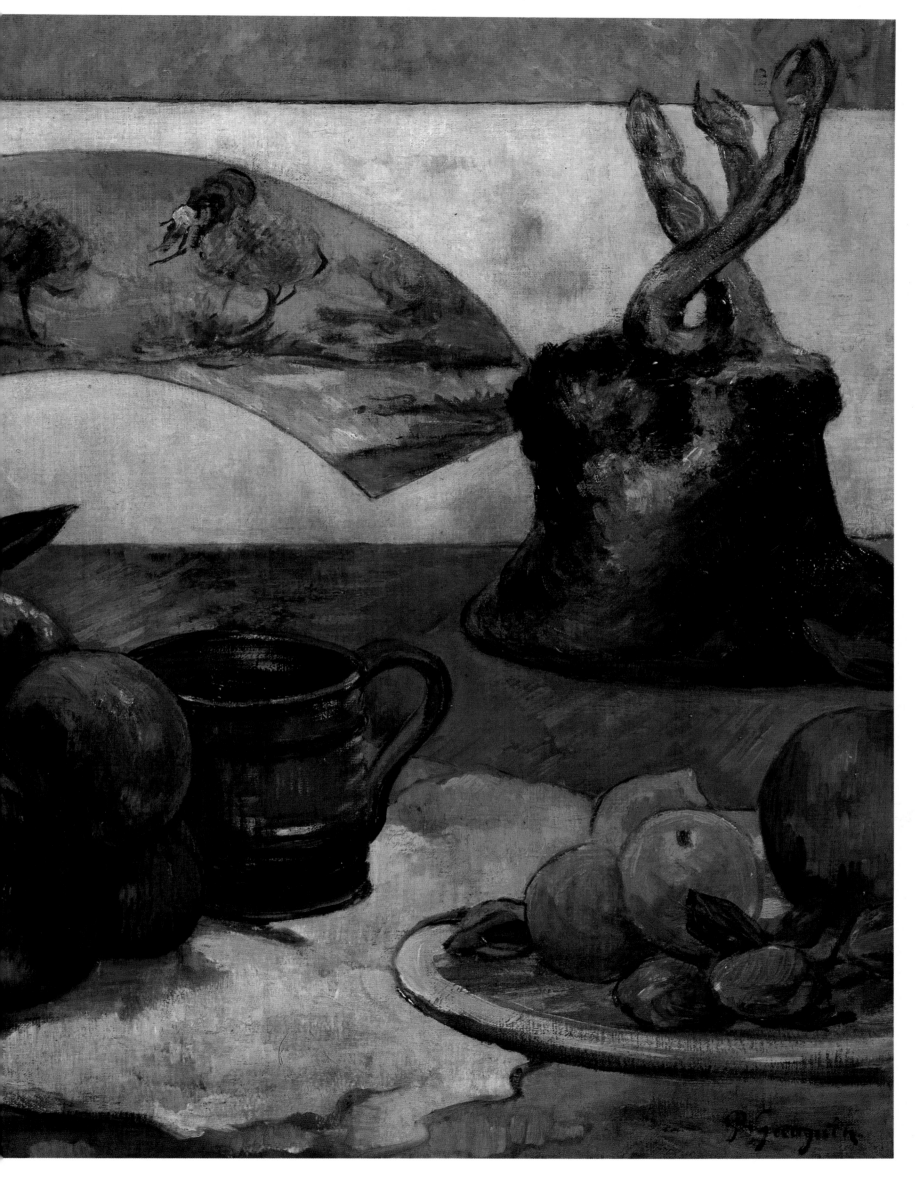

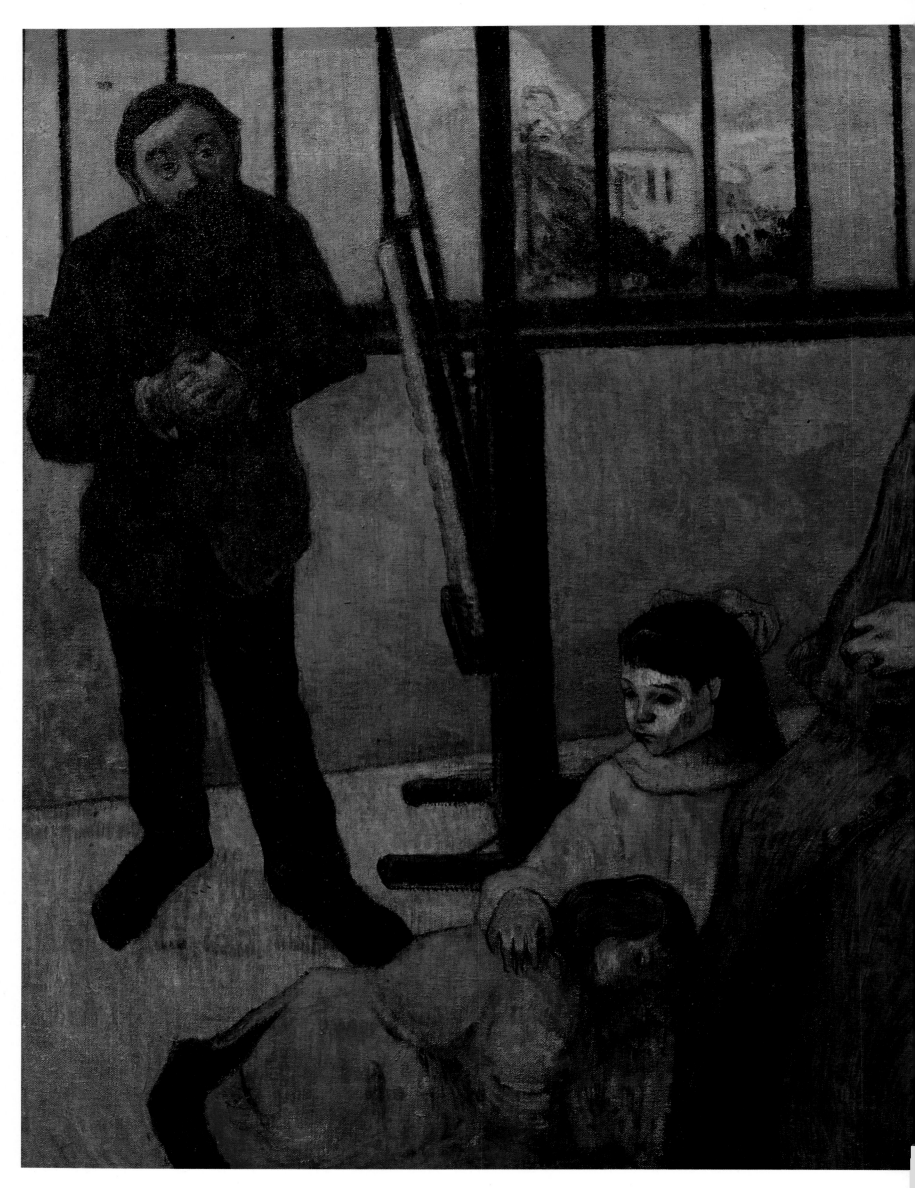

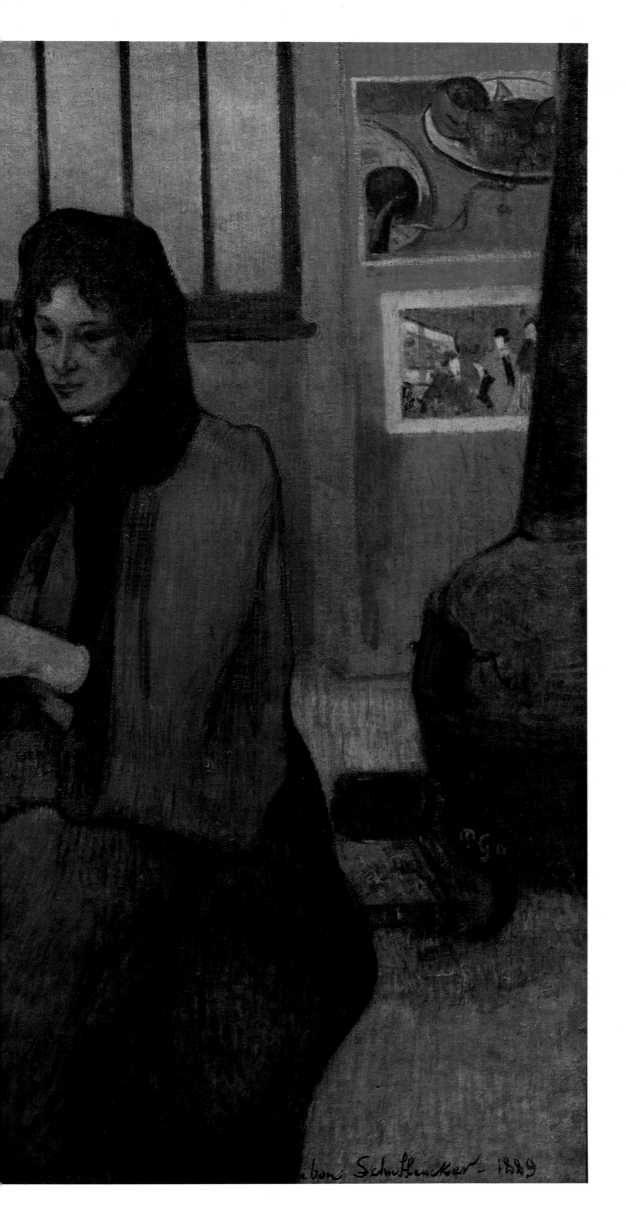

The Schuffenecker Family, 1889

Oil on canvas
28¾×36¼ inches (73×92 cm)
Musée d'Orsay, Paris

After leaving Arles Gauguin spent the next couple of months in Paris, lodging with his friend Emile Schuffenecker (1851-1934) whom he had known since his stock-broking days and who had been an early supporter of his painting. At difficult times in Gauguin's life, it was Schuffenecker who helped him out with money and to whom he turned with domestic problems. Schuffenecker seems to have been very fond of Mette Gauguin and continued to correspond with her even after she and Gauguin had separated, sometimes acting as go-between. His own marriage to Louise Schuffenecker was not a happy one, and this seems to be implied in Gauguin's portrait of the couple with their daughter and son.

The painting was probably done over several months during which Gauguin was living between Brittany and Paris; he and Schuffenecker were engaged in elaborate plans for the Volpini exhibition, which took up much of their energy at this time. It was probably begun in the winter, hence Madame Schuffenecker's heavy outdoor clothing and the burning stove, but finished in the early summer when the exhibition opened, to judge by the fresh green landscape in the background.

Group portraiture was an unusual subject for Gauguin and had not really been tackled since the rue Carcel paintings of his family (pages 34 and 40); he perhaps undertook it out of politeness to his hosts. The work seems to be a thinly veiled comment on his friends' marriage – Madame Schuffenecker is seated, wearing a voluminous indeterminate garment, holding her two children within her orbit like a latter-day Madonna, the three of them forming a tight triangle. The 'good Schuffenecker' to whom the painting is dedicated stands apologetic and isolated beside his easel. The Japanese print on the rear wall attests to one of the main non-western pictorial influences on Gauguin, Schuffenecker and other independent artists at this stage.

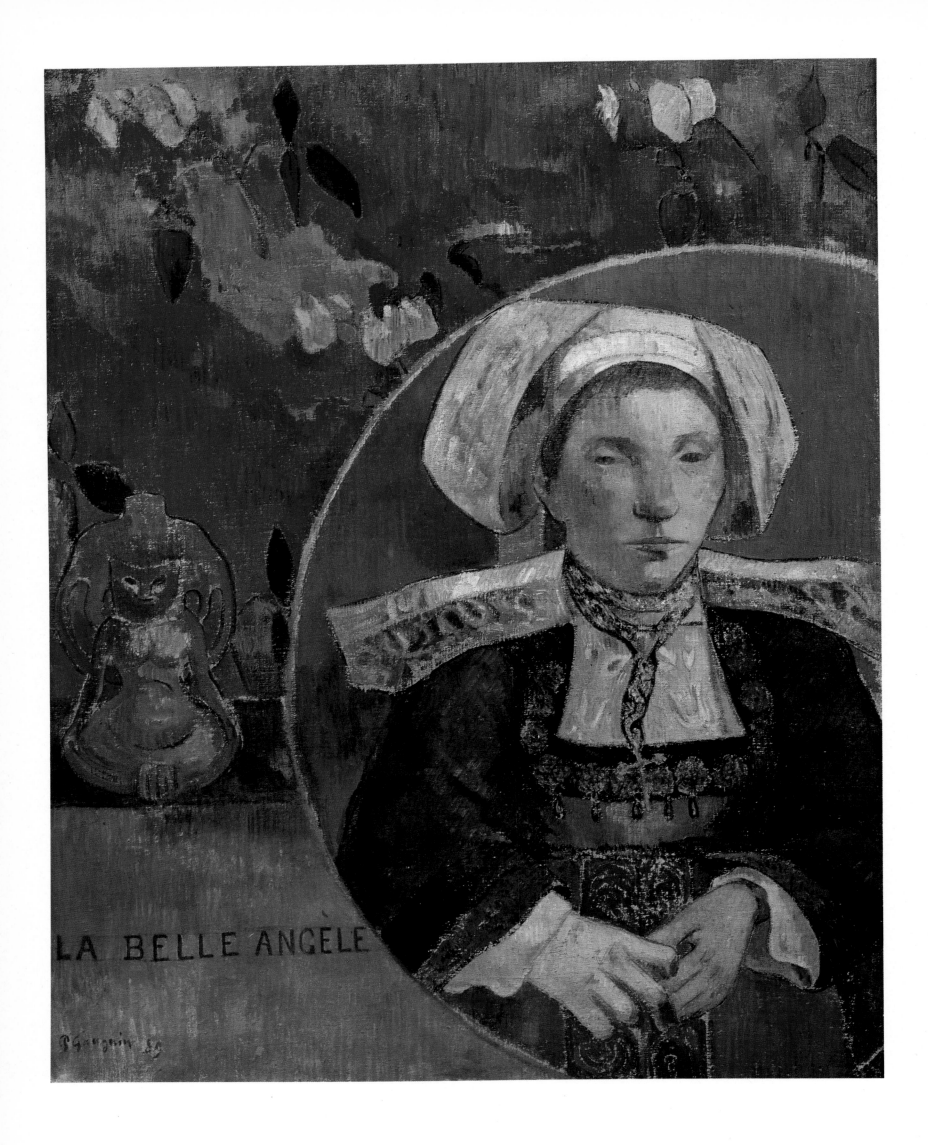

La Belle Angèle, 1889

Oil on canvas
36¼×28¾ inches (92×73 cm)
Musée d'Orsay, Paris

On 5 September 1889 Theo Van Gogh wrote to Vincent:

Gauguin has sent me several new canvases. He says that he hesitated before sending them because they weren't what he had been looking for . . . There's one among them which is a very fine Gauguin. He calls it 'La belle Angèle'. It's a portrait positioned on the canvas like those large heads in Japanese *crépons*, there's the portrait bust and then the background. It's a seated Breton woman, with clasped hands, black costume, lilac apron and small white collar, the frame is gray and the background a beautiful lilac blue with pink and red flowers. The woman rather resembles a young cow, but there is something so fresh and yet at the same time so rustic, that it is very pleasant to look at.

The portrait depicts Madame Marie-Angélique Satre (1868-1932), who gave one of Gauguin's early biographers an account of the sittings. Apparently she was prevailed upon by Gauguin to pose for her portrait, which took him some time to complete and which he seems to have done largely from the model rather than from memory. When he showed it to Madame Satre, she was so appalled at the crude image that she refused to have the work. Clearly Gauguin's so-called primitive Breton works did not impress the natives.

Theo's assessment of the woman's bovine appearance is a fair one; Gauguin certainly seems to be interested in conveying her passivity, giving her an almost icon-like quality in the devotional pose and the meticulous detail of her garments. The circular image of the young woman has been set in front of, or more strictly alongside (for western spatial conventions are inappropriate here), an exotic idol and an area composed of flowers reminiscent of the background of *Les Misérables* (page 74), where a similar floral area denoted innocence. Theo's description of the work is interesting for the way in which he has tried to conjure up the image to his absent brother. He has laid great emphasis on the role of color in the work, as in Gauguin's own descriptions of his paintings, where it occupies a central place to convey feelings and emotions.

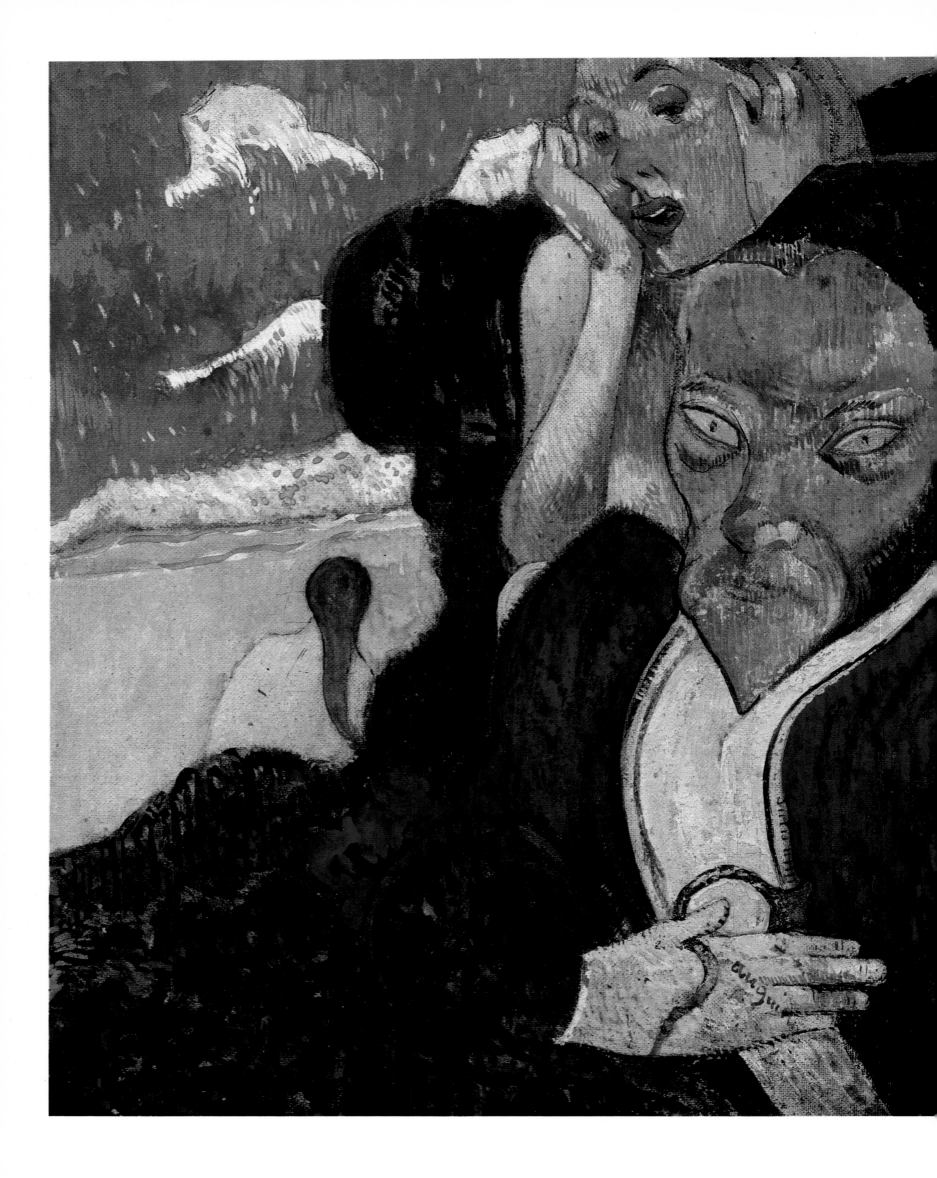

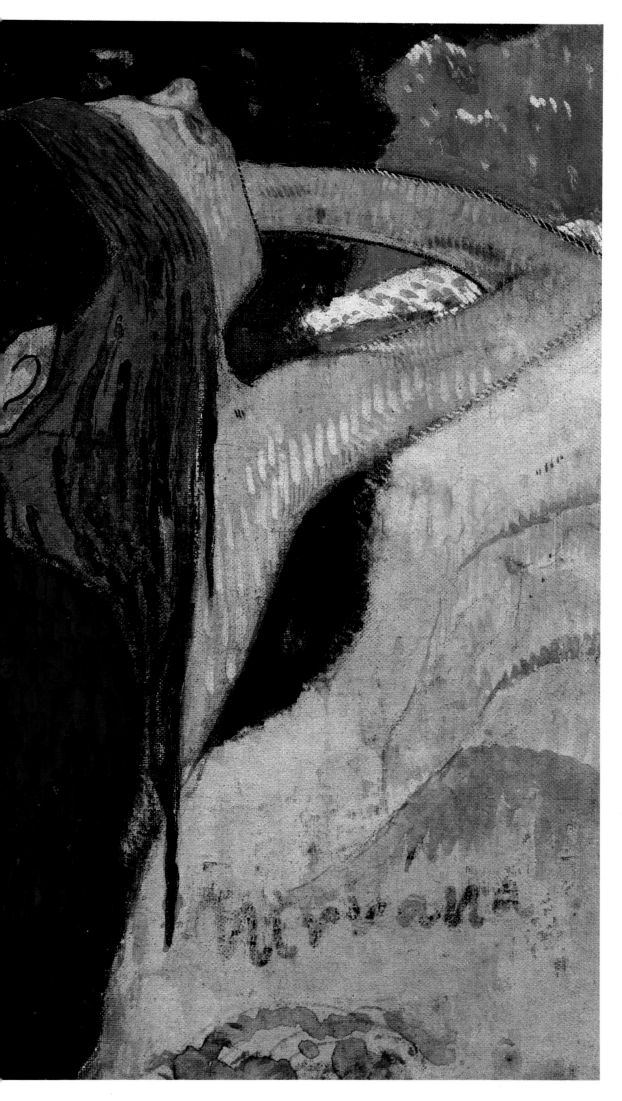

Nirvana, Portrait of Meyer de Haan, 1889

Essence on silk
8×11½ inches (20×29 cm)
Wadsworth Atheneum, Hartford

This small work is painted on silk in *essence*, oil thinned with turpentine and used like watercolor, a favorite medium of Degas. It represents Gauguin's friend Jacob Meyer de Haan (1852-95), who joined him and Sérusier in Le Pouldu, a remote village 15 kilometres from Pont-Aven, in the summer of 1889. The work was probably painted then, or it may date from 1890. This is one of a number of portraits which Gauguin made of the Belgian, who continued to reappear in his work until the end of his life. The last instance was in 1902, in *Contes Barbares* (page 170), when Meyer de Haan had been dead for some time. In this work Gauguin has caricatured his friend; he appears demonic, with slanting staring eyes and his beard and ear sharpened to points. The background women against whom Meyer de Haan leans are in fact derived from a composite of two other paintings by Gauguin, *Woman in the Waves (Ondine)* (page 106) and *Women Bathing, Life and Death*, both painted in 1889.

Gauguin has signed the work on the sitter's hand, and the capital 'G' of 'Gauguin' is composed of the head and body of the serpent which Meyer de Haan holds. The use of a snake, with its reference to temptation and the Fall of Man, was widely used by the artist at this time, notably in the *Self-Portrait* (page 102), which is itself linked to another portrait of Meyer de Haan. On the bottom right-hand side the work's title has been inscribed: 'Nirvana'. The use of this Buddhist term gives some indication of the philosophical interests of the people in Gauguin's circle at this time, which were closely aligned with Symbolist theories.

Bonjour Monsieur Gauguin, 1889

Oil on canvas
44½×36¼ inches (113×92 cm)
Narodni Gallery, Prague

'Gauguin and I went yesterday to Montpellier to see the museum there and especially the Brias [Bruyas] room', Vincent Van Gogh wrote to Theo in December 1888. 'There are lots of portraits of Brias, by Delacroix, Ricard, Courbet . . .' In the museum they saw Courbet's *Bonjour M. Courbet* (page 18), which represents Bruyas and his servant, accompanied by a dog, greeting the artist, who is in the guise of a wandering Jew. Gauguin's work, painted in response to this after a gap of some months, bears little overt resemblance to its prototype; instead the artist encounters a woman in Breton clothing and there is none of the meeting of personalities which occurs in the Courbet. Gauguin has, however, preserved some of the feeling of the original. The sense of the artist as outsider, which Courbet had suggested by his depiction of the wandering

Jew, was transposed in Gauguin to the bohemian outcast, suggested by his jaunty beret, his heavy overcoat and clogs. It is also hinted at by the gate between the two figures, similar in intention to that in *Old Women at Arles* (page 87), which suggests a psychological divide between the figures and the viewer. The rather hostile landscape in *Bonjour M. Gauguin* may also have roots in the Arles work. The dog in Courbet is here reduced in size, which adds to the slightly comic touch of the work.

This is one of a number of self-portraits from this time, and two versions treat this particular theme. The work clearly assumed an important place in Gauguin's oeuvre; when he returned from Tahiti in 1893 and held a one-man exhibition at Durand-Ruel's gallery, the vast majority of his works were from Tahiti, but he felt compelled to include this picture.

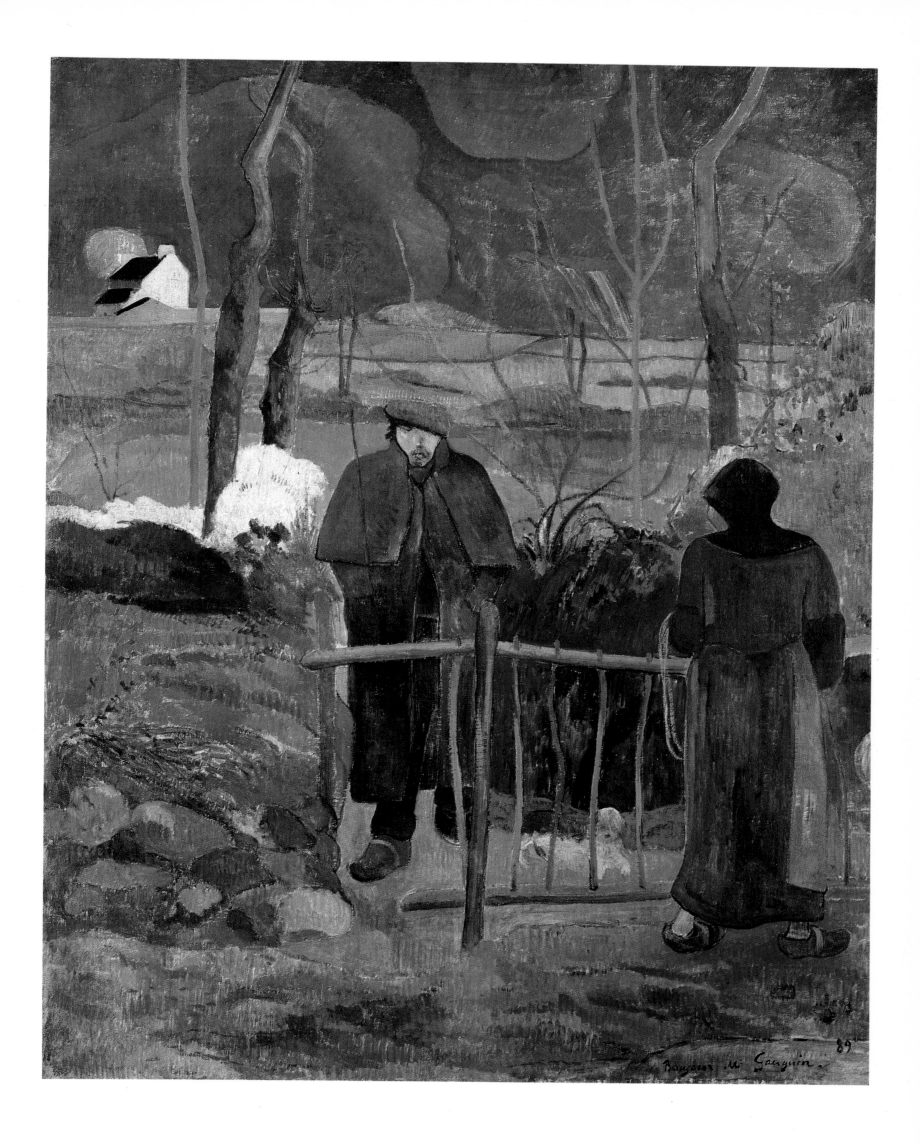

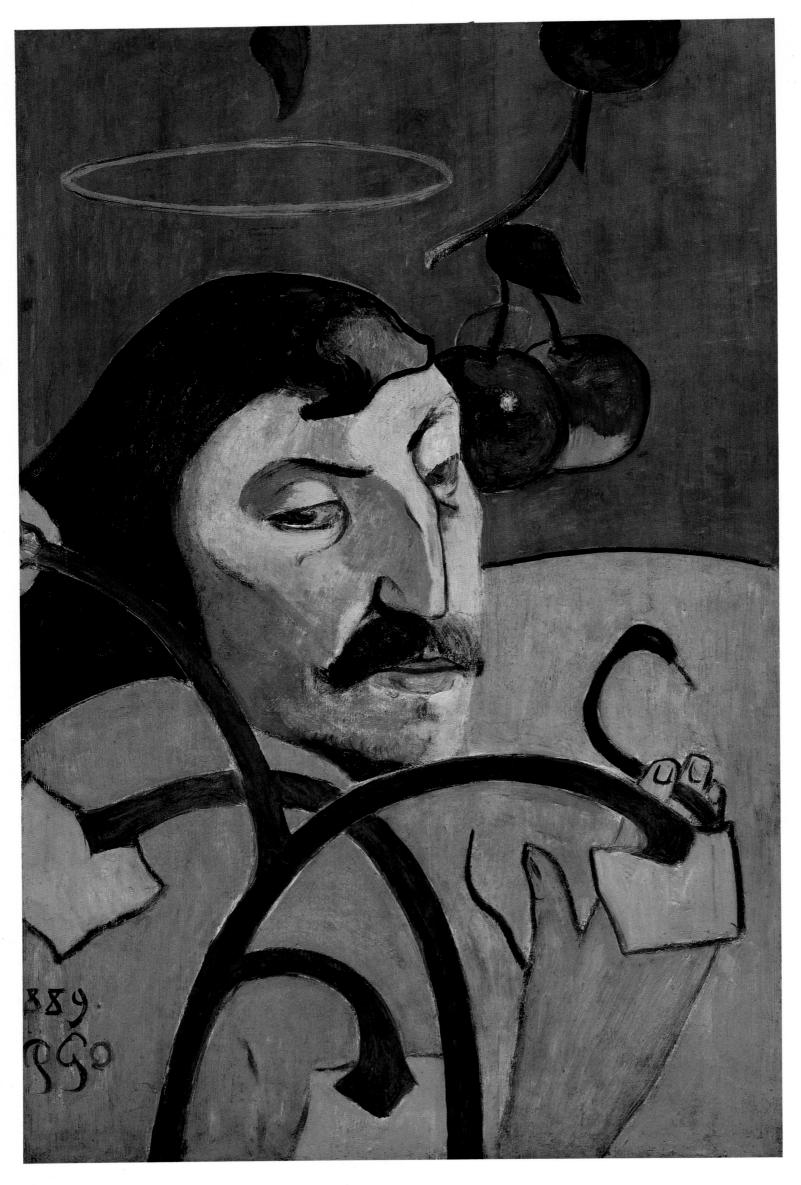

Self-Portrait with Halo, 1889

Oil on wood
31¾×20¼ inches (79.2×51.3 cm)
National Gallery of Art, Washington

In the summer of 1889 Gauguin was working at Le Pouldu with Sérusier and Meyer de Haan and stayed at an inn in the village run by Marie Henry, with whom Meyer de Haan was having an affair. Towards the end of the year they decorated the dining room with a series of paintings which were later removed and sold piecemeal. Gauguin painted this work on the wooden door of a cupboard, with a portrait of Meyer de Haan on the opposite door. The works function together as a pair; their treatment is very similar and the symbols used in each are inextricably linked. In both there is a great degree of simplification, partly because of the synthetist methods which Gauguin had adopted at the time, but also because of his rapid working procedures and the constraints of decorating on wood.

The paint is applied with broad sweeps of brilliant color, the intense reds and yellows echoed in the portrait of his friend. The bright red ground, similar to that in the *Vision after the Sermon* (page 76), symbolizes the demonic aspect of Gauguin's nature, while the yellow represents greatly simplified angel wings. This duality is echoed in the halo and the apples of temptation. Gauguin's role as the controler of temptation is underlined by the serpent that he holds, similar to that in *Nirvana* (page 98). The apples refer to the Fall of Man and woman's responsibility for the dismissal from Paradise. The apples recur in the portrait of Meyer de Haan on the other door, and may therefore also allude more specifically to Marie Henry and hence to sexual jealousy.

The graceful curving lines and the caricatural aspect of the features, coupled with the flat application of colors, resemble Japanese prints which Gauguin studied at this time.

Christic in the Garden of Olives (Agony in the Garden), 1889

Oil on canvas
28¾×36¼ inches (73×92 cm)
Norton Gallery of Art, West Palm Beach,
Florida

The critic Aurier found much to illustrate
his Symbolist theories in this work and
wrote of:

. . . the sublime *Garden of Olives* where a Christ
with rosy hair, seated in a desolate site, seems
to cry with the inexpressible sadness of dream,
the agony of fantasy, the treachery of contin-
gencies . . .

After completing the work toward the end
of 1889, Gauguin sent a sketch and
description of it to Vincent Van Gogh, who
wrote to Theo:

The thing is that I have worked this month in
the olive groves, because they [Gauguin and
Emile Bernard] have maddened me with their
Christs in the Garden, with nothing really
observed. Of course with me, there is no
question of doing anything from the Bible –
and I have written to Bernard and Gauguin too
that I considered that to think, not to dream,
was our duty, so that I was astonished looking
at their work that they had let themselves go so
far. For Bernard has sent me photographs of the
canvases. The trouble about them is that they
are a sort of dream or nightmare . . . How I
would like to see Gauguin's and Bernard's
studies from nature . . .

In this painting Gauguin has developed
the theme of artist as martyr, which he had
first explored in *Self-Portrait (Les Misérables)* (page 74), but here he has disguised
the self-portrait as a religious work. The
idea of comparing himself to Christ was
not new. At an exhibition of his work and
other paintings from his collection held in
Copenhagen in 1889, a Danish critic wrote
an assessment of Cézanne's *Castle at
Médan* which clearly benefited from remembered conversations with Gauguin
rather than from his own assessment of the
picture:

. . . the path winding across the broken ground
through the young trees reminded a French
painter – the owner of the picture – of the
lonely path along which Christ wandered in
somber thought towards the Mount of Olives.

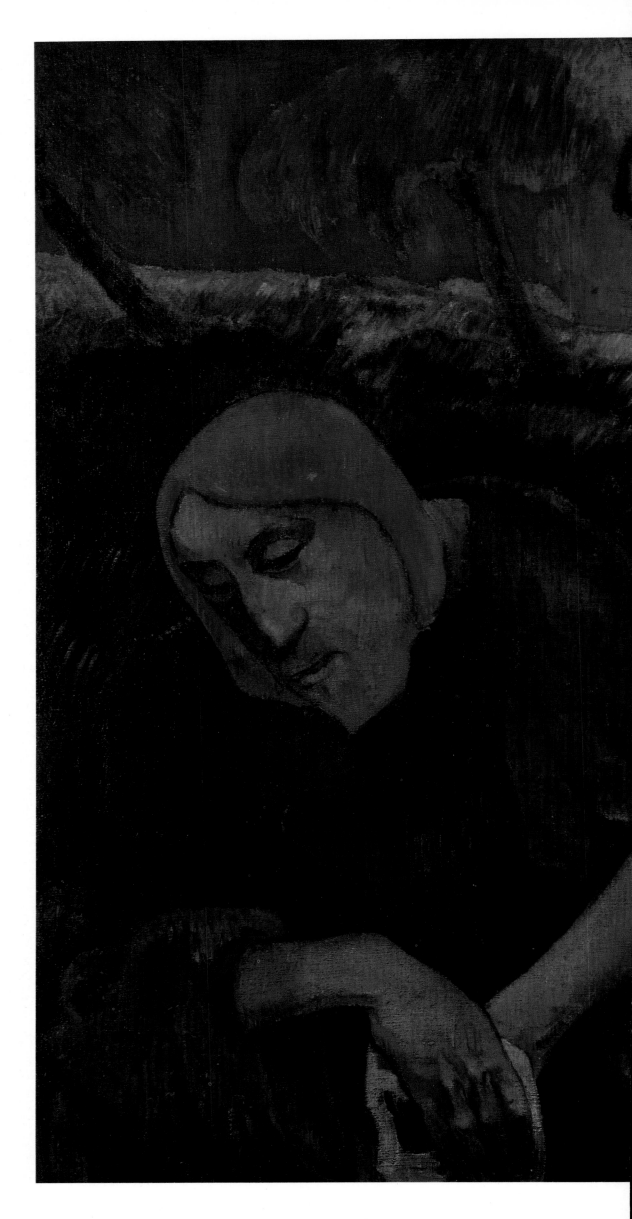

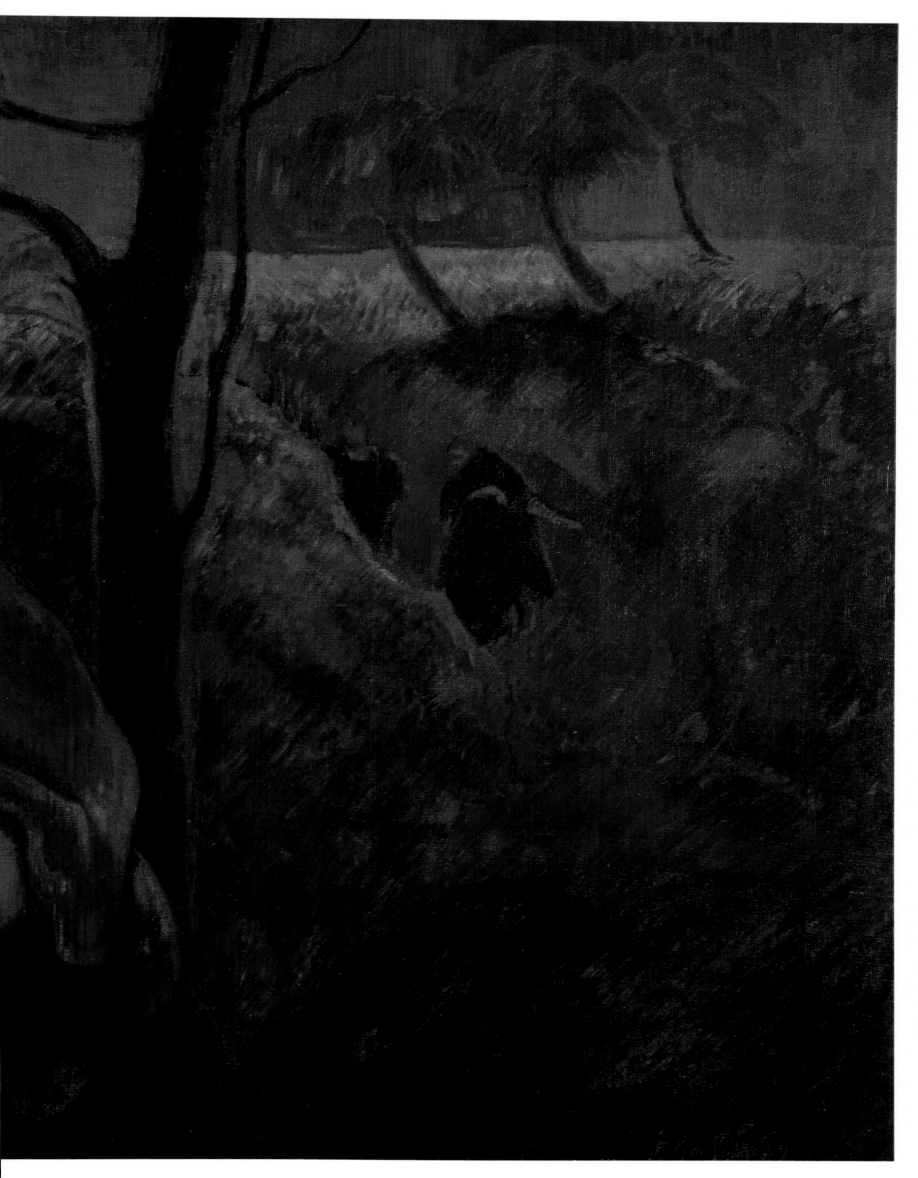

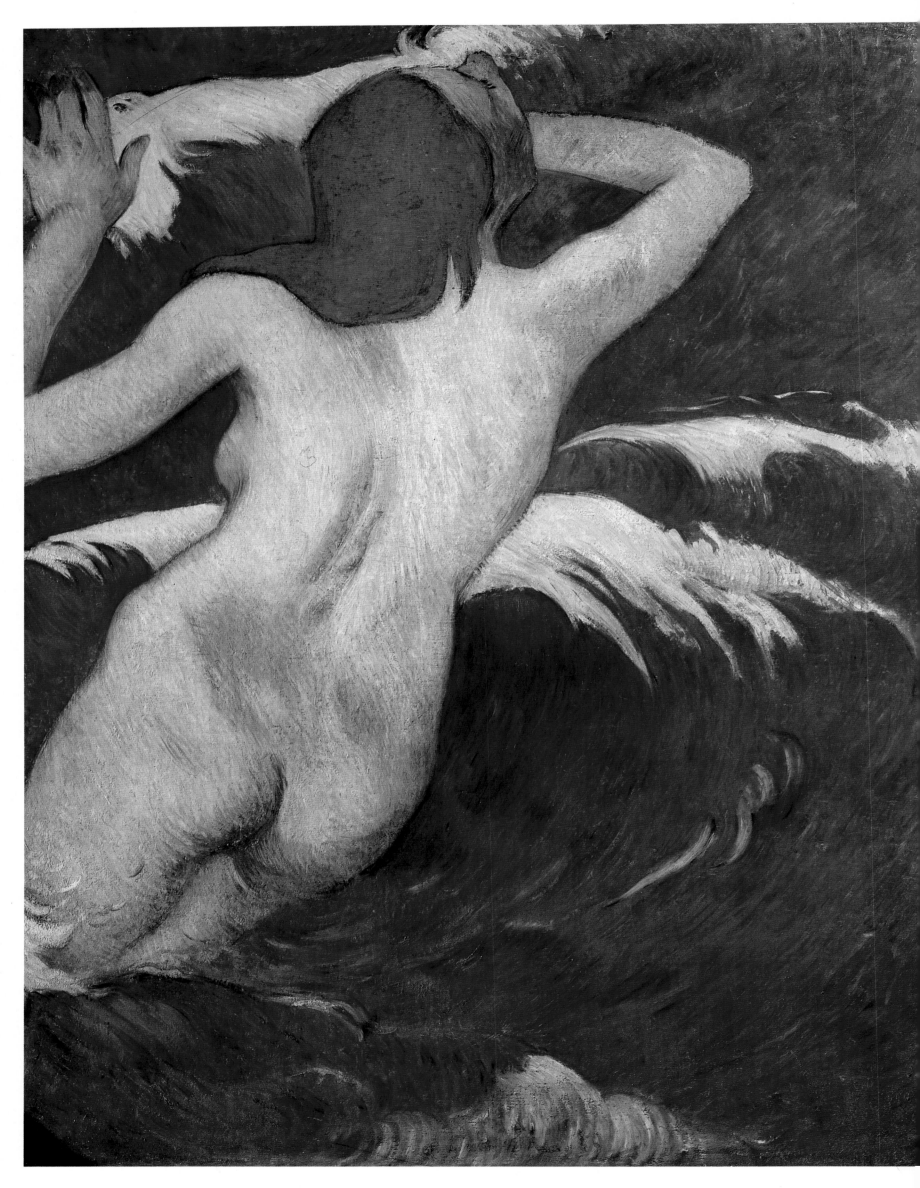

Woman in the Waves (Ondine),
1889

Oil on canvas
36¼×28⅜ inches (92×72 cm)
Cleveland Museum of Art

With its companion, *Women Bathing, Life and Death, Woman in the Waves (Ondine)* was exhibited with Gauguin's most important recent work at the Volpini exhibition in Paris in the early summer of 1889, and the image of *Life and Death* was used on the cover of the catalog; clearly Gauguin regarded these as outstanding works in his oeuvre. The theme of women and the evolutionary process is common to both, but the paintings' iconography defies any straightforward explanation and is rather an attempt to explore central questions of existence. The female nude had not been a favorite subject for the artist since the heavy realism of *Suzanne Sewing* (page 32) and here her re-emergence suggests a sexual theme. The suggestion of fear in the crouching woman in *Life and Death* contrasts with the exhilaration of *Ondine*; this theme of the duality of woman's nature was frequent in Gauguin's art.

The symbolic intentions of *Ondine* are quite overt. Gauguin has looked to the myth of the water-sprite that can only become human by bearing a child fathered by a human. The life-giving nature of sexual love is treated in a symbolic way: abandonment is suggested by the woman outstretched in the frothy waves. There is none of the angst-ridden tension of *Life and Death*, and the woman's ostentatiously upheld arms and the curves of her body suggest that Gauguin may have looked to current theories about upsweeping lines as being an effective way of suggesting joyousness.

At the same time the painting must be regarded as more than merely an exposition of literary Symbolism. Gauguin has worked using the synthetic method, abstracting the essentials of the subject to form a coherent composition. The flattening of the body, with its curves echoed in the sweeping waves, owes much to Japanese precedents. The choice of a red-headed woman to sharpen the intensity of the bluey-green waters is deliberate, as is the prominent red signature and date.

This woman was to recur in later works, and in each further treatment she became simpler and more synthetic. She reappeared in a pastel drawing, and on a fan. In the former Gauguin gave her dark hair, but on the decorative fan he retained the pairing of orangey-red and bluey-green.

Yellow Christ, 1889

Oil on canvas
36¼×28¾ inches (92×73 cm)
Albright-Knox Art Gallery, Buffalo

In the *Yellow Christ* Gauguin returned to religious subject-matter for the first time since the *Vision after the Sermon* (page 76), painted a year previously, and the two works have certain similarities. Gauguin has focused on the kneeling Breton peasant women who are grouped around a simple wooden crucifix, but the whole is reminiscent of the three Maries at the foot of the cross on Calvary. The division between reality and imagination is blurred, or rather the imaginary experience becomes real because of the faith of the simple peasant women, much as in the *Vision*. The autumnal background, with its acid yellows and oranges, is not faithful to the biblical version of the crucifixion, but helps to convey a strong impression of sadness. The three Breton figures crossing the wall in the middle distance are quite unaware of the religious experience in the foreground.

In this painting Gauguin worked in a synthetic fashion, gradually distilling and simplifying his subject-matter and trying to convey his message as forcibly as possible. The figure of Christ on the cross was initially suggested to him when he saw a small seventeenth-century polychromed crucifix in the church at Trémalo near Pont-Aven. He sketched this and then worked on the finished oil painting from the rough drawing. The undulating lines of the figures are echoed in the landscape and tie the whole together, while the foliage on the trees is reduced to simple organic shapes. Octave Mirbeau in the *Echo de Paris* wrote about this work:

In a completely yellow landscape, a dying yellow, on top of a Breton hillside which the end of autumn turns a sad yellow, under a heavy sky, there is a wooden calvary, clumsy, rotting, disjointed, which stretches its warped arms into the air. Christ . . . roughly cut from a tree-trunk by a local artist, a pitiful and barbaric Christ, is daubed in yellow. At the foot of the Calvary, some peasants are kneeling. Unconcerned, their bodies collapsing heavily into the earth, they have come there because it is customary to go there on Pardon days . . . the sadness of this wooden Christ is inexpressible, his head is full of awful sadnesses . . . he seems to say to himself, seeing these miserable and ignorant creatures at his feet "What if my martyrdom has been in vain?"

The head of Christ is similar to that in *Christ in the Garden of Olives* (page 104) and invites a similarly autobiographical interpretation.

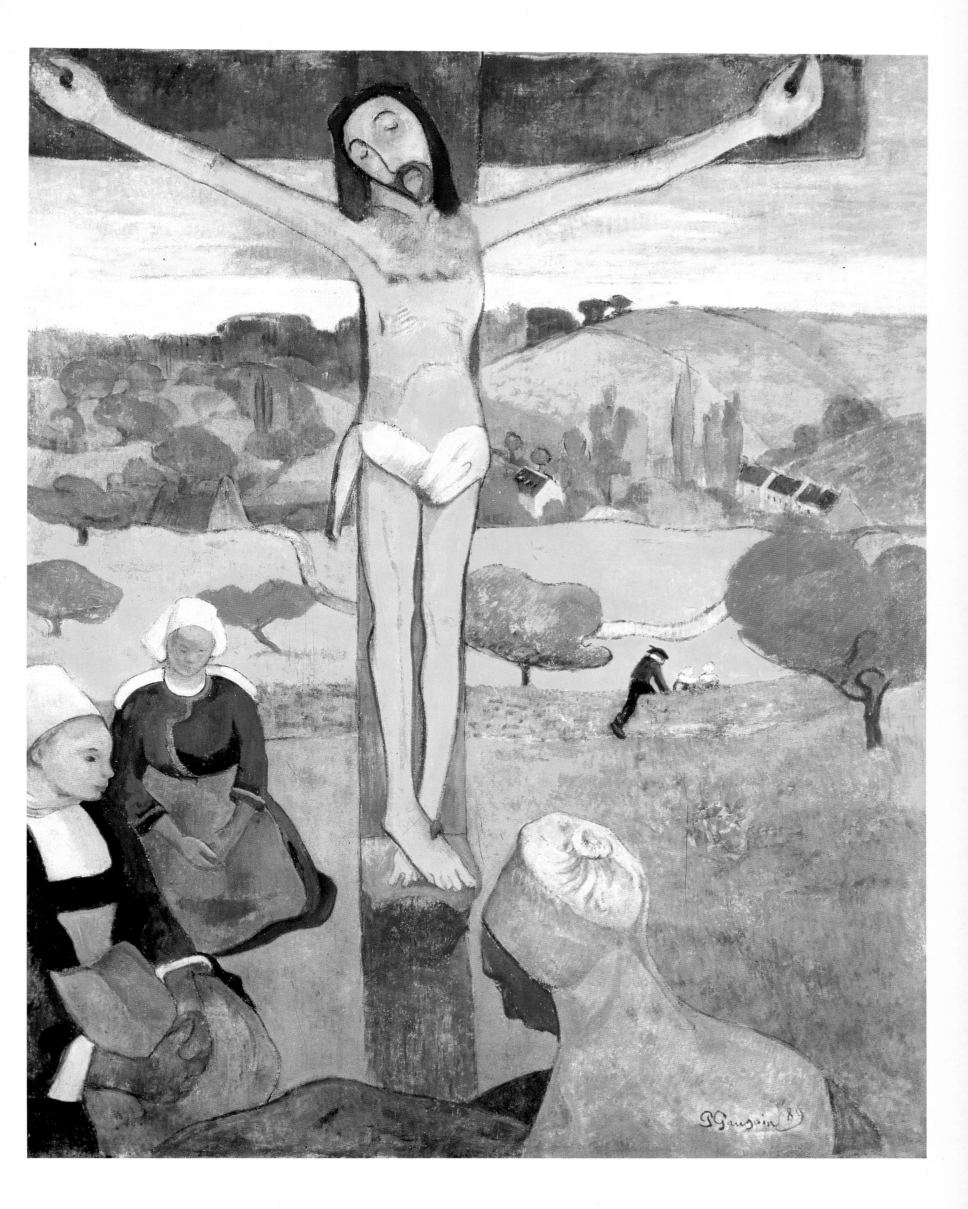

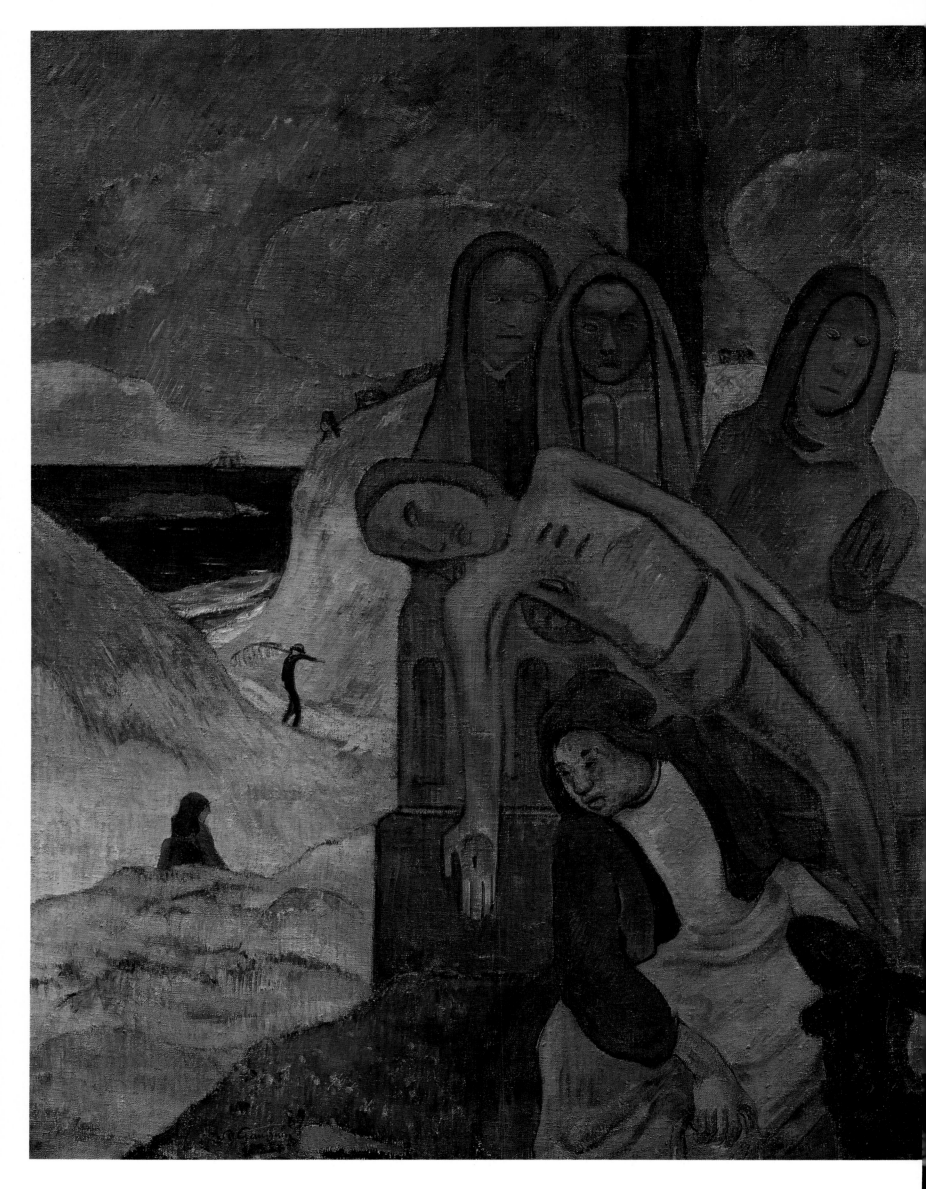

Green Christ (Breton Calvary), 1889

Oil on canvas
36¼×28¾ inches (92×73 cm)
Musées Royaux des Beaux-Arts de Belgique, Brussels

Returning once again to the religious theme explored in the *Vision after the Sermon* (page 76) and the *Yellow Christ* (page 108), Gauguin has tried to penetrate what he perceived as the 'savage' character of Brittany and its religious rituals. Together with the *Yellow Christ, Green Christ* is Gauguin's most highly developed synthetist work, in which he progressed by a process of elimination towards a strong, simple image. The somber mood of the deposition is carried through into the violets and blues of the sky and the oval clouds duplicate the circular faces of the stone figures. It was only towards the end of 1889 that Gauguin abandoned the rather superficial aspects of Brittany which he had depicted until then, and went in search of traditional native art as a source of imagery. The sense of continuity, and of a people rooted to a cyclical progression, is echoed in the dramatic and moody landscape.

As in the *Yellow Christ* Gauguin has looked to Breton folk art for inspiration, in this case a calvary which he found at Nizon, near Pont-Aven. The stone monument was covered in moss, hence the lurid green color. The real and the fictional combine into a powerful image; the Breton peasant woman in the foreground merges into the stone carving of the slumped Christ and the three Maries. The sense of everyday life continues in the background, with the lone figure returning from the beach. As in his other depictions of Christ at the same time, Gauguin has attempted to transpose his own features on to the stone statue as an image of suffering. The suggestion that martyrdom was necessary for the creative process had been a frequent one in his art since *Self-Portrait (Les Misérables)* (page 74). The theme of the artist as an outsider looking in on reality with a necessary detachment had been a common one in the nineteenth century, and one which Gauguin had been quick to spot in his version of Courbet's *Bonjour M. Courbet* (pages 18 and 100). Vincent Van Gogh recognized this when he wrote to his brother a few months after the completion of this work '[Gauguin] has a sort of need for expansion and he finds, and there's some justification for it, the artistic life ignoble'.

111

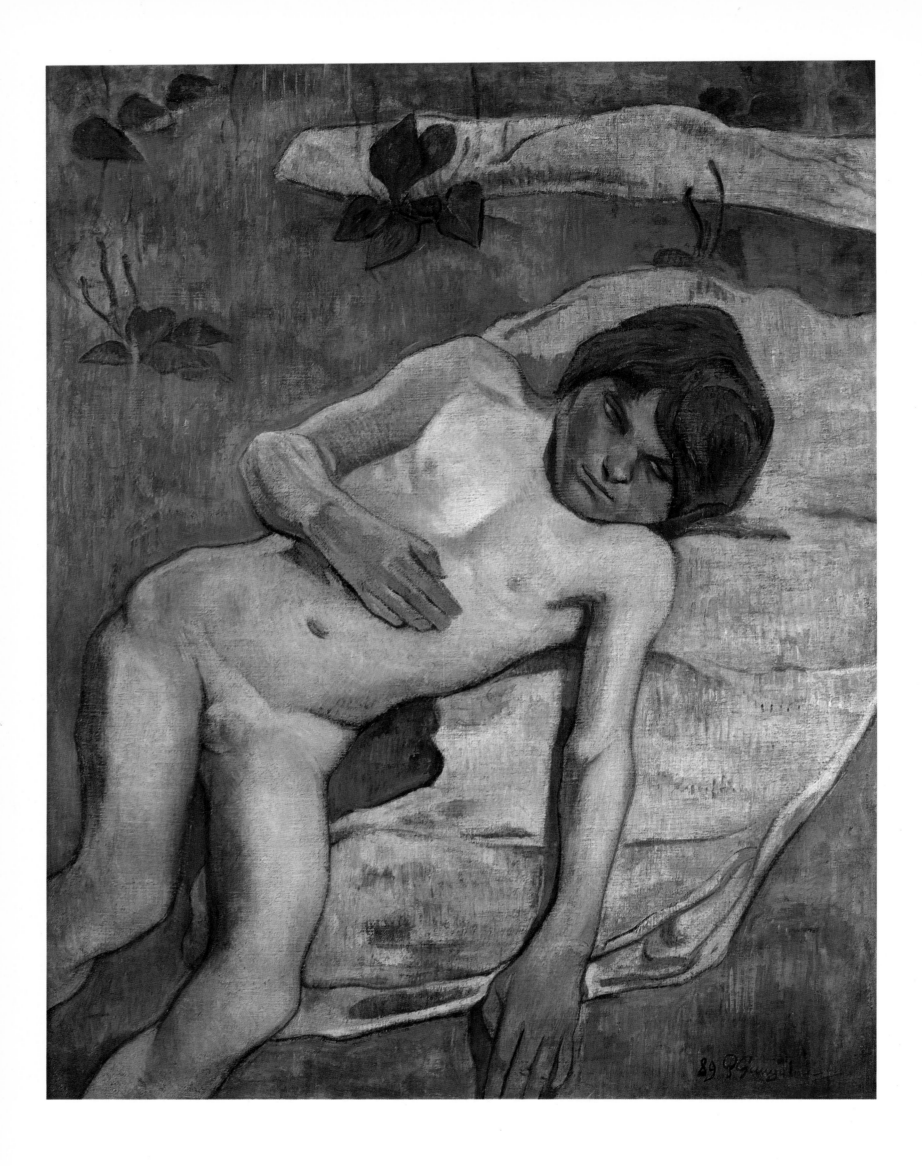

112

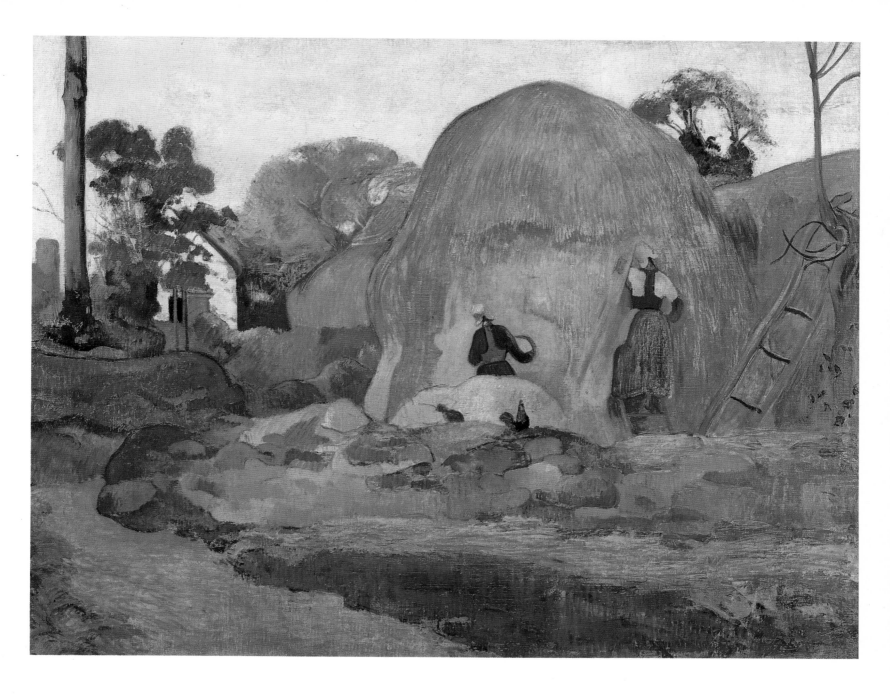

Naked Breton Boy, 1889

Oil on canvas
36⅝×29 inches (93×73.5 cm)
Wallraf-Richartz Museum, Cologne

This is one in a series of naked youths which Gauguin had begun the previous year with *Young Bretons Bathing* (page 70). Gauguin perhaps had to fall back on the male nude as a subject because of limited access to female models in Brittany. Opportunities for studying the male nude were much greater, with the wrestling match contributing an important part to the elaborate rituals surrounding the religious festivals and pardons.

This work is unusual in that it is one of the few canvases from this period which is known to have been painted from the model, but it shares with other works an interest in the burgeoning male body, here all gauche angles and sunburned face. Gauguin's interest in youthful models was reflected not only in his choice of conspicuously young native girls as companions when he went to Polynesia, but also in the followers, such as Emile Bernard, with whom he chose to surround himself throughout his career. The tender-

ness with which he has treated his awkward model is rather touching. A hint of his relative innocence is suggested by the fresh young plants strewn on the grass around his head which are reminiscent of the flowers in *Self-Portrait (Les Misérables)* (page 74), where they serve the same role. At the same time the flattening and the total absence of any kind of horizon in this work suggests the artist towering above his subject. He has treated the nude rather like a still-life painting, with the subject positioned on a white linen cloth.

Yellow Haystacks, 1889

Oil on canvas
29×36⅝ inches (73.5×93 cm)
Musée d'Orsay, Paris

1888 and 1889 were by far Gauguin's most productive years when he painted a vast number of canvases, many of them drawing on the Breton countryside and its people and chronicling their everyday pursuits. In this landscape, which he reworked in *Haymaking* (page 114), he has depicted the rural activity of stacking hay, which employed a number of women.

The figures are turned away from the viewer, working on the large dome of yellow hay in the background. Coupled with the oddly-truncated tree to the left-hand side of the composition, this has the general effect of excluding the viewer from participation in the scene. Instead Gauguin has dwelt upon the almost abstract shapes of the composition and the bright yellow colors of the hay. The use of a wide variety of tones is reminiscent of the work of Van Gogh, who had extoled the expressive qualities of saturated yellows when the two artists had worked together in Arles the previous year.

Haymaking, 1889

Oil on canvas
36¼×28¾ inches (92×73 cm)
Courtauld Institute Galleries, London

In this canvas, painted in Pont-Aven in the summer of 1889, Gauguin has returned to the same subject as *Yellow Haystacks* (page 113), and the two works were probably painted at the same time. He used the same size of canvas for both, a size 30, and has here turned it on its side, using the less common vertical format.

In his treatment of Breton subjects Gauguin has stressed the timelessness of such activities as stacking hay. The figures are dressed in their traditional costumes and there is no hint that this is the rapidly industrializing late nineteenth century. In selecting such subject-matter, Gauguin has deliberately flouted the convention established by the landscape impressionists, which conveyed specific information both about the time of day, season and weather conditions, and about the place depicted. There is little suggestion of labor here; the figures are treated as if engaged in a more relaxing pastime and the decorative, curving lines of the women's bodies are exploited at the expense of any description of toil. The protective arms of the large haystacks at the back of the picture space and the broad backs of the cattle across which the viewer looks strengthen the rather static quality of the painting.

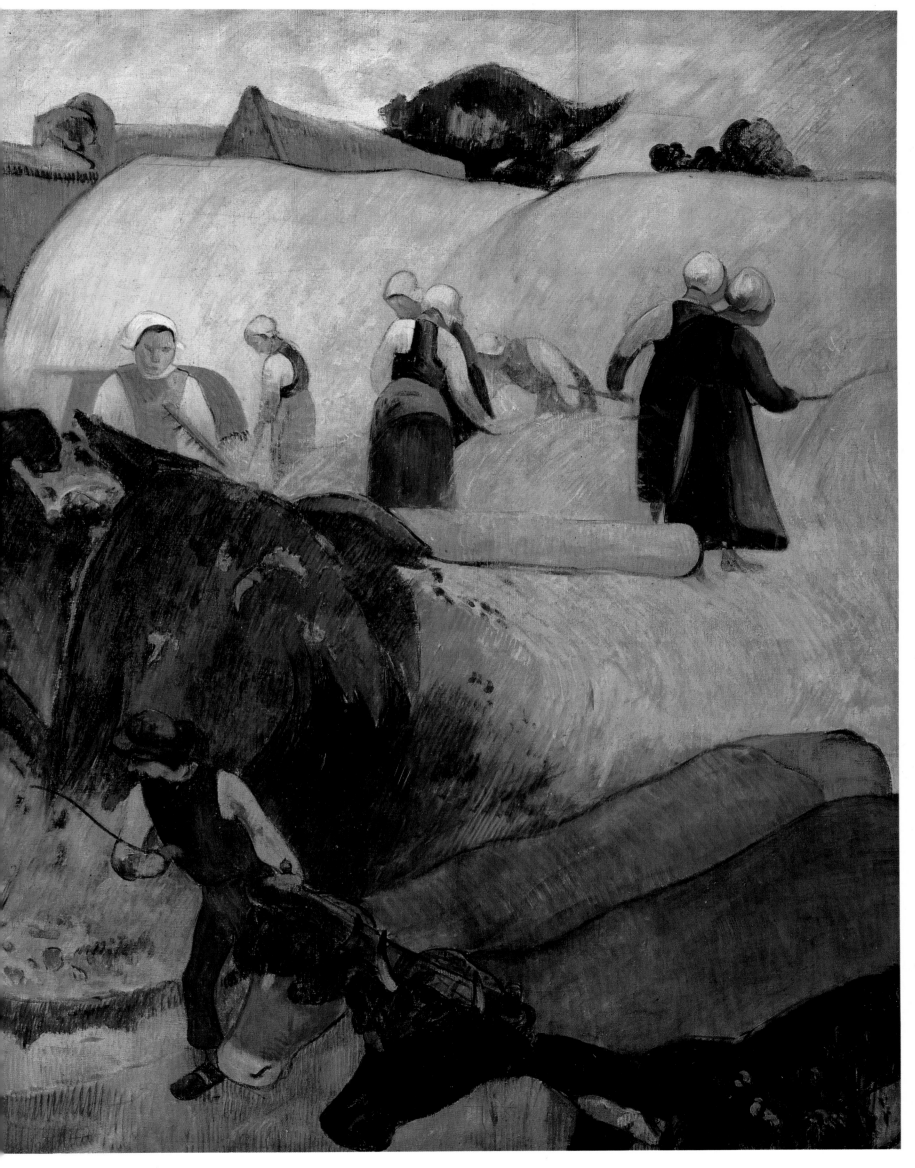

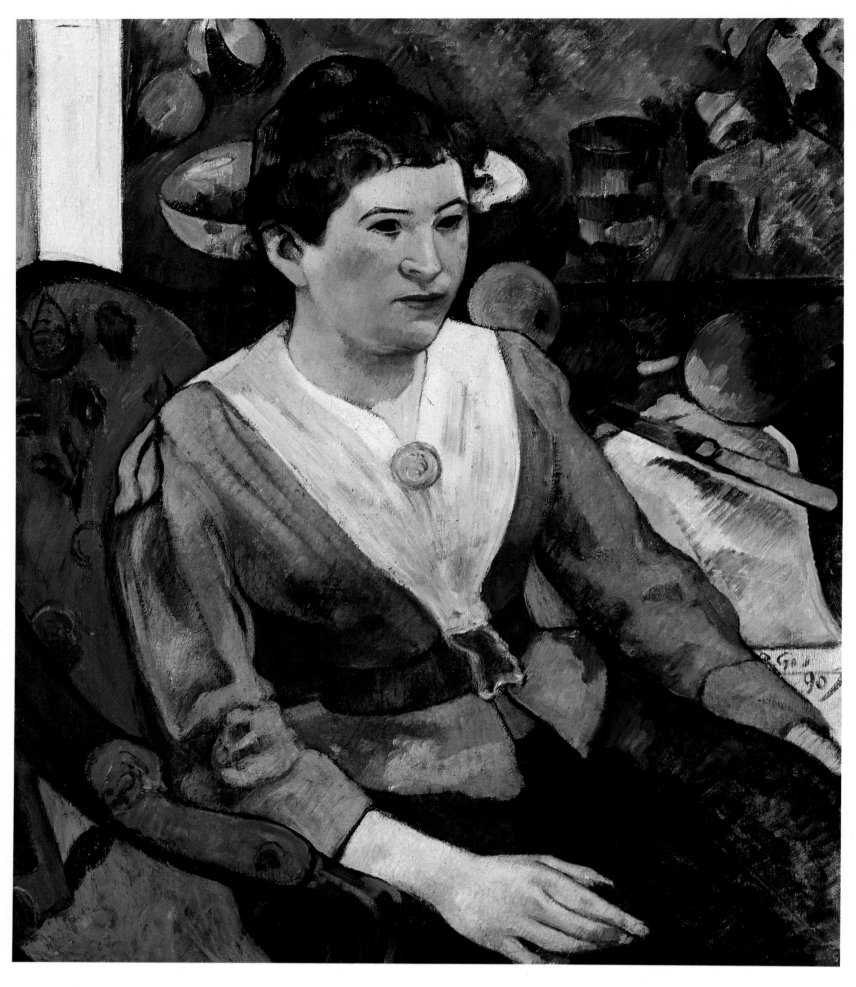

Portrait of a Woman, with Still Life by Cézanne, 1890

Oil on canvas
25¾×21⅝ inches (65.3×54.9 cm)
Art Institute of Chicago

According to Sérusier, before Gauguin began painting a still life he would exclaim 'Let's do a Cézanne!', a remark suggesting the respect in which he held the other artist, but one not without its ironies – he felt that Cézanne's work could be reduced to a formula which begged imitation. By this time Gauguin was much more confident than the young amateur who had only half-jokingly asked Pissarro to obtain

the secrets of Cézanne's formula. The still life included in this work was an important part of his collection.

From his letters it is clear that Gauguin prized his collection of Cézanne paintings above his other impressionist works; even when impoverished he refused to sell them to the collectors who had recently become interested in the work of the southern artist, which was not widely available in

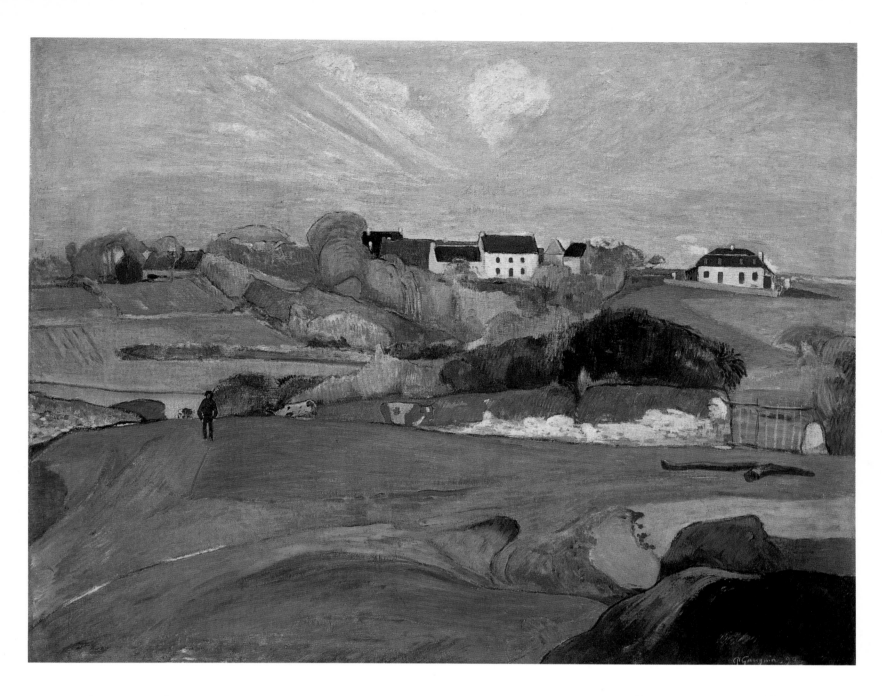

Paris in the 1880s. The painting, which forms the background of this work, the *Still Life with Compotier*, was sold only after Gauguin had gone to Tahiti for ever. Schuffenecker had made enquiries about the work in 1888, but Gauguin had refused to consider selling it:

...the Cézanne you enquire about is a pearl of great value, and I've already refused 300 francs for it; I regard it as the apple of my eye and short of absolute necessity I will part with it only after my last shirt...

Gauguin has reproduced the still-life painting in the background, increasing its size in relation to the figure and altering the angle of the knife, with the effect that it seems like an actual tabletop behind the woman. In addition the woman depicted bears similarities to a number of portraits of Madame Cézanne. Her position in the chair and her mask-like face with its almond-shaped eyes is a direct homage to paintings of the other artist's wife.

The woman has been variously identified as Marie Henry, the companion of Meyer de Haan, and as Marie Derrien, referred to as Marie Lagadu because of her black eyes.

Landscape at Le Pouldu, 1890
Oil on canvas
28⅞×36⅜ inches (73.3×92.4 cm)
National Gallery of Art, Washington

The subject was painted in the summer of 1890, when Meyer de Haan and Gauguin worked side by side on the same motif. To compare this work with the former's landscape is to see the degree to which Gauguin has distanced himself from the conventions of landscape painting. Meyer de Haan provided a network of trees in the foreground which act as *repoussoir* elements, leading the viewer gently into the picture space. Gauguin, on the other hand, has painted an ill-defined foreground area of alternating organic patches of reds and greens, which fails to give any sense of scale to the picture. The interlocking shapes of red and green, however, provide one of the best examples of synthetism. The strange landscape with its bright, non-naturalistic colors gives a sense of the 'primitive' elements that Gauguin was seeking in Brittany, and the reason why he abandoned Pont-Aven with its tourists and Sunday painters for the much more rugged landscape around Le Pouldu.

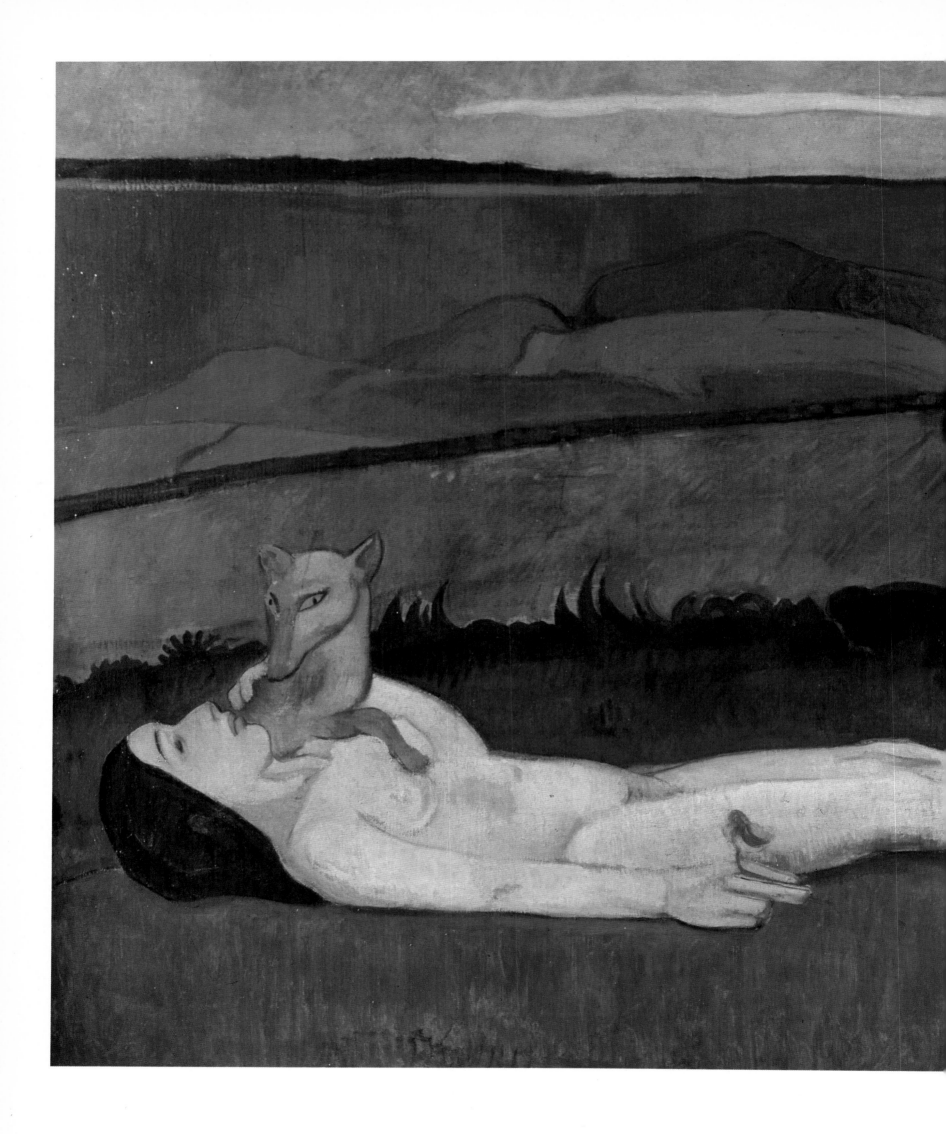

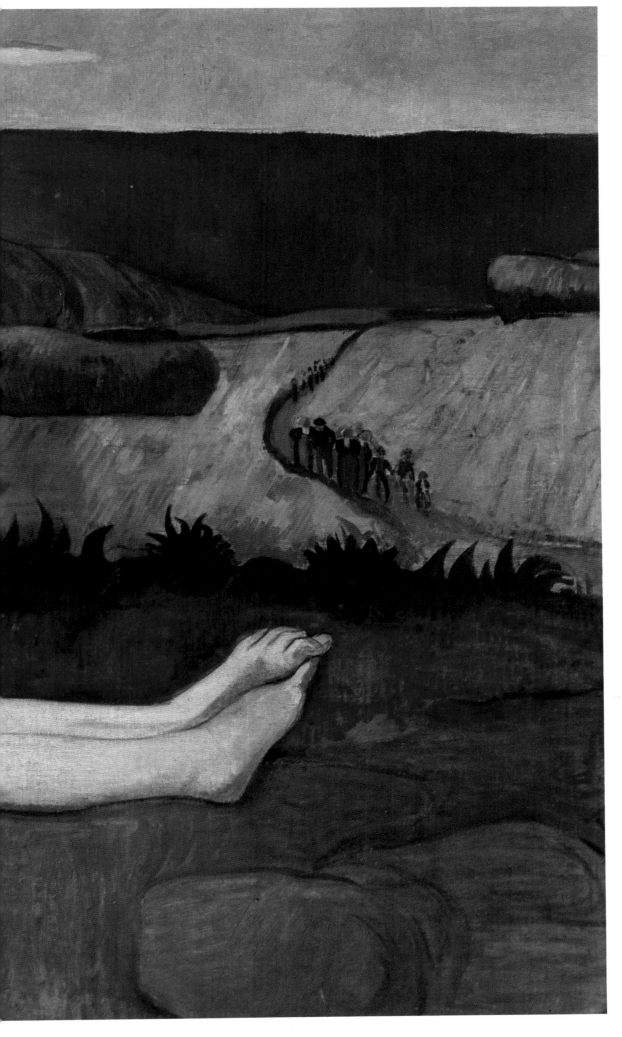

The Loss of Virginity or The Awakening of Spring, 1890

Oil on canvas
35½×51¼ inches (90×130 cm)
Chrysler Museum, Norfolk, Virginia

The model for this painting was the 20-year-old Juliette Huet, Gauguin's mistress, who was pregnant with his child when he left for Tahiti. The Manet painting of *Olympia* (page 21), which had entered the Luxembourg Museum and which Gauguin had copied at the beginning of 1891, is an obvious precedent for the figure of the reclining female nude. The black cat in the Manet becomes a lascivious fox in Gauguin, which he referred to as the 'Indian symbol of perversity', and the ostentatious bouquet in *Olympia* becomes a single red-tipped flower, alluding to the maiden's defloration. The alternative title gives some idea of the wealth of interpretation offered for the work; *The Awakening of Spring* conveys the idea of personal liberation offered by sex, a theme which Gauguin also explored in *Woman in the Waves (Ondine)* (page 106).

The work was painted in Paris and is therefore a memory of Brittany, in which the countryside is simplified and strongly rendered. The nude is set against a highly schematic landscape which is painted in a series of brightly colored planes, with little stick-like figures in the distance. These are sometimes identified as a traditional Breton wedding procession. If this interpretation is correct, then the symbolism of the work becomes much more personal and Gauguin has tried to come to terms with his relationship with Juliette in the painting.

At the same time the work is a blatant attempt to woo the avant-garde literary Symbolists to whom he was particularly close at the beginning of 1891, just prior to his departure for Tahiti. The rather contrived placing of the flower and the fox suggest that Gauguin is producing work for a small circle of initiates.

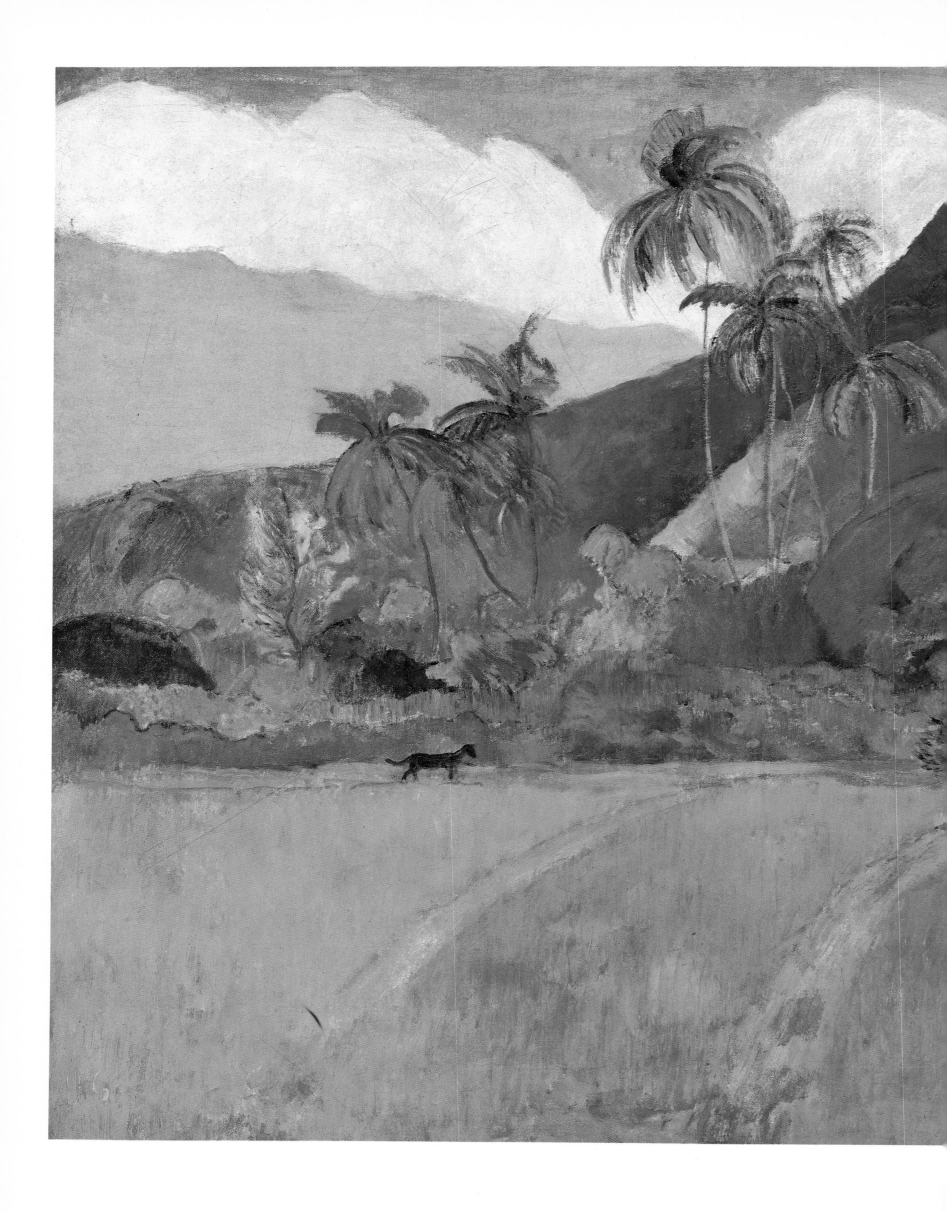

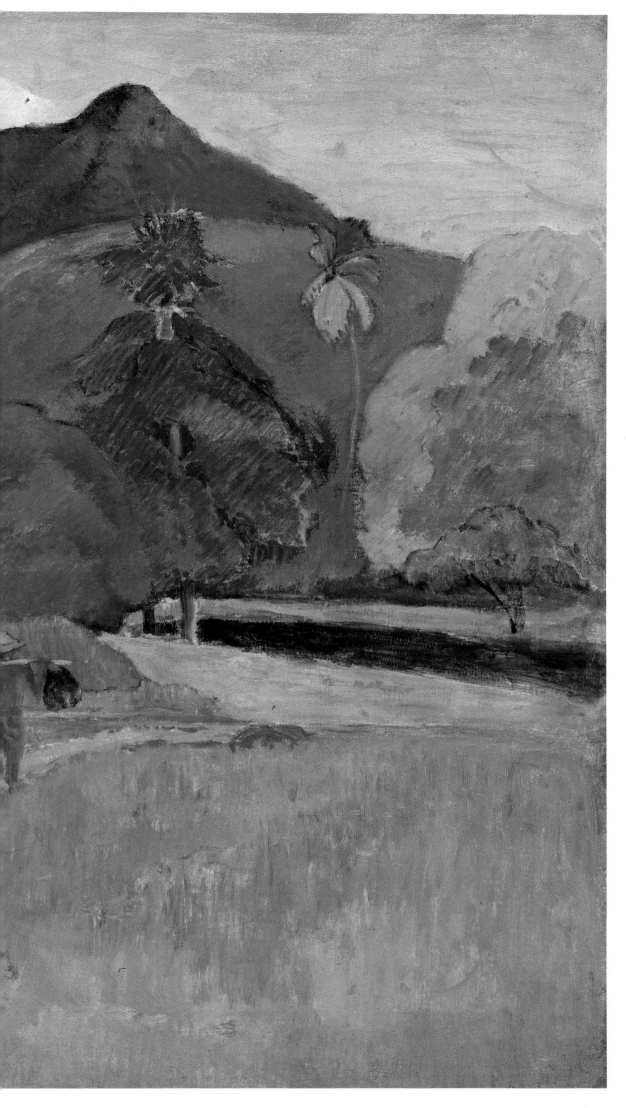

Tahitian Landscape, 1891
Oil on canvas
26¾×36⅜ inches (68×92 cm)
Minneapolis Institute of Arts

'The Tahitian soil is becoming quite French, and the old order is gradually disappearing', Gauguin wrote to his wife in July 1891, 20 days after his arrival. At first Gauguin lived in Papeete, the capital of French Polynesia which, as he recognized, was rapidly becoming a Europeanized town. This landscape was probably painted not long after his arrival, perhaps as a part of his semi-official commission from the Ministry of Public Education from which he had received help with his passage in return for providing views of Tahiti and its people; an exercise in colonial public relations.

Gauguin has depicted a scene outside Papeete with all the ingredients of a tropical Eden: jagged mountains, tall palm trees and a single native crossing into the background. The work is one of only a handful of such landscapes that he made on his first trip to Tahiti. He quickly abandoned the idea of painting pure landscapes and henceforth the landscape became a decorative backdrop to his paintings of the exotic natives of Tahiti. As in Brittany, Gauguin expressed the 'savage' and 'primitive' aspects of life in Tahiti by painting the people dressed in their traditional costumes, despite the fact that many had adopted westernized dress by this time. Similarly very few aspects of colonial rule are apparent in his work. His view of the country and its inhabitants, like his view of Brittany, was highly selective, intended to conform to his previous notions of life in the tropics.

Gauguin's letters on his arrival in Tahiti make it clear that he was simultaneously charmed by the place and disappointed at not finding what he had expected in the way of ancient customs and religious rituals. A work such as Tahitian Landscape may have been painted while he looked for more appropriate subject-matter.

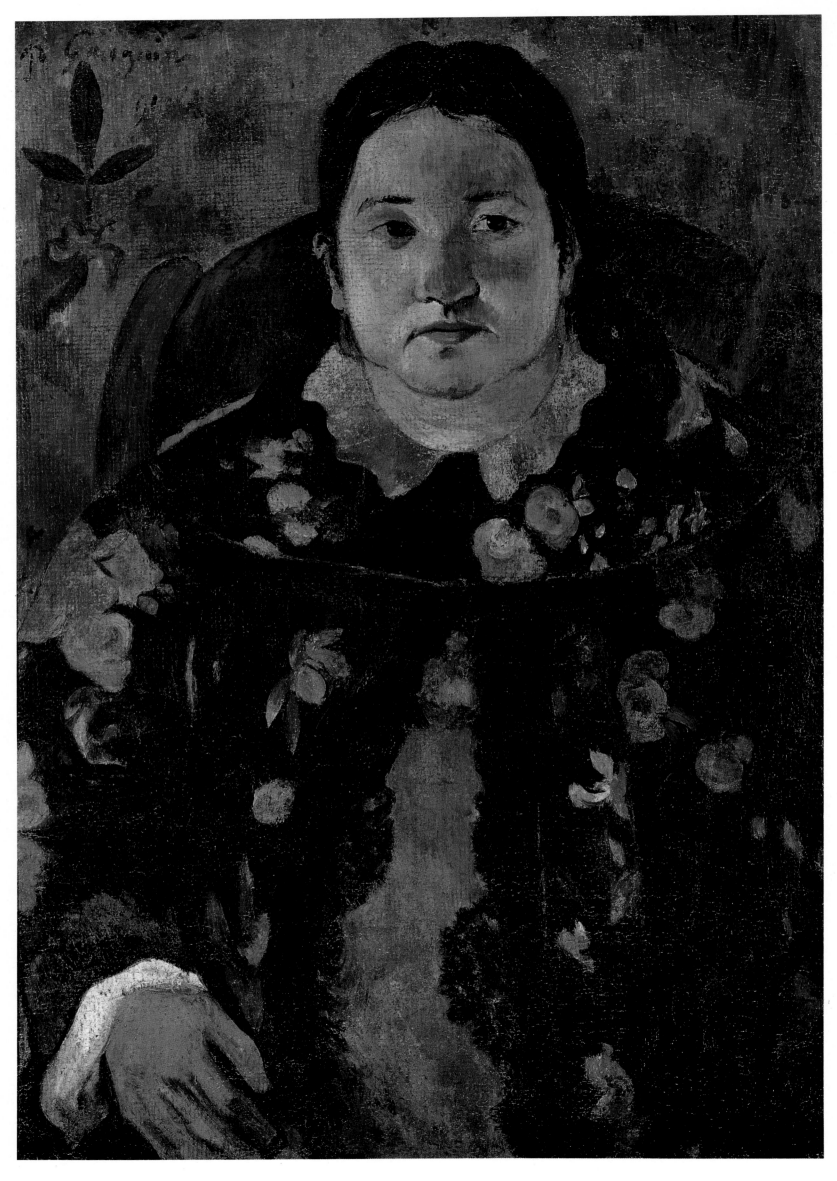

122

Suzanne Bambridge, 1891

Oil on canvas
27½×19¾ inches (70×50 cm)
Musées Royeaux des Beaux-Arts de
Belgiques, Brussels

On 4 June 1891 Gauguin wrote to Mette from Tahiti just after his arrival, 'I think I shall soon have some well-paid commissions for portraits. I am bombarded with requests to do them'. He had arrived in Papeete without a clear idea of how to make money, other than an informal commitment from the Ministry of Public Education and Fine Arts that it would buy some of his works. His plan of seeking patronage from King Pomare V was abandoned because of the king's death, which had occurred just after Gauguin's arrival in Tahiti and forced him to turn to commissioned portraits, which are rare in his oeuvre. Other portraits are normally of friends and family, works which he chose

to paint, rather than subjecting himself to the constraints of commissioned paintings, where a degree of flattery is normal.

The portrait of *Suzanne Bambridge*, an Englishwoman married to a Tahitian chief and who served as an interpreter, cannot have pleased his sitter. Gauguin was only paid 200 francs and the numerous portrait requests which he had anticipated in writing to Mette appear never to have materialized. He has painted the middle-aged sitter in a similar way to *La Belle Angèle* (page 96), as a passive, rather bland creature in a fancy costume, set against a background enlivened by wallpaper which is reminiscent of the wallpaper in some of Cézanne's still lifes.

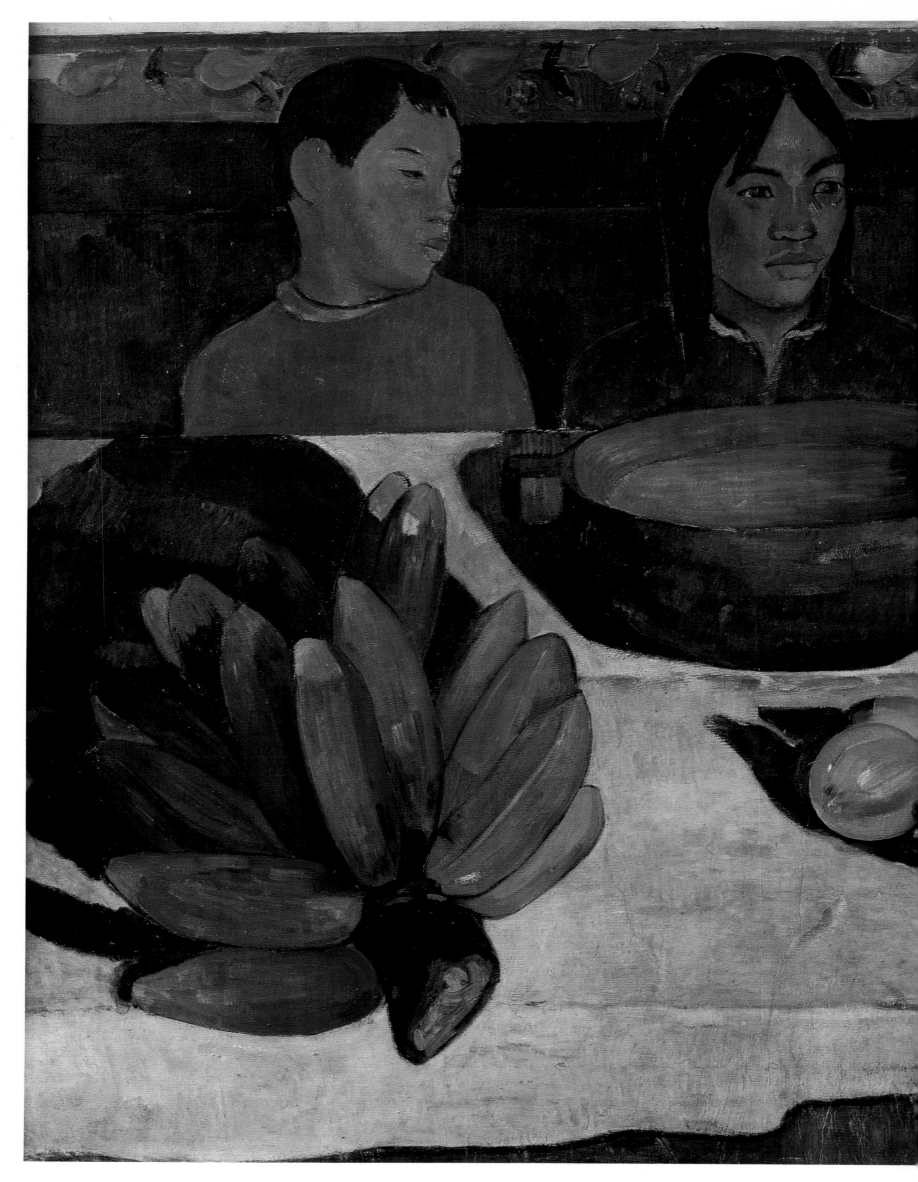

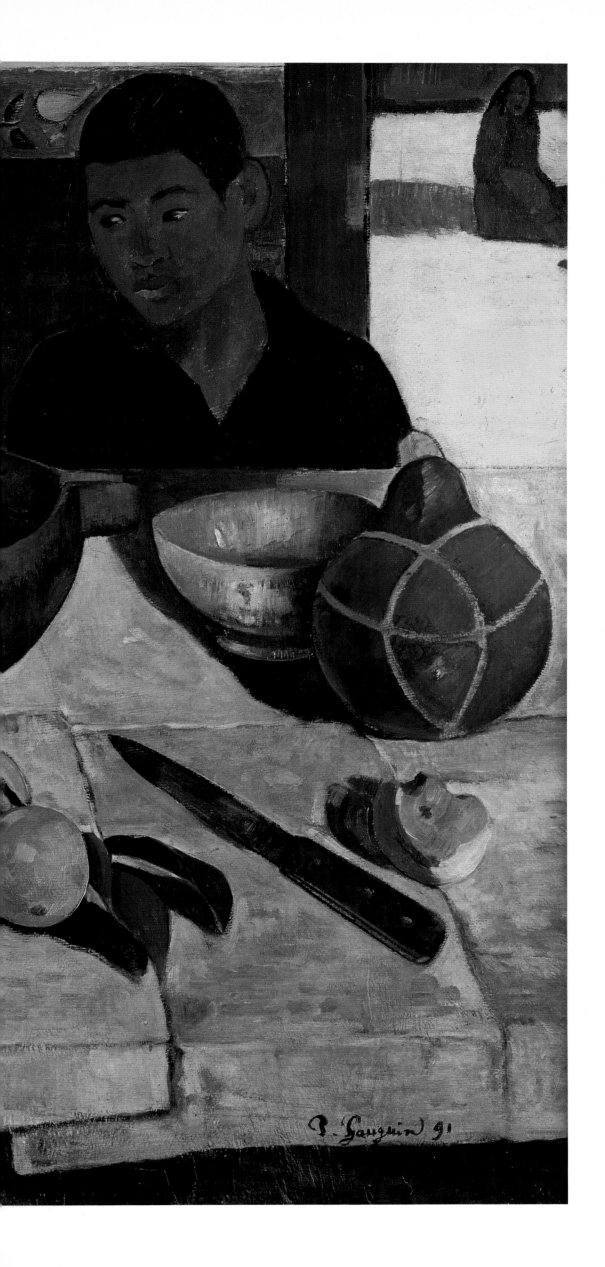

The Meal, 1891
Oil on canvas
28⅞×36⅜ inches (73×92 cm)
Musée d'Orsay, Paris

The work may originally have started out as a simple still life of exotic and decorative Tahitian fruits, placed on a table with other household implements. The knife placed at an angle and the wide bowl are reminiscent of objects in the still life by Cézanne, which Gauguin owned and which he depicted in the background of *Portrait of a Woman with Still Life by Cézanne* (page 118). The glowing, jewel-like colors are also similar to Cézanne's painting, but Gauguin has transformed the simple still life into a genre scene by the inclusion of three children in the background, who contemplate the fruit. This development of the still life into another genre by the addition of figures is characteristic of many of Gauguin's works, for example *Flowers, Still Life* (page 34). The relatively somber tones with which the children have been painted means that much of the viewer's attention is directed to the brilliant foreground fruit.

Behind the children on the upper right-hand side of the composition, there is a doorway through which can be glimpsed a seated figure. This person is presumably represented out of doors in strong sunlight, to judge by the intense yellow ground and the shadow cast, but is wrapped up with a hood around the head and is reminiscent of some of the figures of foreboding which Gauguin had used in earlier works such as *Old Women at Arles* (page 87).

125

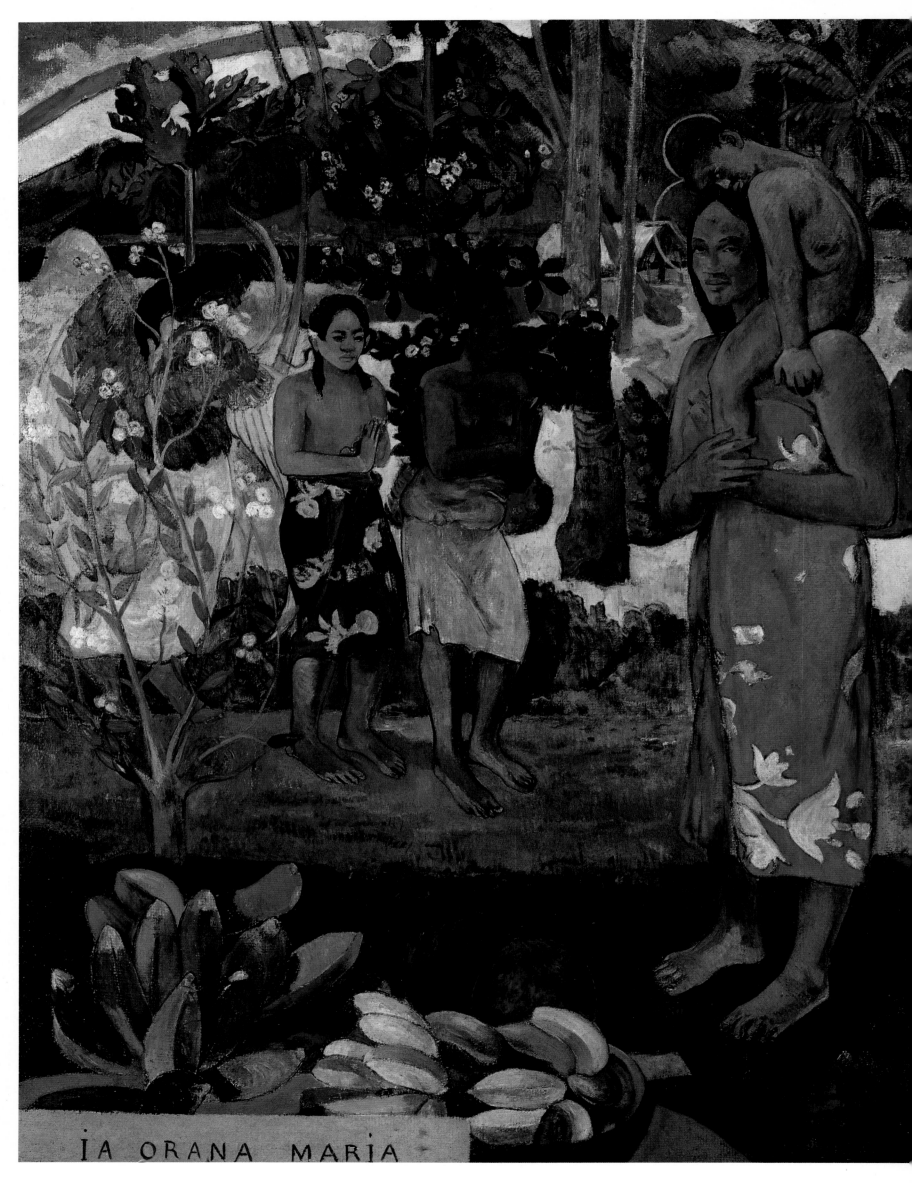

Ia Orana Maria (Hail Mary),

1891

Oil on canvas
44¾×34½ inches (113.7×87.7 cm)
Metropolitan Museum of Art, New York

In this work Gauguin returned to the religious themes explored in Brittany, such as *The Vision after the Sermon* (page 76), *Yellow Christ* (page 108) and *Green Christ* (page 110). It is unusual, however, in that it deals with the incursion of western culture into the lives of Tahitians, which Gauguin tended to ignore in his paintings, preferring to look for something more exotic and alien. He had told Mette in a letter not long after his arrival about the effect of Protestant religion on the native inhabitants, but here he deals with the Catholic image of the Madonna and Child, albeit one where they are only distinguishable from the two worshipping Tahitian women in the middle-distance by their interlocked haloes. Like the Breton religious works, this painting examines the effect of an almost superstitious faith on the two native women who witness Mary and the young Jesus. Behind them, almost lost in the mass of vegetation, is an angel.

This painting, slightly larger than the majority of Gauguin's works and more highly finished, with a great deal of detail, is the summation of all that he had experienced and achieved in his first year in Tahiti. He wrote to his friend Daniel de Monfreid on 11 March 1892:

An Angel with yellow wings reveals Mary and Jesus, Tahitians just the same, to two Tahitian women, nudes dressed in *pareus*, a sort of cotton cloth printed with flowers. . . Very somber mountainous background and flowering trees. Dark violet path and emerald green foreground, with bananas at the left. I am rather happy with it.

Although the work is ostensibly a religious one, it is treated like a Tahitian genre scene, and the pose of the two worshipping women is very different from that in traditional western devotional images. In fact Gauguin has borrowed it from photographs of the Buddhist temple at Borobudur in Java, reliefs from which he had seen at the Exposition Universelle. His subject-matter, although drawn from western conventions, has been transposed to a much more exotic location, and the final result is a composite of East and West.

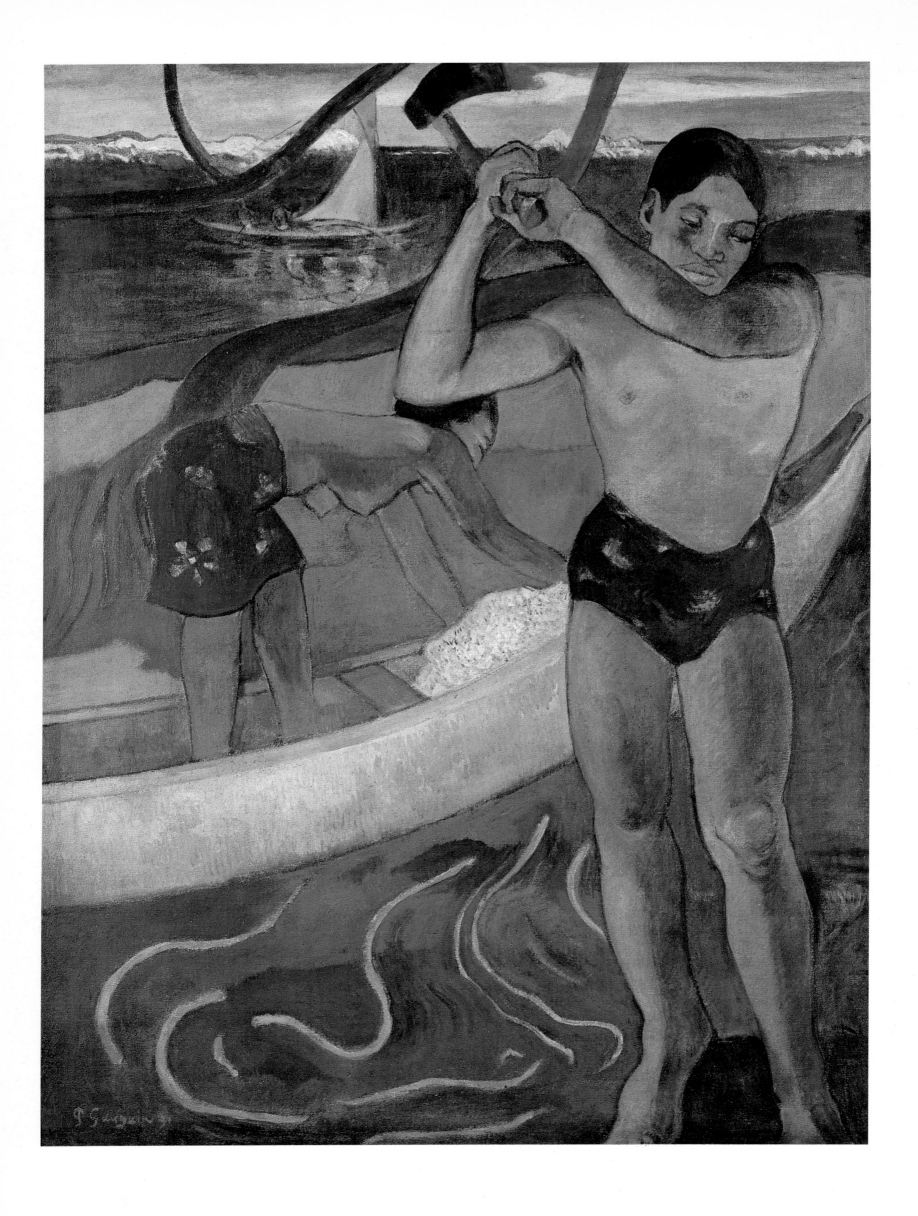

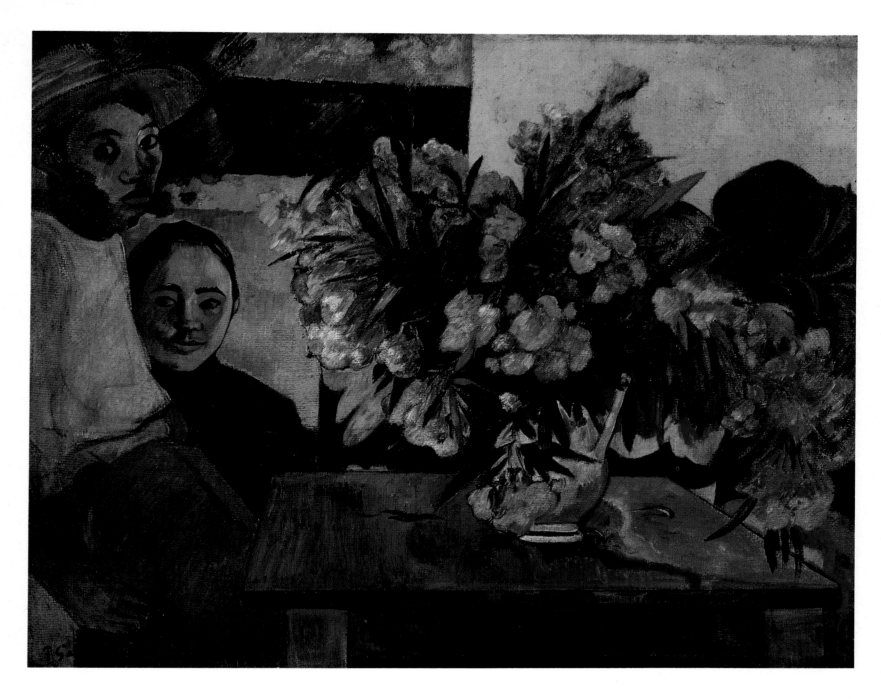

Man with an Ax, 1891

Oil on canvas
36¼×27½ inches (92×70 cm)
Private collection

It is morning. On the sea, close to the sea front, I see a canoe and in it a woman; at the shore, an almost naked man. The man lifts a weighty ax in his two hands, in a gesture at once harmonious and supple . . .

Gauguin described *Man with an Ax* thus in *Noa Noa*. The description is in pictorial terms rather than of a scene remembered. In an alternative version of *Noa Noa* he wrote:

A woman arranged some nets in the canoe and the horizon of the blue sea was often broken by the green of the crest of the waves on the coral reefs.

The purpose of *Noa Noa* was partly to elucidate and explain his Tahitian works to an unsympathetic Parisian audience, but also partly to weave a number of half-truths around a personal vision of life in the South Seas, and thereby create a much

wider theoretical framework for his pictures. Typically he has dwelt upon those aspects of the scene which make the work romantically 'primitive': the alien coral reefs, the virtually naked man, who is in tune with nature in his approach to work, and the reference to a simple way of life in which the natives fish and chop wood.

The work gives the impression of having been posed in the studio rather than glimpsed on the sea shore. The horizon is unnaturalistically high and seems about to push the sky completely out of the picture space. At the same time as we are invited to look up to the sea, we look down onto the tops of the man's feet, giving the sense of a dual perspective. The two foreground bodies are locked together and their limbs and boldly patterned clothes echo each other.

Te Tiare Farani (The Flowers of France), 1891

Oil on canvas
28⅜×36¼ inches (72×92 cm)
Hermitage Museum, Leningrad

This work was included in the auction sale of Gauguin's paintings in 1895, which was intended to finance his second trip to Tahiti, but, like many of the other pictures, *Te Tiare Farani* was bought back by the artist under an assumed name. The relative failure of that sale, compared with the one held in 1891 before the first trip, is partially explained by the change in subject-matter since Gauguin's departure from France. Certainly the work defies an easy explanation. Like many of Gauguin's other paintings, such as *The Meal* (page 126), it is neither still life nor genre scene. The large bouquet on the table dwarfs the heads of the figures to the left-hand side and they assume a secondary role within the composition. The traditional still life combines uneasily with the Tahitian figures and the meeting of the two cultures must have appeared odd to a Parisian audience.

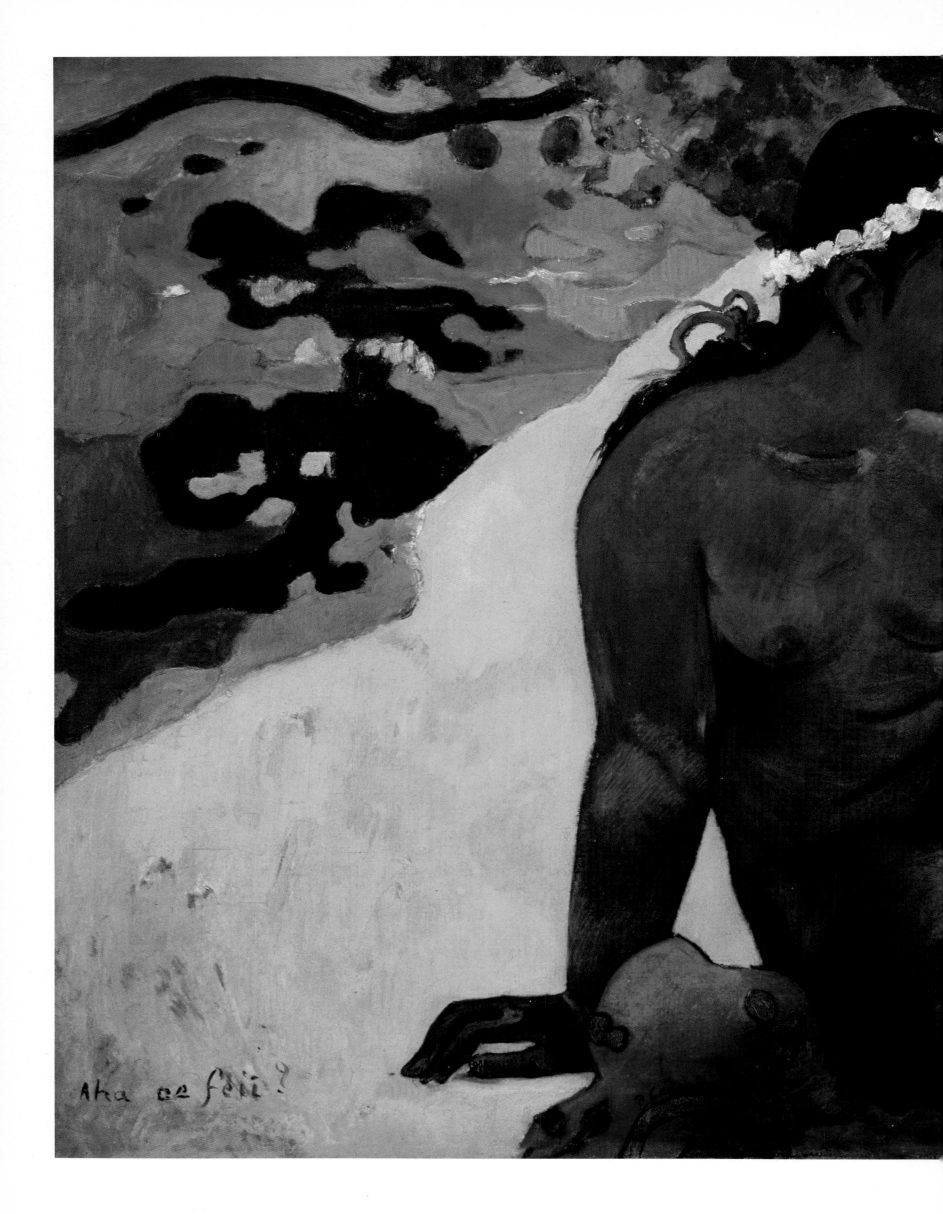

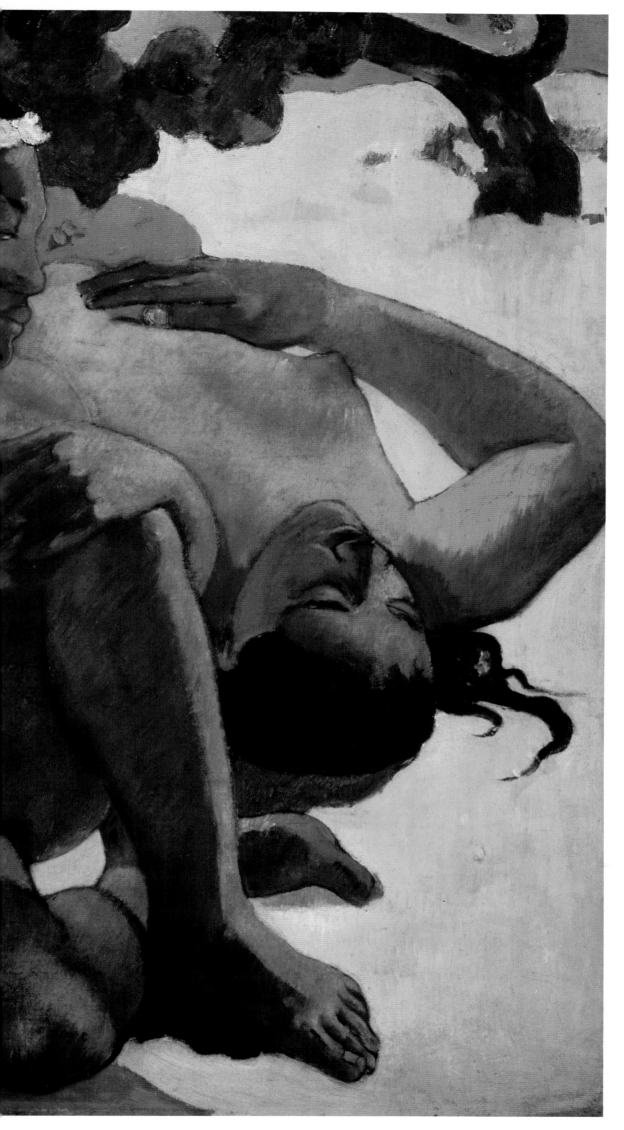

Aha eo Feii? (What! Are you jealous?), 1892

Oil on canvas
26×35 inches (66.6×89.6 cm)
Moscow, Pushkin Museum

'I recently did a nude without using a model, two women at the edge of the sea, I think that it is still my best thing to date', Gauguin wrote to Daniel de Monfreid in the fall of 1892, and it was most probably to this canvas that he referred. The two women are placed against a highly decorative and schematic representation of waves crashing against the shore, with the sensuous curves of their bodies echoed in the landscape. They are depicted as indolent creatures who appear to have little to do, and the tension suggested by the title is not to be found in the work itself. The importance which Gauguin attached to these titles is demonstrated in a letter he wrote to his wife in Copenhagen on 8 December 1892:

'I found an opportunity to send eight canvases to France... Below is the translation of the titles I have put on the canvases. This translation is for you only so that you may give it to those who ask for it. But I want the titles in the catalogue to be the same as those in the pictures. This language is fantastic and has several meanings ... *Eaha oe Feei? (What are you jealous/envious?).*'

Gauguin went on to say that, when the works went on exhibition in Copenhagen, Mette could fix the prices but that *Aha oe Feii?* was to be sold for no less than 800 francs. This relatively high price gives some indication of the value Gauguin placed on this picture.

Once again, the artist has been eclectic in his subject-matter. He may well not have used a model for the seated nude, since the pose is borrowed from a figure on the frieze of the Theater of Dionysus in Athens, a photograph of which Gauguin took with him to Tahiti.

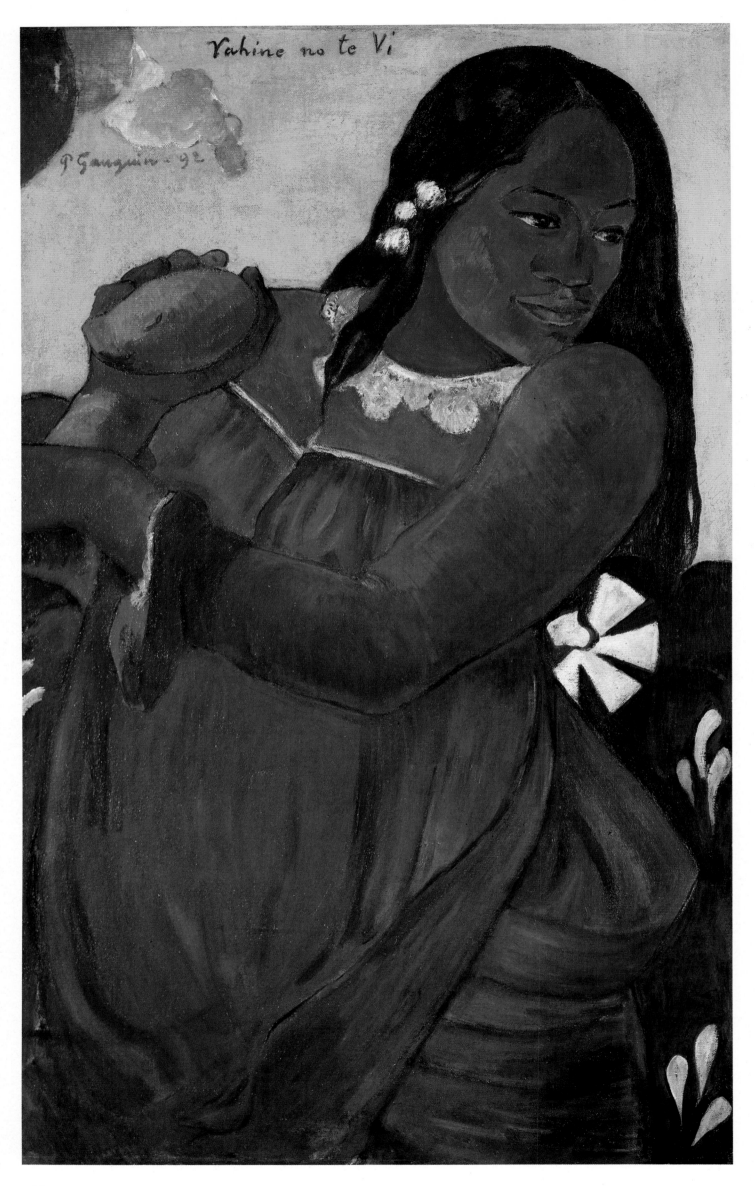

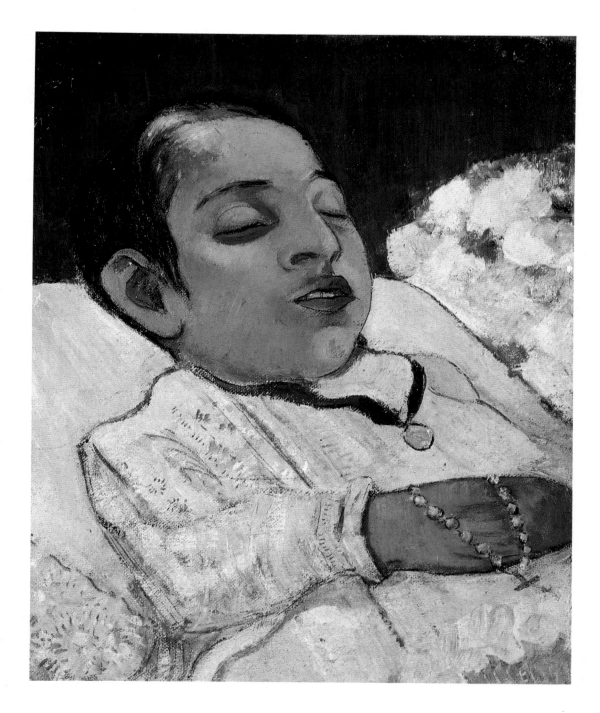

Vahine no te Vi (Woman with a Mango), 1892

Oil on canvas
28⅝×17½ inches (72.7×44.5 cm)
Baltimore Museum of Art

This work is apparently a portrait of Teha-mana, the first in a succession of young native girls with whom Gauguin lived while in Polynesia. Tehamana was 13 when she was given by her parents to Gauguin at the end of 1891 in a native marriage and was subsequently to become pregnant with his child, which may explain the round-ness of her body under her flowing west-ernized dress. The ripe fruit which she holds in her hand may also be a reference to her fertility. Tehamana was immortal-ized and perhaps idealized in Gauguin's account of his first voyage to Tahiti, *Noa Noa*, which drew on *The Marriage of Loti*, a fictionalized account of a similar marriage between a European and a native girl. The rather generalized treatment of the woman, her apparently unconcerned gaze and the ostentatious holding of the fruit makes the work more like a genre painting than a portrait of the woman who shared his life at this time. The bright yellow back-ground is intensified by the purple of the sitter's dress, and the work is a harmony of colors and decorative patterning. It was in-cluded in the sale of Gauguin's work before his second visit to Tahiti, where it was bought for 450 francs by the painter Degas.

Portrait of Atiti, 1892

Oil on canvas
11¾×9¾ inches (30×25 cm)
State Museum Kröller-Müller, Otterlo

This portrait is of Aristide Suhas, son of Gauguin's neighbors in Mataiea in Tahiti, the English bacteriologist Jean-Jacques Suhas and Helen Burns. At the time of his death, on 5 March 1892, the child was 18 months old but he appears oddly mature in this work, his head grossly inflated in com-parison with his small hands holding a crucifix. It was perhaps for this reason that the child's mother rejected the portrait.

When Gauguin first arrived in Tahiti, he wrote to his wife that he intended making some money by seeking commissions for portraits among the colonials. He appears only to have painted *Suzanne Bambridge* (page 124), however, and this work was re-portedly not well liked. Presumably Gau-guin did not have the necessary tact to make a successful portrait painter; he was much more interested in the idea of pro-ducing a strong, simplified image incor-porating the essentials of the sitter than in producing a flattering representation.

The idea of producing a deathbed repre-sentation of a loved one was common enough in the nineteenth century. Monet had painted his dead wife and the artist hero in Zola's novel *The Masterpiece* por-trayed his son after his death. However, the idea of confronting death in all its im-mediacy was much more central to the Realist doctrine of the previous generation, and one can only assume that Gauguin undertook the work at the parents' re-quest.

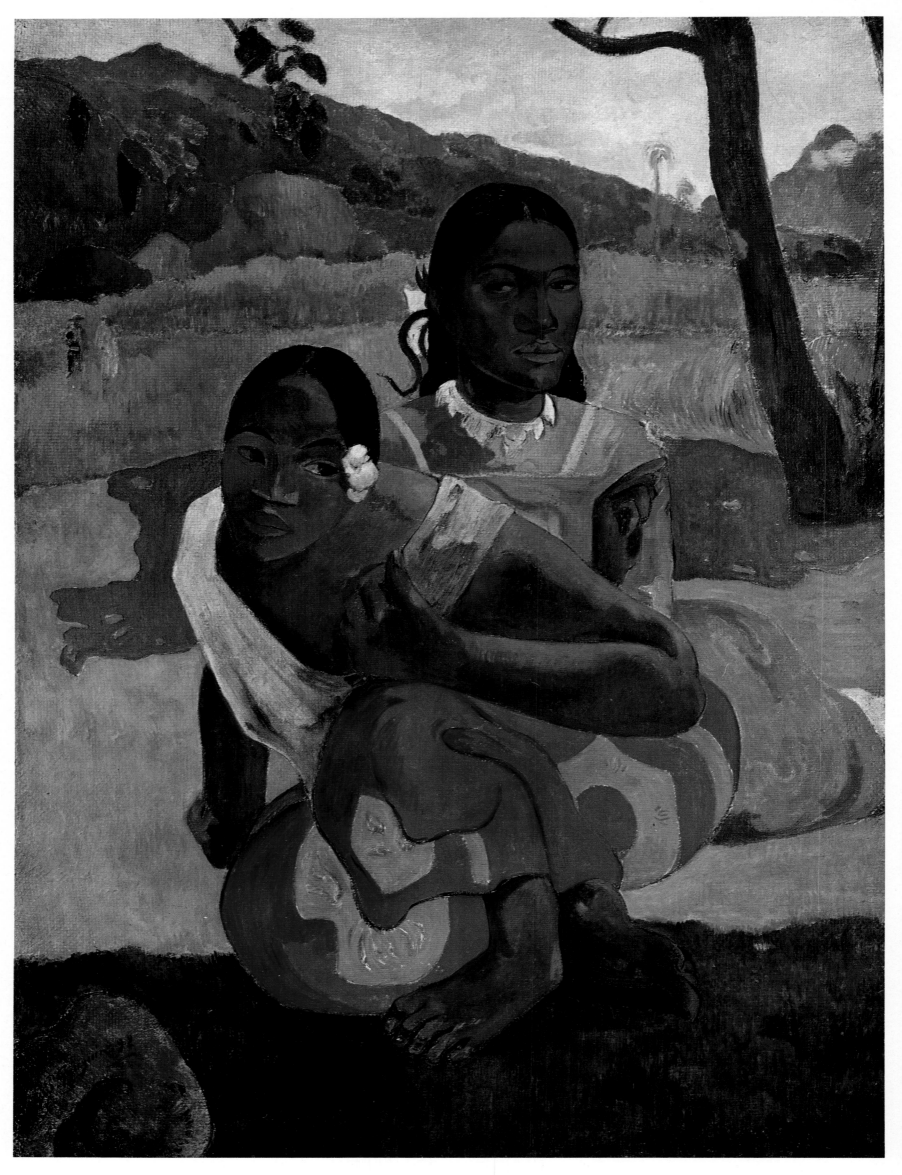

Nafea Faa Ipoipo (When will you Marry?), 1892

Oil on canvas
40×30½ inches (101.5×77.5 cm)
Rudolf Staechelin Foundation, Basle

This work uses a rhetorical question as a title, perhaps as a concession to Gauguin's Symbolist audience back in Paris. Like the contemporary *Aha oe Feii*, it includes two figures within a greatly simplified Tahitian landscape, with the foreground woman in a crouching position. Despite the fact that there is a question posed, however, there is no apparent interaction between the two figures.

Gauguin derived much of his information, and prejudices, about Tahitian marriage rituals from the hugely popular *Marriage of Loti*, which he had read before leaving Paris and which colored his view of native women as passive and hedonistic creatures. The woman in the foreground may be represented as being in search of a husband, suggested by the bloom behind her ear. The work may therefore be construed as a dialogue between the maiden and the figure of a matron in westernized dress in the background. If this is so, then Gauguin may have intended a more general contrast between relative states of innocence and knowledge.

The painting draws its strength from judicious juxtapositions of bright patches of color and from a static, triangular composition. The women's bodies are heavy and sculptural and the work takes on a feeling of monumentality. That Gauguin regarded this as one of the most important works from his first period in Tahiti is demonstrated by the fact that when the work was on display in Durand-Ruel's gallery in 1893 he asked 1500 francs for it, more than any of his other paintings.

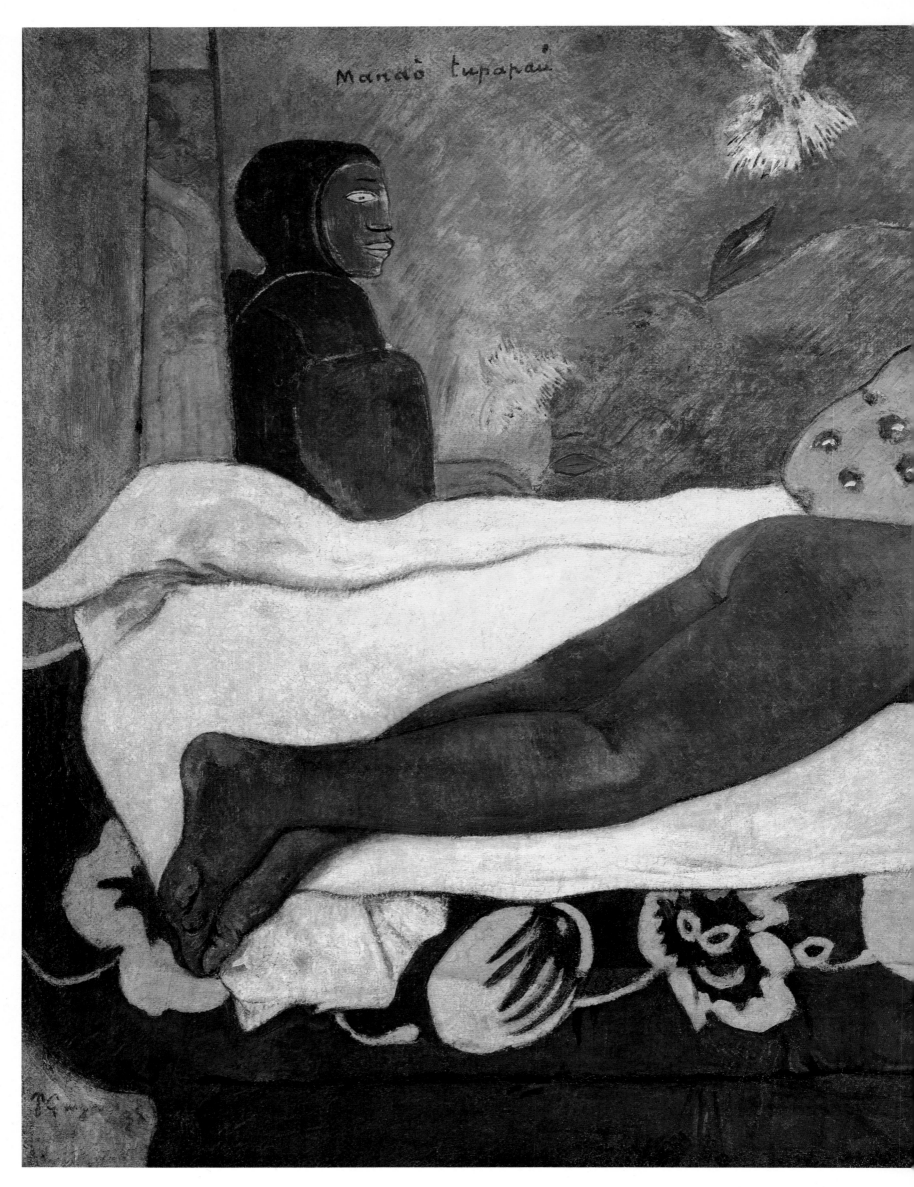

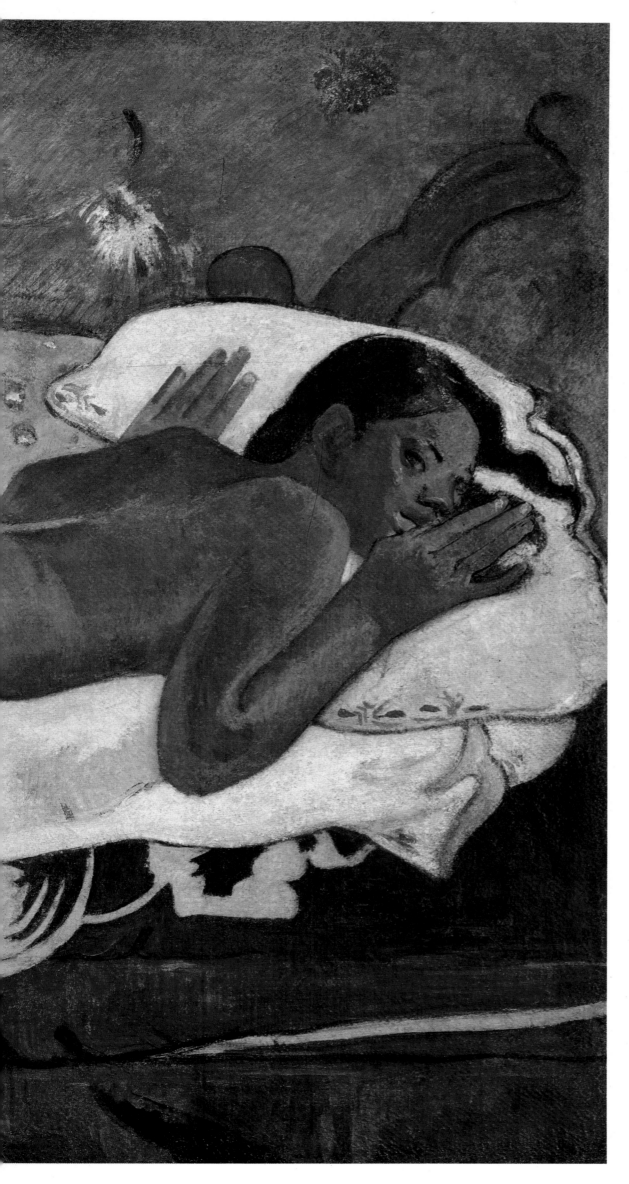

Manao Tupapau (The Spirit of the Dead keeps Watch), 1892

Oil on burlap mounted on canvas
28½×36⅜ inches (73×92 cm)
Albright-Knox Art Gallery, Buffalo

In 1892 Gauguin read J-A Moerenhout's *Voyages aux Iles du Grand Océan*, which dealt with the ancient, and largely vanished, customs and rituals of Polynesia. From this important source he found much of the inspiration for his art and his writings. In his text *Noa Noa*, which he wrote on returning from Tahiti and which drew largely on Moerenhout, Gauguin relates the story of this painting, which depicts his young companion Tehamana whom he calls Tehura. On returning from a trip, he entered his hut to be confronted by the image of his young bride:

I lit some matches and I saw . . . motionless, naked, lying on her stomach on the bed, her eyes greatly widened by fear, Tehura, who looked at me apparently without recognition. . . Never had I seen her so beautiful, especially not with such a moving beauty.

He gave an account of the work to Mette at the end of 1892, since it was to be included in an exhibition of his work in Copenhagen in 1893, discreetly omitting to mention his relationship with the model:

Manao tupapau. I have painted a young girl in the nude. In this position, a trifle more, and she becomes indecent. However, I want it in this way as the lines and movement interest me. So I must make her look a little frightened. . . This people have, by tradition, a great fear of the spirit of the dead. . . General harmony, somber, mournful, startled look in the eye like a funeral knell. Violet, dark blue and orange yellow. . . . There are some flowers in the background, but they are not real, only imaginary, and I make them resemble sparks. The Kanaka believe the phosphorescences of the night are the spirits of the dead and they are afraid of them. To finish, I make the ghost only a good little woman, because the young girl . . . could not visualize death itself except as a person like herself. . . . To end up, the painting has been done quite simply, the motive being savage, childlike.

The more immediate artistic source for the work is Manet's *Olympia* (page 21), which Gauguin had copied before leaving Paris and a photograph of which he had with him in Tahiti.

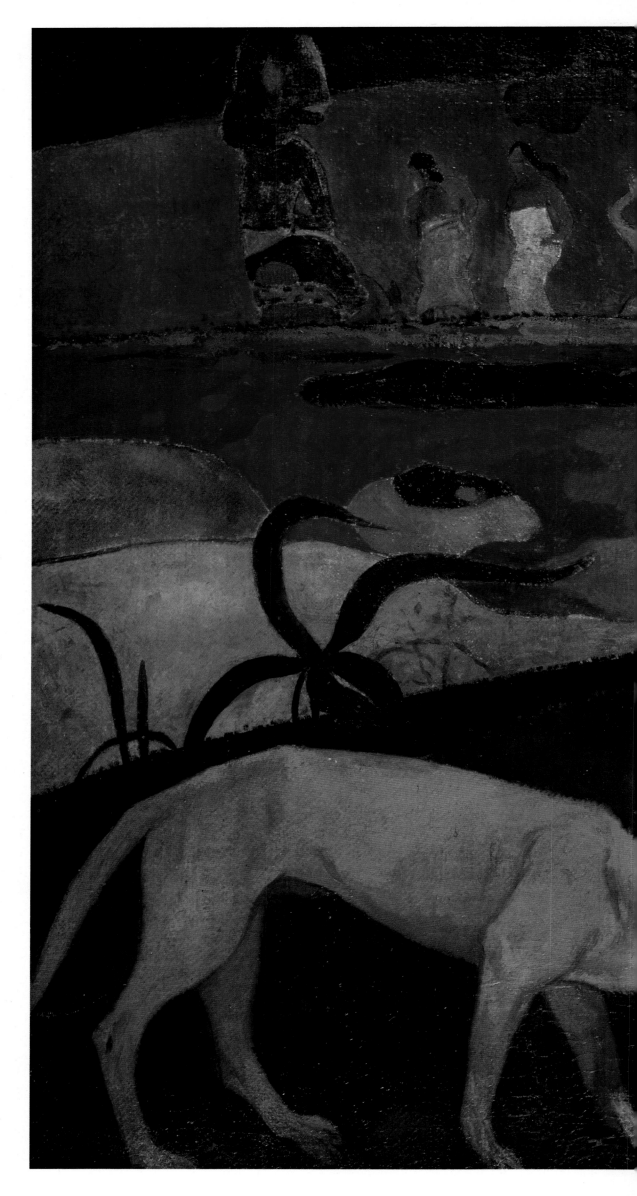

Arearea (Pranks), 1892

Oil on canvas
29½×37 inches (75×94 cm)
Musée d'Orsay, Paris

This is another work from his first trip to
Tahiti in which Gauguin used the theme of
two Tahitian women and explored the relationship between them, which is hinted
at by his use of an enigmatic title. In these
paintings the titles played an important
role, often inscribed in sizeable capital
letters, as here. They add a further layer of
meaning to works which are already complex, and it would appear that they were
intended to mystify and appeal to his
Symbolist friends back in Paris. Gauguin
was adamant, when he sent Mette instructions about recent Tahitian works to be exhibited, that no translations were to appear
in the catalog. This failure to provide any
solution for the works may rather have
backfired on him and he later recognized
the need to provide some kind of inter-
mediary text between the work and its
audience, when he began work on *Noa Noa*
back in Paris. This painting was included
in the exhibition of the artist's recent work
at his one-man show at Durand-Ruel's gallery in 1893.

Gauguin was to reuse parts of this work;
the same subject was used on a fan and the
background dancers reappeared in
Mahana no Atua (page 147), painted when
he was back in Paris. The hieratic pose of
the foreground woman points to the
artist's use of a wide variety of sources,
which he hoped would ultimately give the
work its 'primitive' flavor. When it was included in the 1895 auction sale held to
finance Gauguin's second trip to Tahiti, he
was forced to buy it in, like many of the
other Tahitian paintings.

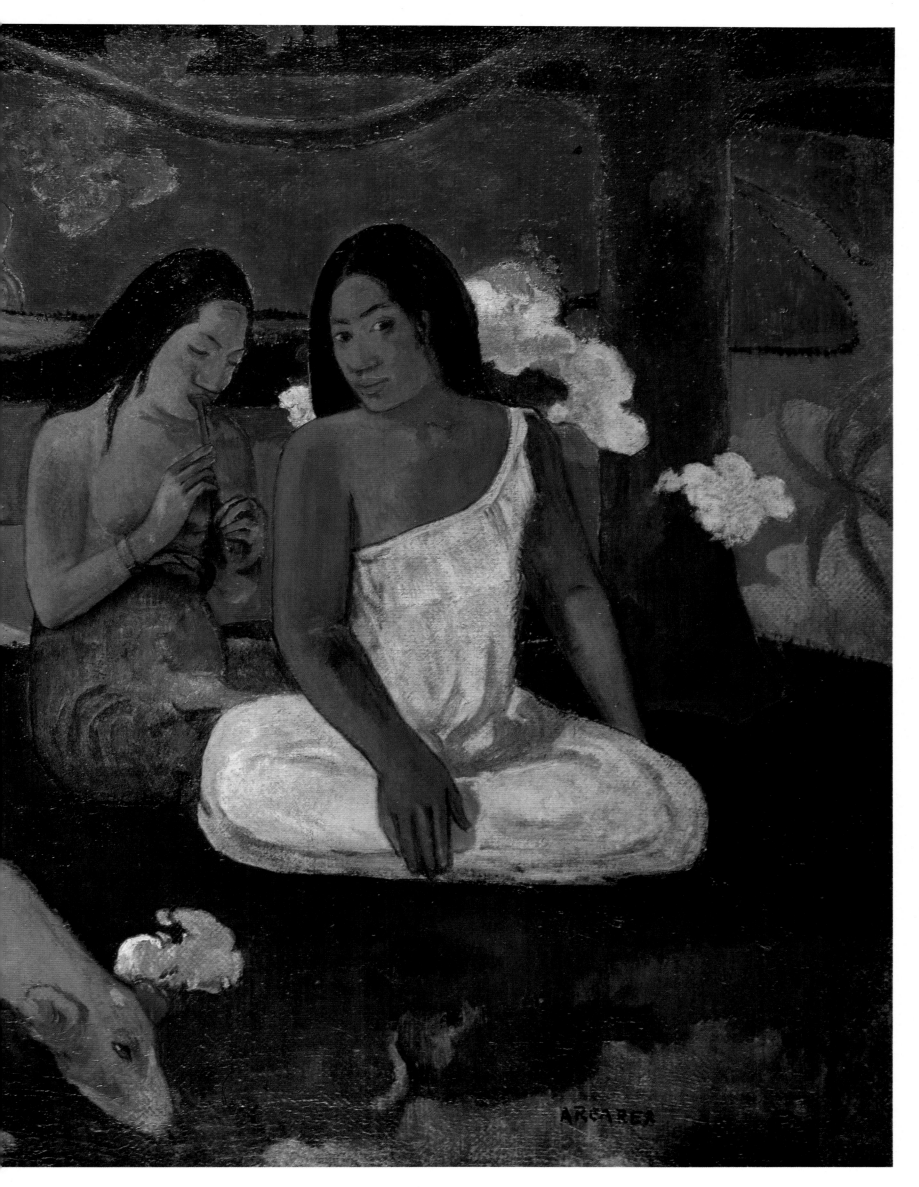

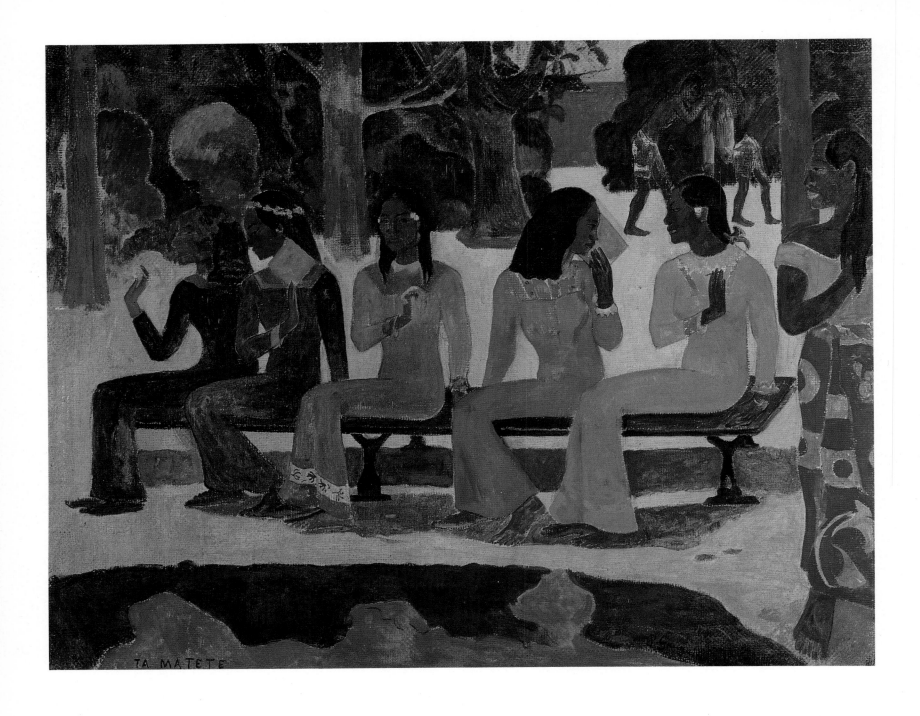

Ta Matete (The Market), 1892

Tempera on canvas
28¾×36¼ inches (73×92 cm)
Kunstmuseum, Basle

Gauguin's letters back to Europe from Tahiti make it clear that he was only too aware of the damaging effect of western society on Tahitian life, brought about by over-zealous missionaries and also by the sexually-transmitted diseases introduced by the colonial population. The demand for prostitutes was only one of many changes introduced by western culture, and it is these women whom Gauguin has depicted here. Their profession is made clear in the title, which is perhaps better translated as 'We shall not go to market today'. They are depicted in the main market square in Papeete where they plied their trade.

While these women are clearly prostitutes, they have been depicted in a chaste fashion, wearing concealing missionary dresses and with contrived rigid postures.

Their poses were derived from a photograph in Gauguin's possession of an Egyptian fresco on a tomb from Thebes, in the British Museum (page 20). He has retained the frieze-like composition of the original, and the figures' lack of depth is emphasized by their encasing costumes and the rigid profiles of five of the figures. A colorful and schematic landscape provides a backdrop to the two-dimensional figures, whose flatness contrasts with the sculptural quality of Gauguin's treatment of other Tahitian women, as in *Nafea Faa Ipoipo* (page 134). Here the insistent flattening is partly an attempt to render the figure 'primitive', but may also be intended as a comment on the constraints imposed by the European settlers on what Gauguin perceived as the uninhibited sexuality of the natives in their 'natural' state.

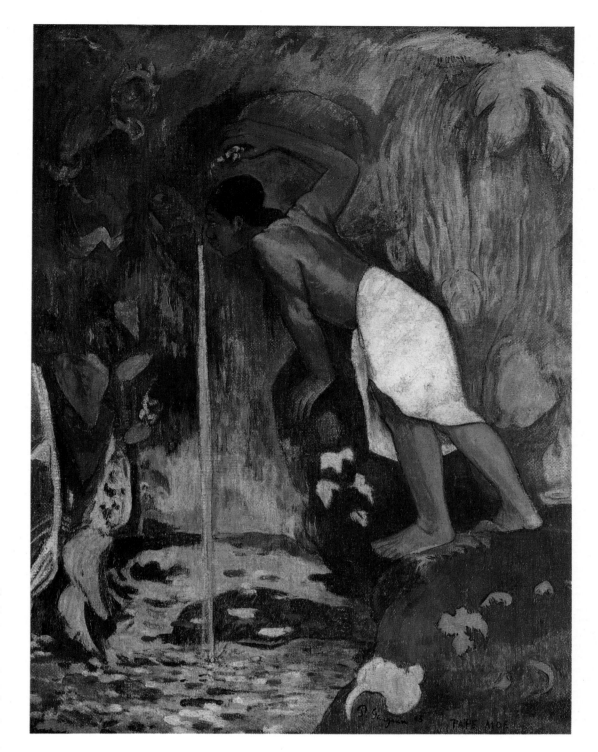

Pape Moe (Mysterious Water),
1893

Oil on canvas
39×29½ inches (99×75 cm)
Private collection, Switzerland

This work is mentioned by Gauguin in *Noa Noa*, the text he began in 1893 to 'facilitate an understanding of [his] Tahitian paintings'. He wrote:

Suddenly, after a sharp turning, I spotted a naked girl pressed against the rock face, which she caressed rather than holding it in her hands; she was drinking from a spring gushing from a great height in the rocks. When she had finished drinking she took some water in her hands and allowed it to run between her breasts.

In fact in the painting the girl is neither naked nor unsupported by her hand. This is because the written account is fictional and the painting did not derive from an actual scene which Gauguin had observed in Tahiti, but rather from a photograph of a Tahitian woman drinking from a waterfall. The erotic tone of the written account demonstrates the lengths to which Gauguin would go in order to interest his largely male audience.

The work is rather somber in color, relieved by the light-colored *pareu* the girl wears and the bright red flowers in the foreground. The dark colors lend emphasis to the mysterious feeling of the work which Gauguin tried to convey. At the end of 1893, when he was back in Paris and working on the manuscript of *Noa Noa*, he held his first one-man show at Durand-Ruel's gallery in which this work was included.

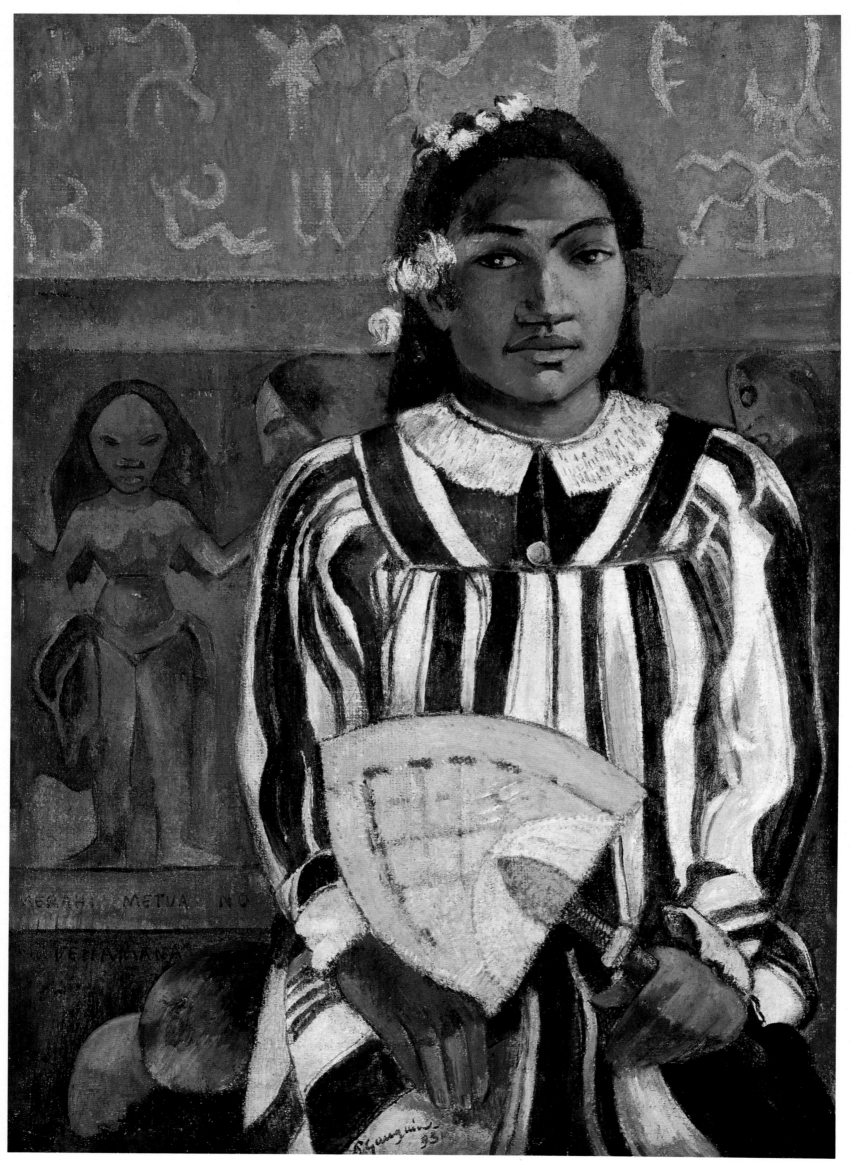

**Merahi Metua no Tehamana
(The Ancestors of Tehamana),**
1893
Oil on canvas
30×21⅜ inches (76.3×54.3 cm)
Art Institute of Chicago

This portrait is of Tehamana, the 13-year-old girl whom Gauguin took as his *vahine* or native bride when he first went to Tahiti in 1891. The work was painted shortly before he took leave of her, when she was probably pregnant with his child. The two ripe mangos in the background may refer to her fertility, a personal symbol which had occurred in *Vahine no te Vi* (page 132).

In his depiction of Tahitian customs, Gauguin turned to Moerenhout's *Voyages aux Iles du Grand Océan*, which he had read in 1892 and large sections of which he had copied into a notebook. Even when there is no overt reference to Moerenhout in his paintings, much of the flavor of the work is retained in Gauguin's depiction of ancient Tahitian customs and rituals which had largely disappeared by this time. The title of the work, sometimes translated as 'Tehamana has many parents', refers to the old belief that all Tahitians were descended from the gods Hina and Taaroa. Tehamana has been portrayed wearing a missionary dress but the setting of the remainder of the painting is Tahitian.

The hieroglyphs at the top of the composition, intended to allude to the unfathomable mysteries of Polynesian culture, are similar to examples which had aroused a great deal of interest at the Exposition Universelle in 1889.

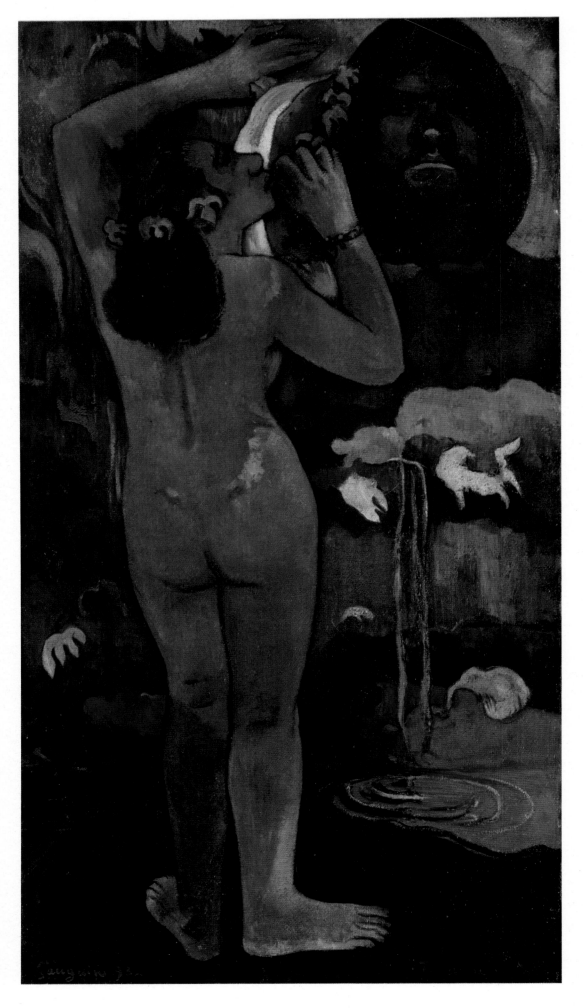

Ancien Culte Mahorie and from there into *Noa Noa*:

Hina said to Tefatou
– Make man live again after his death.
The God of the Earth replied to the Goddess of the Moon
– No I shall not revive him.
Man will die, the vegetation will die, as will those that live from it, the earth will die,
The earth will be finished, finished never to be reborn.

This work and *Pape Moe* illustrate Gauguin's difficulty in finding any extant native tradition on which to base his art, and the extent to which he was prepared to look to other sources in order to find the kind of subject he wished to depict in his painting.

When the painting was included in the one-man exhibition at Durand-Ruel's gallery towards the end of 1893, it was bought by the artist Degas who was one of Gauguin's few admirers from the original Impressionist circle.

Ea Haere Ia Oe? (Where are you Going?), 1893

Oil on canvas
35¾×28 inches (91×71 cm)
Hermitage Museum, Leningrad

Once again Gauguin has given his painting a prominent title which raises more questions than it answers. It is difficult to imagine which, if any, of the women in the picture is posing the question; they all appear to be regarding the viewer with a mixture of coyness and mistrust. It is perhaps to Gauguin's imminent departure from Tahiti that the title refers. Certainly he has included all those aspects of Polynesia which he would most miss; beautiful, available women, luscious vegetation and fruit, and the traditional native hut in the background.

The crouching woman in the middle distance is the same as in *Nafea Faa Ipoipo* (page 134), and there is also a full-scale squared drawing of her, without the prominent flower behind her ear. Gauguin's eclecticism was so great that he was not above reworking motifs from earlier works, a practice that was to become increasingly evident in his Tahitian paintings.

Hina Tefatou (The Moon and the Earth), 1893

Oil on burlap
45×24½ inches (114×62 cm)
Museum of Modern Art, New York

This work deals with the same theme as *Pape Moe* (page 141), which Gauguin had written about in *Noa Noa*. Here the girl is completely naked and clings to a large male head instead of to the rock face, as in the other work. The canvas represents the Polynesian deity Tefatou, who refused to grant the goddess Hina's request to guarantee immortality to humanity. The legend was recounted in Moerenhout and Gauguin copied it into the manuscript of

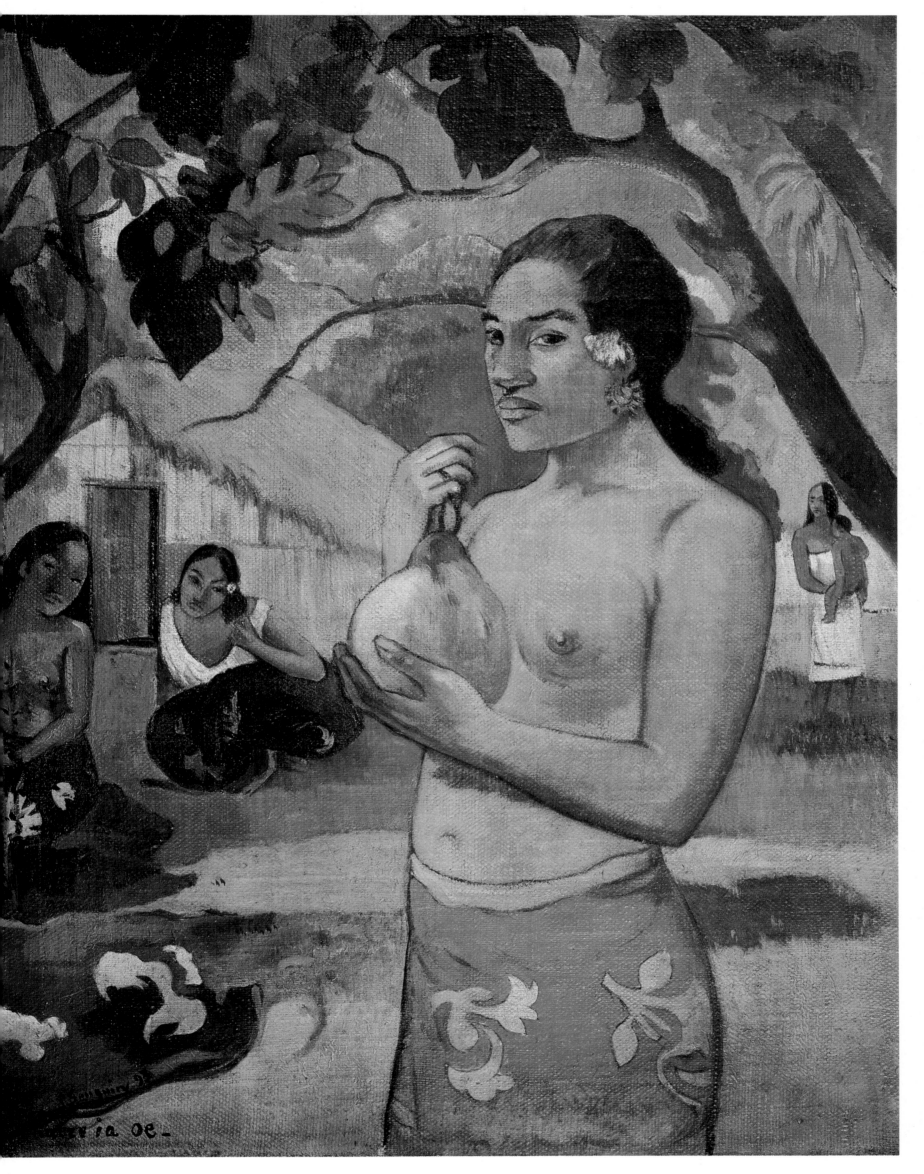

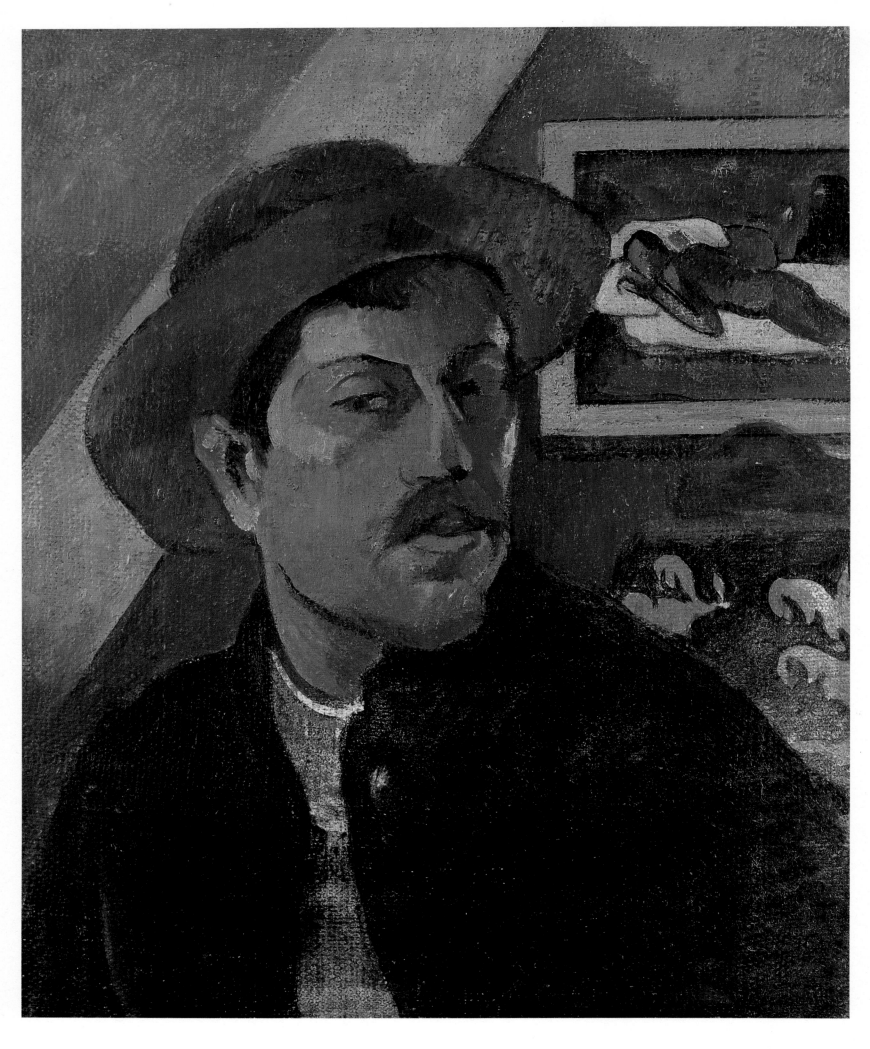

Self-Portrait Wearing a Hat, 1893

Oil on canvas
18⅛×15 inches (46×38 cm)
Musée d'Orsay, Paris

Gauguin moved into an apartment at number 6 rue Vercingétorix in Paris in the winter of 1893-4 and this work was painted there. There are many eyewitness accounts of this exotic residence, where Gauguin entertained Symbolist writers. The walls were painted in chrome yellow, visible

here, and were hung with the remainder of his collection of impressionist works, a number of reproductions and some of his own works. *Manao Tupapau* (page 136) is seen in the background, in reverse since it has been viewed in a mirror. This had been included in the recent exhibition of Gau-

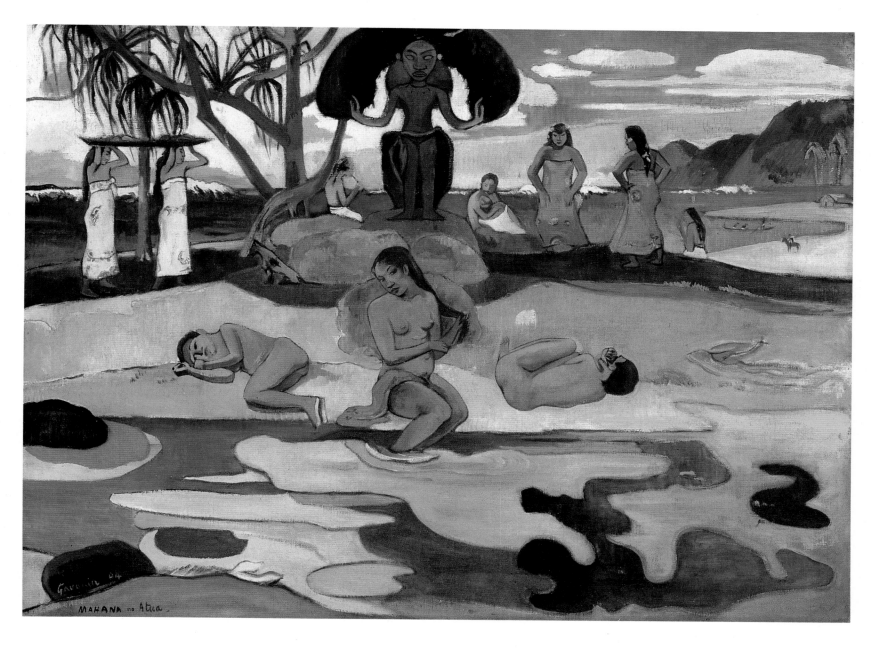

guin's works at Durand-Ruel's gallery, and he considered it to be one of the most important records of his time in Tahiti. It is framed in bright yellow, rather than the simple white Gauguin had used since his days exhibiting with the Impressionists. Presumably the white frames had been abandoned in order not to provide too stark a contrast with the chrome walls. The painting of *Manao Tupapau*, which in reality was almost a meter in width, is shown very much smaller, at the far side of the room.

In spite of Gauguin's bohemian existence in the rue Vercingétorix, this image is much more self-analytical than the self-portraits from the period 1888-9, when he painted a number of works in which his own physiognomy is often thinly veiled under Symbolist titles. There is none of the posturing of *Bonjour M. Gauguin* (page 100) and his dress is restrained. However, just as the sitter's personality was conveyed in the background of *Self-Portrait* (*Les Misérables* (page 74), the reproduction of one of his own paintings in this work is intended to make a general comment on Gauguin's image of himself at this stage. On the reverse of this canvas is a portrait of his friend the musician William Molard, the first owner of the work.

Mahana no Atua (Day of the God), 1894

Oil on canvas
26⅞ × 36 inches (68.3 × 91.5 cm)
Art Institute of Chicago

After the relative failure of his one-man exhibition at Durand-Ruel's gallery, when he received some laudatory reviews but barely covered his expenses, Gauguin continued working on the text of *Noa Noa* which, as he explained to Mette, he hoped would 'facilitate the understanding of [this] painting [from Tahiti]'. This text, the title of which means 'fragrant', was a reworking of several sources, including the two-volume *Voyages aux Iles du Grand Océan* by the Belgian J-A Moerenhout, which documented ancient Tahitian rituals as well as more mundane customs.

Much of Gauguin's two-year interlude in Paris before returning to Polynesia was spent writing, producing articles and mixing with literary figures. Consequently his painting output was demonstrably lower than before. Those pictures which he did produce, like *Mahana no Atua*, were reworkings and reinterpretations of his time in Tahiti and several of the figures in this painting had occurred in previous Tahitian

works. Gauguin was clearly not looking for new imagery at this time but rather was producing works which should be viewed in the same light as *Noa Noa*; that is, where he assembled the most exotic elements of a fictional Tahiti and presented them to an élite Parisian audience with little regard for their authenticity. The hieratic, frieze-like composition emphasizes the 'savage' aspect of the Tahitian ritual represented and the unreality of the scene is heightened by the abstract quality of the foreground elements, with their interlocking organic shapes and unnaturalistic colors.

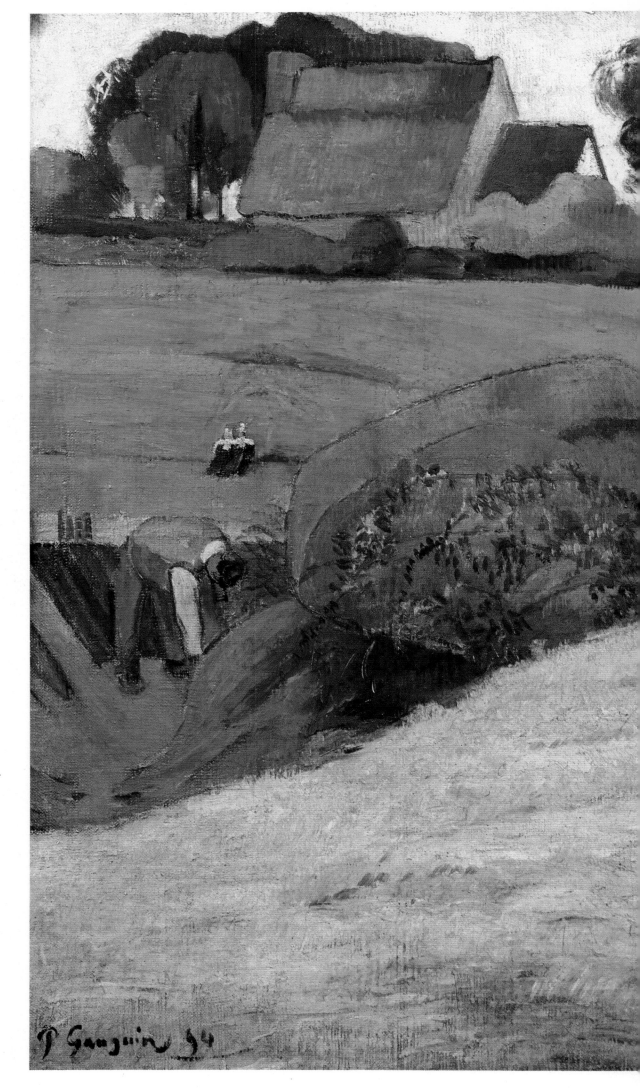

Peasant Women from Brittany,
1894

Oil on canvas
23⅝×36¼ inches (60×92 cm)
Musée d'Orsay, Paris

In the spring of 1894 Gauguin left Paris for
Brittany and visited Le Pouldu and Pont-
Aven, where he worked with a number of
young painters. Towards the end of May he
was badly injured in a brawl with some
sailors and could not paint for two months.
In his two years back in France, Gauguin
painted fewer than three dozen works,
many of them reworkings of Tahitian
themes and motifs, influenced in part by
his writing of *Noa Noa*. This is one of the
few which uses French subject-matter, but
it too is a reinterpretation of previous
works, exploring little that was new in
terms of technique or subject-matter. Instead Gauguin has produced a work in
which he uses the motif of two women,
which he had favored in Tahiti, but transposed to a Breton landscape and dressed in
traditional costume. The enigmatic relationship between the two is akin to that
found in the Tahitian works. Their figures
are locked together to form a solid block,
set against a landscape in which recession
is suggested by a series of planes.

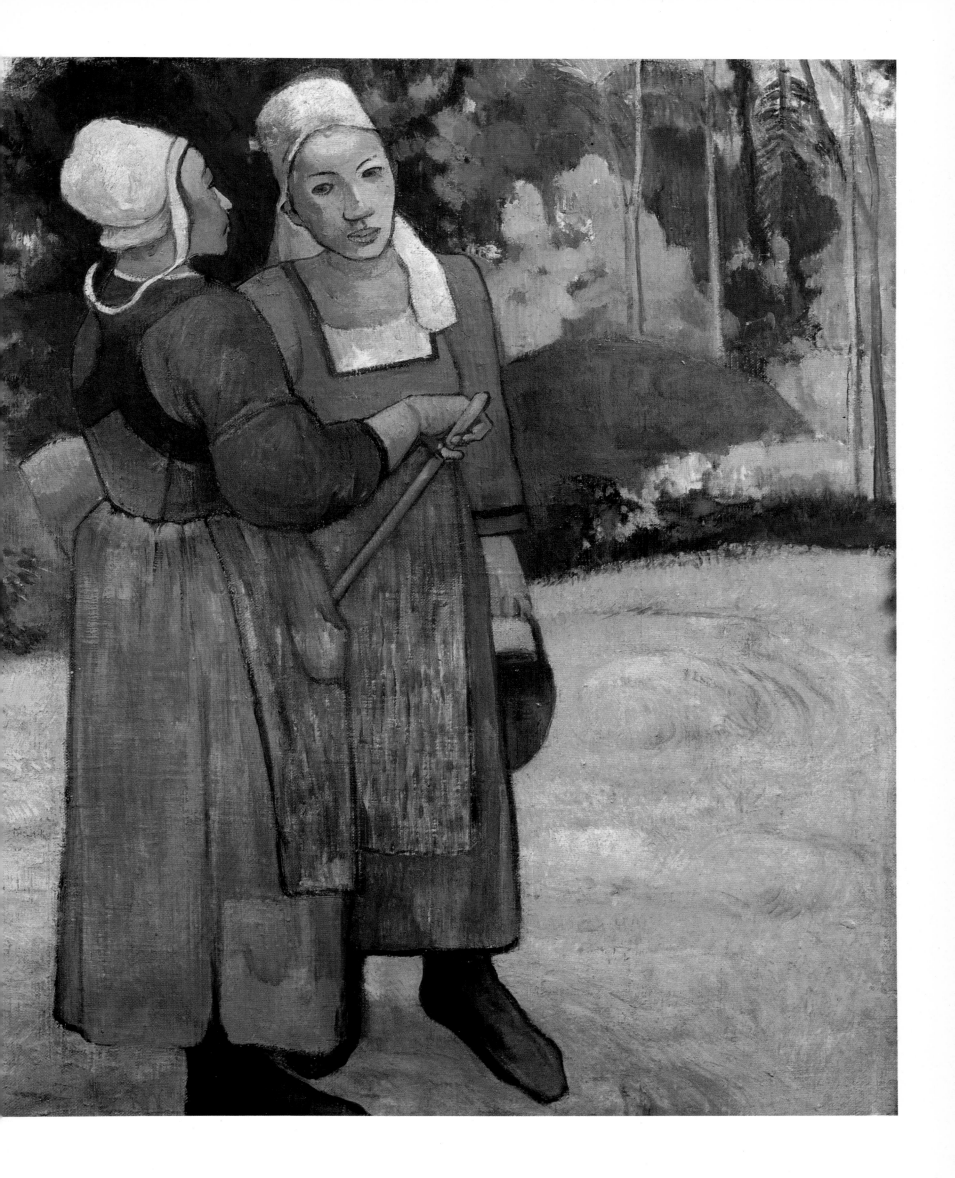

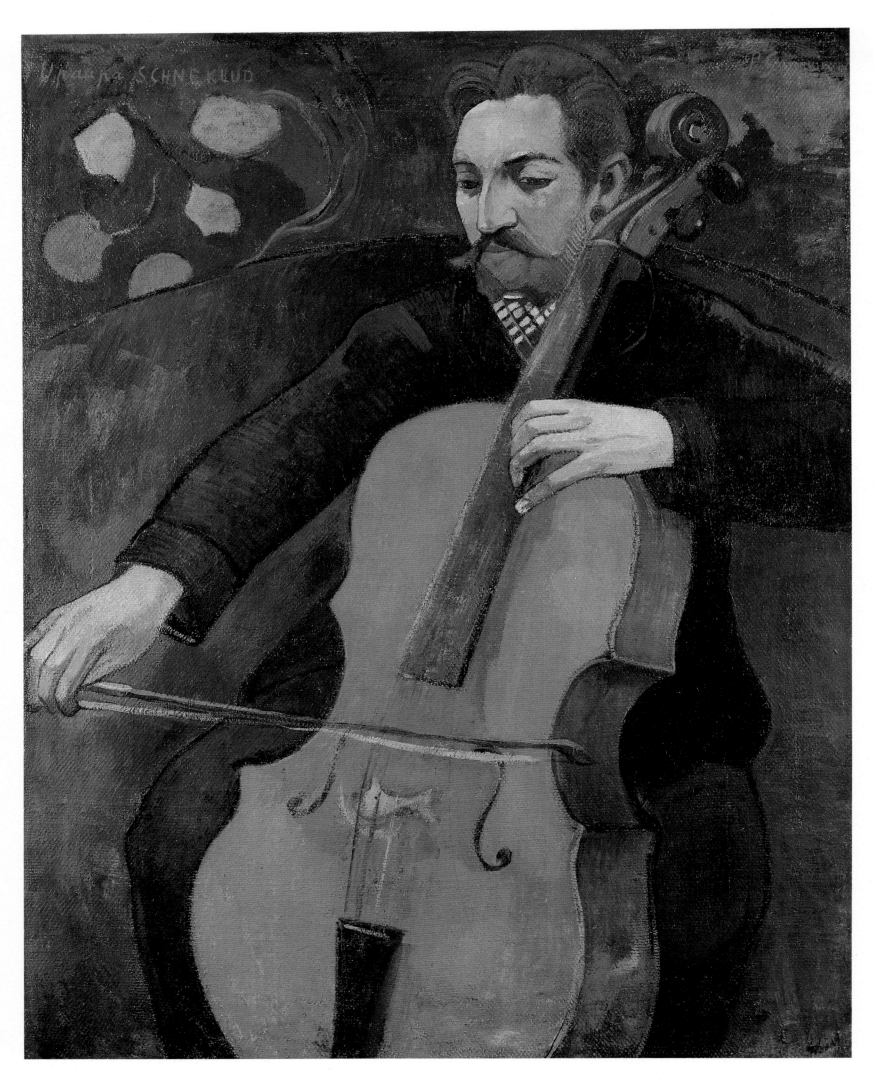

Upaupa Schneklud, 1894
Oil on canvas
36½×28⅞ inches (92.5×73.5 cm)
Baltimore Museum of Art

In this portrait of the Swedish musician Fritz Schneklud, who belonged to the circle of literary and artistic figures that he frequented, Gauguin has painted one of his most forceful portraits. The stunning con

trast between the complementaries, blue and orange, and the flowing rhythms of the cello (echoed by the player's body) and the brown area in which he sits, gives the work a monumental quality. The heavily stylized

150

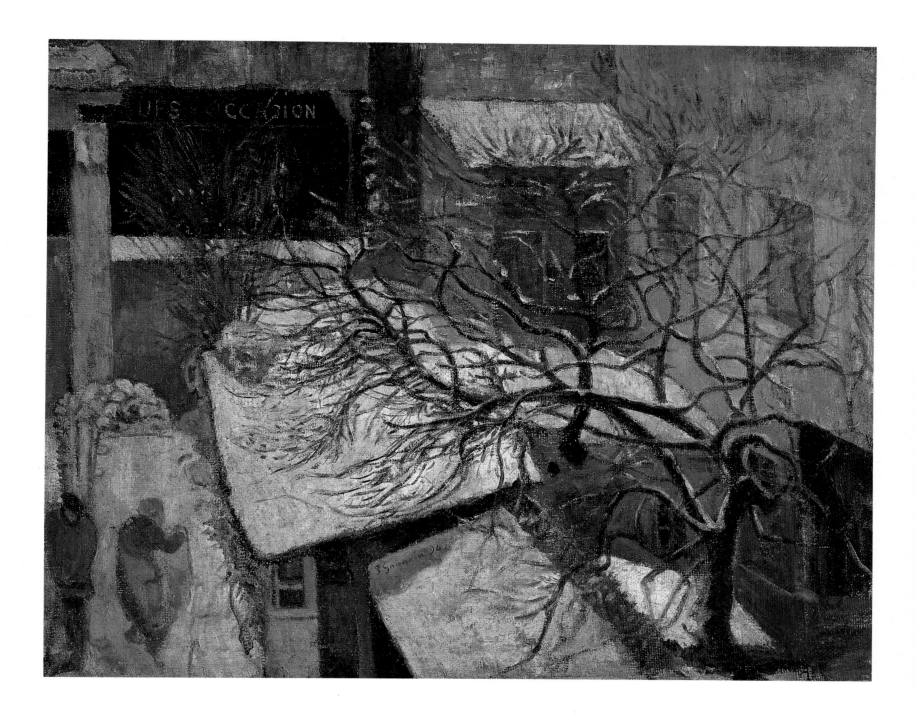

features, with hooded eyes and hooked nose, have led some to identify this as a thinly disguised self-portrait. Certainly Gauguin was an amateur musician – he took his mandoline with him on all his trips – but most of his portraits contain a degree of stylization and simplification which makes them more of a generalized representation than a study of an individual personality, whether his own or that of another.

The work is inscribed on the upper left-hand side with its title, 'Upaupa Schneklud'. Even back in Paris and painting European subjects, Gauguin made continual reference to his time in Polynesia. 'Upaupa' is the name given to the famous native dance of Tahiti. Presumably the use of exotic titles and concepts was out of a desire to create an image of himself as a worldly-wise, bohemian figure.

Paris in the Snow, 1894

Oil on canvas
28⅛×34⅝ inches (71.5×88 cm)
National Museum Vincent Van Gogh, Amsterdam

Painted towards the end of winter in 1894, this is one of a number of works produced on his return to France in which Gauguin has fallen back on previous styles and subjects. He has produced one of his most frankly urban scenes in a manifestly impressionist style and has adopted the favorite impressionist device of depicting a snowscape as a means of studying the effects of light reflexions on a white surface, painting his shadows with bright blue pigment. In this respect, and in the choice of Parisian subject, the work is similar to *The Seine at the Pont d'Iéna* (page 28) of almost 20 years earlier. The brushstrokes

used here are feathery and rapid, with little of the outlining that Gauguin had used in more recent works.

It seems odd that Gauguin should have returned to a style which had certainly been superseded in his own work, and which was becoming increasingly popular and imitated at the Salon as impressionism became widely acceptable. Perhaps the painting was done from a need to assimilate and justify the changes that had taken place in his own oeuvre in the previous 20 years; perhaps it was partly because of a failure to find anything 'savage' in Paris as he had in Brittany and Tahiti, which he could paint in a correspondingly naive fashion. Certainly there is an element of homage to his first artistic style, re-awakened by the famous Caillebotte legacy of Impressionist paintings to the nation that same year.

Self-Portrait (at Golgotha), 1896

Oil on canvas
30×37 inches (76×94 cm)
Museu de Arte, São Paulo

This brooding self-portrait was painted in the summer of 1896, when Gauguin was hospitalized in Papeete and in desperate financial straits. Once again he has identified himself with Christ, and in particular Christ's suffering. The inscription makes it clear that this work is 'near Golgotha', and there may be a suggestion of a calvary in the background, but it is rather a psychological closeness to Christ's Passion to which the title refers. The following year Gauguin apparently attempted suicide and references to his death become more common in his letters.

The painting makes allusion to a number of Old Master prototypes. The very generalized smock and hair has the effect of making the portrait timeless and any comparisons with religious works becomes that much more overt. There may be a suggestion of Watteau's *Gilles*, which Gauguin knew from the Louvre, in the costume and in the theme of the misunderstood social outcast. The gloomy atmosphere and the unflinching rawness of the pose, facial expression and setting is reminiscent of a number of Rembrandt self-portraits. The subject is far removed from the bombast of *Self-Portrait (Les Misérables)* (page 74) or *Self-Portrait with Halo* (page 102) and the treatment is very different, but it is simply a further attempt to explore the theme of the artist as persecuted creator. The work had great personal importance for Gauguin; it is one of the few which was not sent back to Paris but remained with him until his death in Hivaoa, seven years later.

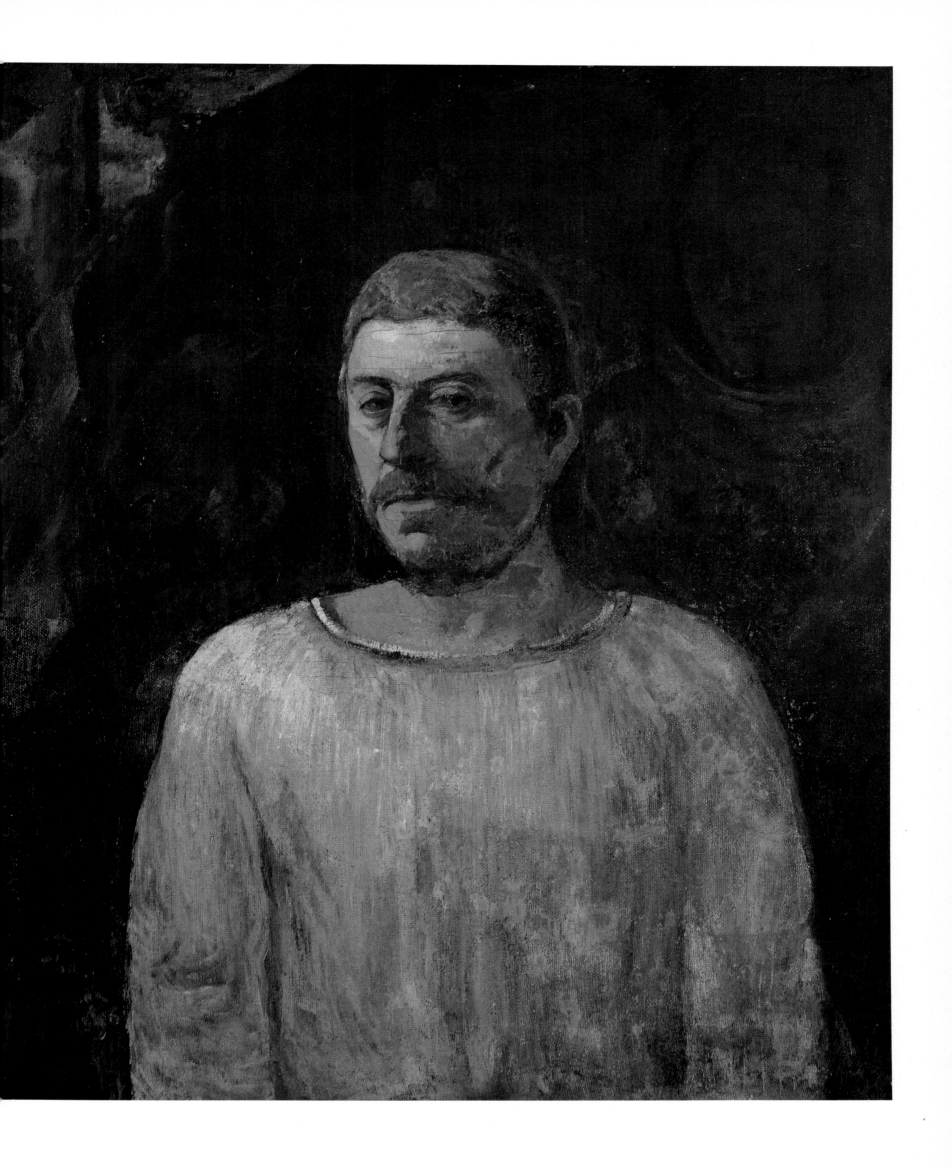

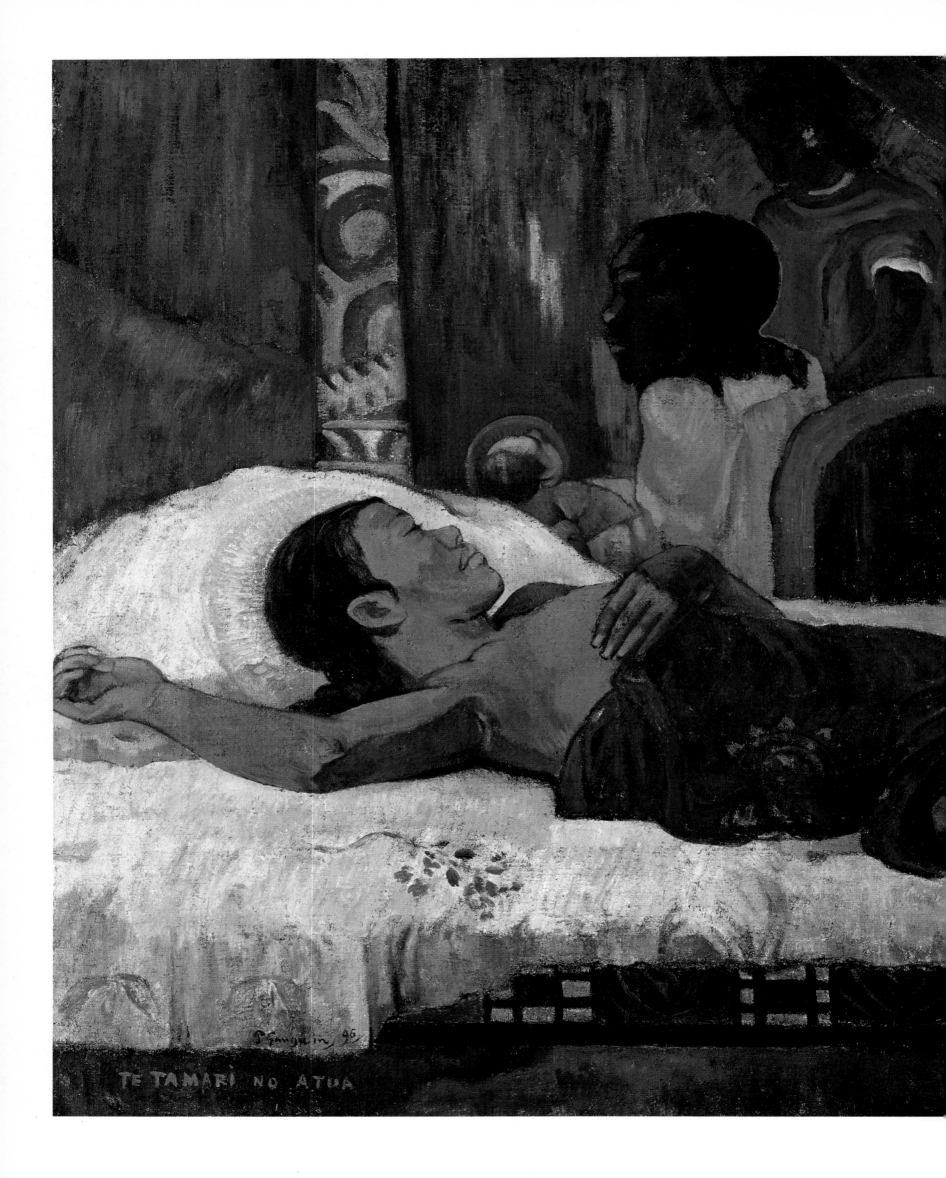

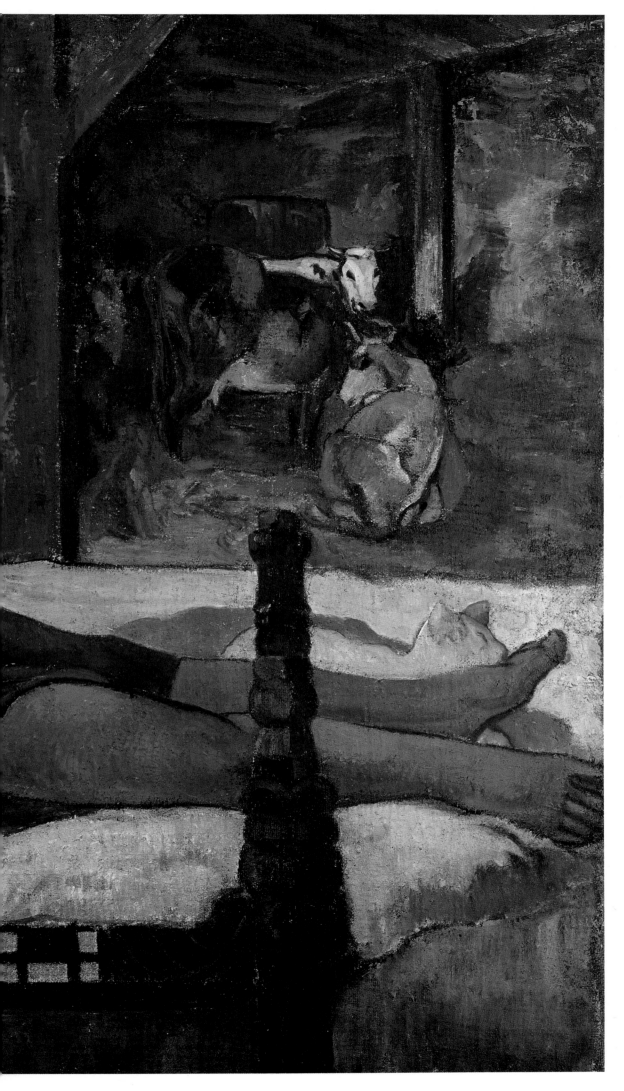

Te Tamari no Atua (The Birth of Christ, Son of God), 1896

Oil on canvas
37¾×50¾ inches (96×129 cm)
Bayerische Staatsgemäldesammlungen,
Munich

This work is the conceptual companion to *Ia Orana Maria* (page 128), painted during Gauguin's first trip to Tahiti. Both deal with Christian themes fused with Polynesian subject-matter and attempt to reconcile eastern and western motifs. The figures are Tahitian women but the elaborate bed and the cattle in the background are transposed from Europe. In fact the upper right-hand side of the work is from a painting by the mid-nineteenth-century artist Octave Tassaert, which had belonged to Gauguin's guardian Arosa and a photograph of which he must have had with him in Tahiti, so close is the similarity. The left-hand side, with the strange hooded figure who holds the infant Christ, is a copy of one of his own paintings of the same year, *Baby*.

While making overt use of these artistic sources, the work is also a loose reinterpretation of Manet's *Olympia* (page 21) which represents a Parisian courtesan. The reclining woman on the bed, the black woman in the background and particularly the cat on the bed at the woman's feet are clearly taken from the photograph of the Manet which Gauguin had with him in Tahiti. This ironical correlation between the Virgin and the prostitute recurs throughout Gauguin's work.

The depiction of a nativity in 1896 may have been occasioned by the pregnancy of Pahura, Gauguin's 14-year-old *vahine*. She bore a daughter who died shortly after birth, probably towards the end of 1896. There are reminders of death in this work, most notably in the black-hooded figure who holds Christ, and who had appeared in a number of earlier works since *Old Women at Arles* (page 87). This allusion to death has, for some reviewers, turned the painting into an elaborate memorial for Gauguin's daughter, but the intimate connexions between life and death had been a common theme in other paintings, and traditional depictions of Christ's nativity often include symbols of His Passion.

Nave Nave Mahana (Wonderful Days), 1896

Oil on canvas
37×51¼ inches (94×130 cm)
Musée des Beaux-Arts, Lyons

Only slightly larger than most of Gauguin's canvases, this painting nevertheless appears very monumental because of its subject-matter and treatment. The use of a number of full-length standing figures was to reach its finest treatment in *Where do we come from?* (page 160) the following year. The rather rough canvas and the chalky application of paint means that the work resembles a fresco, and Gauguin has been inspired by the wall-paintings of the nineteenth-century artist Puvis de Chavannes. The suggestion of a tropical Eden is made clear by intertwining the young women with the saplings. The static and tranquil quality of the work contrasts sharply with the deprivations Gauguin suffered at this time, owing to failing health and lack of money, and the irony of the title cannot have escaped him or the friends back in Paris to whom he sent the work at the beginning of 1897.

The depiction of the women gives some idea of the difference between the concept of female beauty in Europe and Gauguin's more 'primitive' Eve, who is unself-consciously naked. The exchange between Gauguin and Strindberg, used as the introduction to the catalog for his sale in Paris in 1895, makes this contrast clear, Gauguin had written:

. . .The Eve of your civilized imagination makes misogynists of us. . . The Eve I have painted – and she alone – can remain naturally naked before us. Yours, in this simple state, could not move without a feeling of shame, and too beautiful, perhaps, would provoke misfortune and suffering.

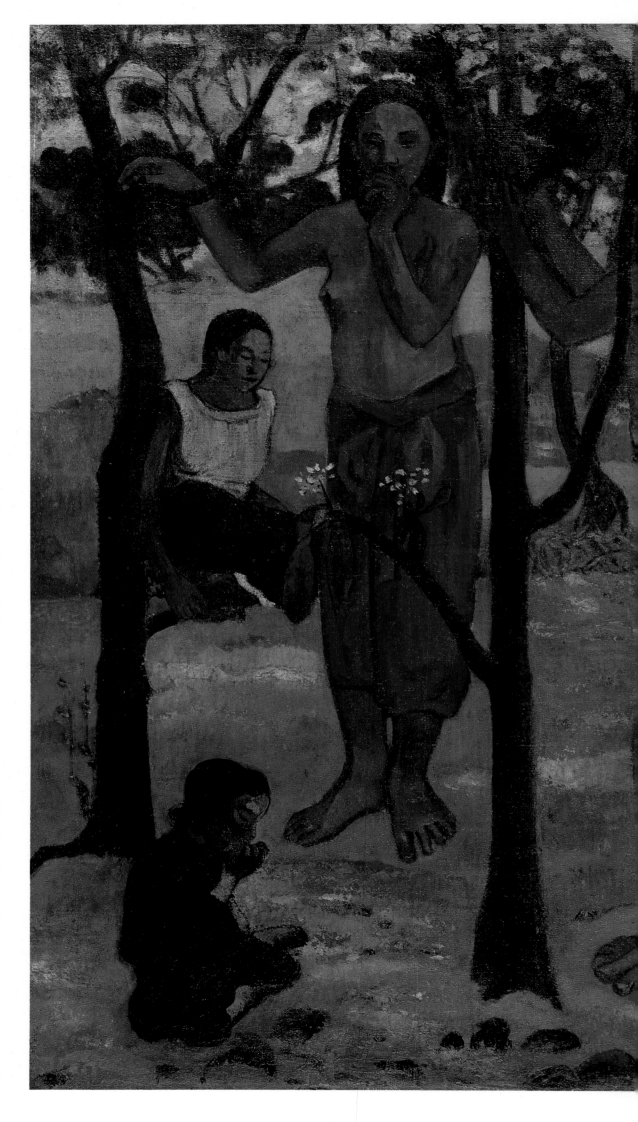

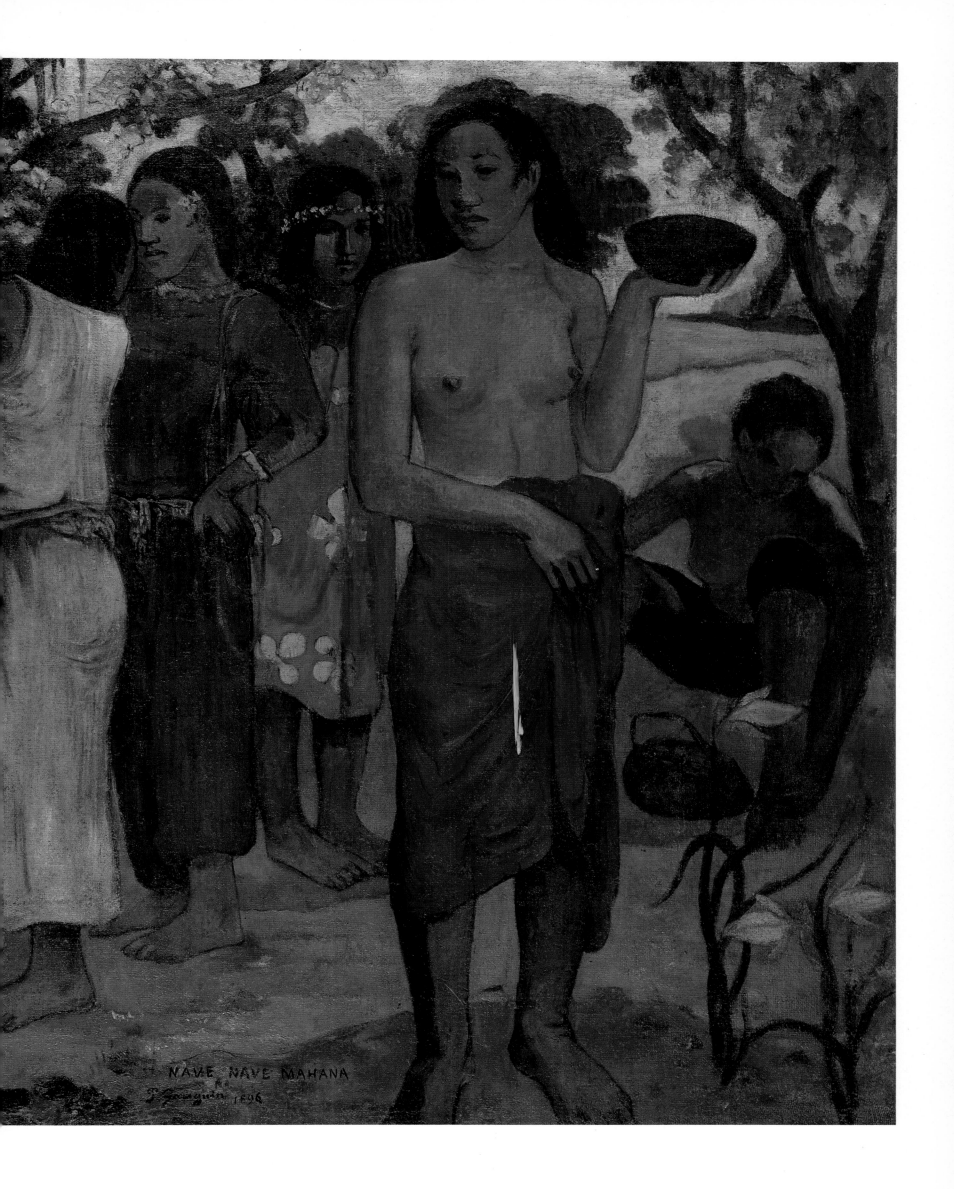

NAVE NAVE MAHANA

P. Gauguin 1896

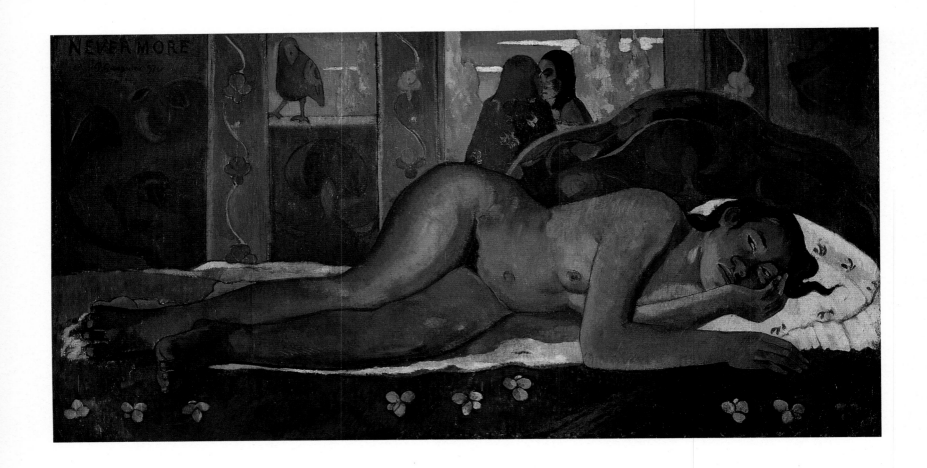

Te Rerioa (The Dream), 1897

Oil on canvas
37⅜×52 inches (95×132 cm)
Courtauld Institute Galleries, London

Painted just after *Nevermore* (page 159), Gauguin explained the painting in a letter to Daniel de Monfreid:

Everything in this canvas is dreamlike; is it the child, the mother, the horseman on the track, or better still is it the painter's dream? All that has nothing to do with the painting, they will say. Maybe, but also perhaps not.

Although he mentions only one woman, the work is one in the series showing two solidly-constructed and interlocking female figures, such as *Nafea Faa Ipoipo* (page 134). The forward-facing woman is seated like a Buddha and gazes at the spectator. The decorations around the walls of the room in which the women are seated have aroused some interest. They may be carved panels or painted to resemble a three-dimensional frieze but are presum-ably the work of Gauguin's imagination, for nothing similar existed in Tahitian domestic decoration. Two panels incorporate idols akin to some of Gauguin's wood-carvings, and the figure to the upper right-hand side of the composition is similar to that in *Mahana no Atua* (page 147). The landscape behind the woman viewed in profile may be the view through an open doorway, or possibly one of Gauguin's canvases propped against the wall of the hut. In subject-matter the picture is similar to *Tahitian Landscape* (page 122).

The role of the imagination and the importance of dreams was one of the central tenets of Symbolism. The relatively large size of this canvas and the sense of mystery with which it is infused suggests that it represents a significant artistic statement by Gauguin.

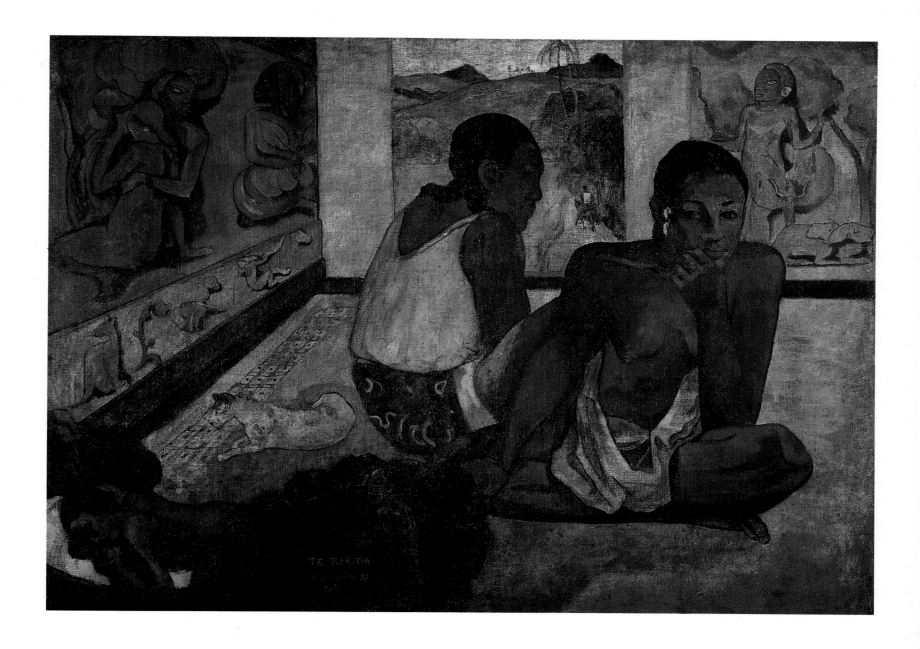

Nevermore O Tahiti, 1897
Oil on canvas
26¾×45¾ inches (68×116 cm)
Courtauld Institute Galleries, London

In a letter to his friend Daniel de Monfreid in Paris, who took care of Gauguin's business arrangements during his second trip to Polynesia, the artist wrote:

I'm attempting to finish a canvas to send with the others, but shall I have enough time? . . I don't know if I'm mistaken, but I believe it to be good. With a simple nude I wished to suggest a certain long-gone barbaric luxury. It is all drowned in colors which are deliberately somber and melancholy; it is neither silk, velvet, muslin, nor gold that creates this luxury but merely the material made rich by the artist's handling. . . For its title, *Nevermore*, not exactly the raven from Edgar [Allen] Poe, but the bird of the devil which keeps watch. It's badly painted (I am so nervous and I am working in fits and starts), never mind, I think that it's a good canvas. . .

This was the latest of a number in which Gauguin referred to Manet's *Olympia* (page 21), with the reclining nude on a bed

in the foreground, and begins to parody some of his earlier workings of the same theme, particularly *Manao Tupapau* (page 136) with its ominous background specter, and *Te Tamari no Atua* (page 154). The latter uses the same device of the bed, unknown in Tahiti, and the same intense chrome yellow to offset the coffee-colored skin of the nude. Here, however, the artist has taken great anatomical liberties. The woman's hip is grossly distended to echo the curve of the bedstead and the arm which protects her face apparently springs from her chest.

Although the title *Nevermore* is conspicuous on the canvas and the raven is unmistakable, Gauguin was at pains in the letter to de Monfreid to dissociate himself from too literary a reading of the work. However, the links between the painting and Poe's poem of 1875, which was a favorite in Symbolist circles, was too close to be overlooked.

159

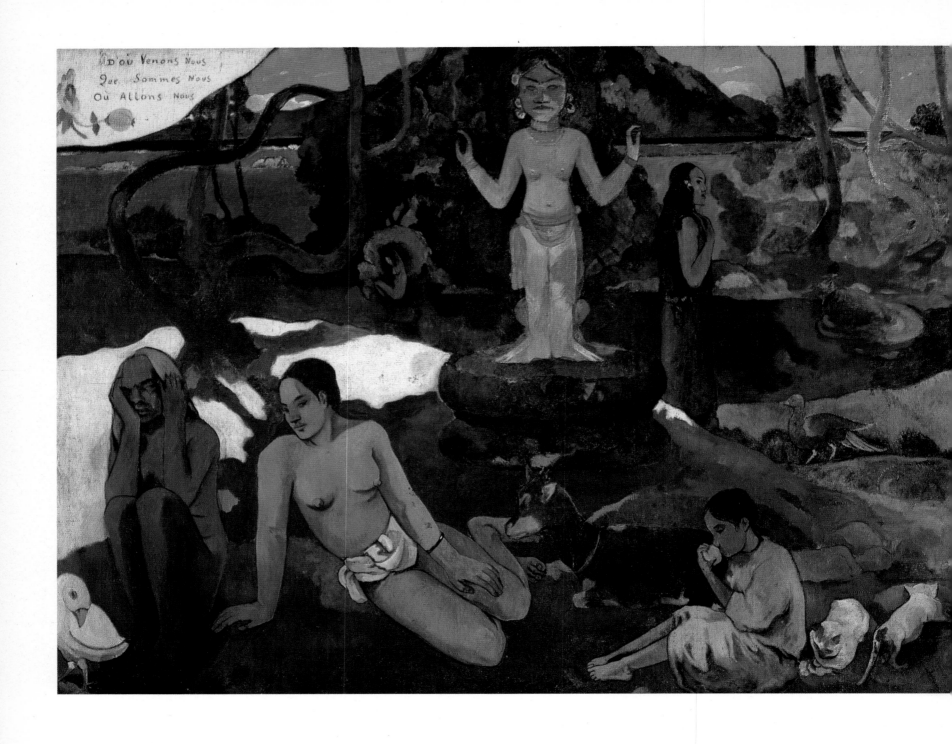

Where do we come from? What are we? Where are we going?,

1897
Oil on canvas
54¾×147½ inches (139.1×374.6 cm)
Museum of Fine Arts, Boston

By far the largest of Gauguin's canvases, this has long been considered the most important work from the second Tahitian period, in which he attempted to embody his artistic philosophy before trying to commit suicide. When he painted the work Gauguin was in poor health, had severe financial worries and had just received news of the death of Aline, his favorite child. In 1901 he wrote to Morice that he had produced the work very quickly in a

burst of feverish activity without recourse to any preparatory studies, painting directly onto the coarse sackcloth. After its completion he retired to the mountains and took arsenic, but his body rejected the poison and the attempt to take his own life was unsuccessful. The motivation behind this story needs to be regarded with a degree of scepticism. Gauguin was fond of making elaborate gestures, he recognized the importance of this work, and realized

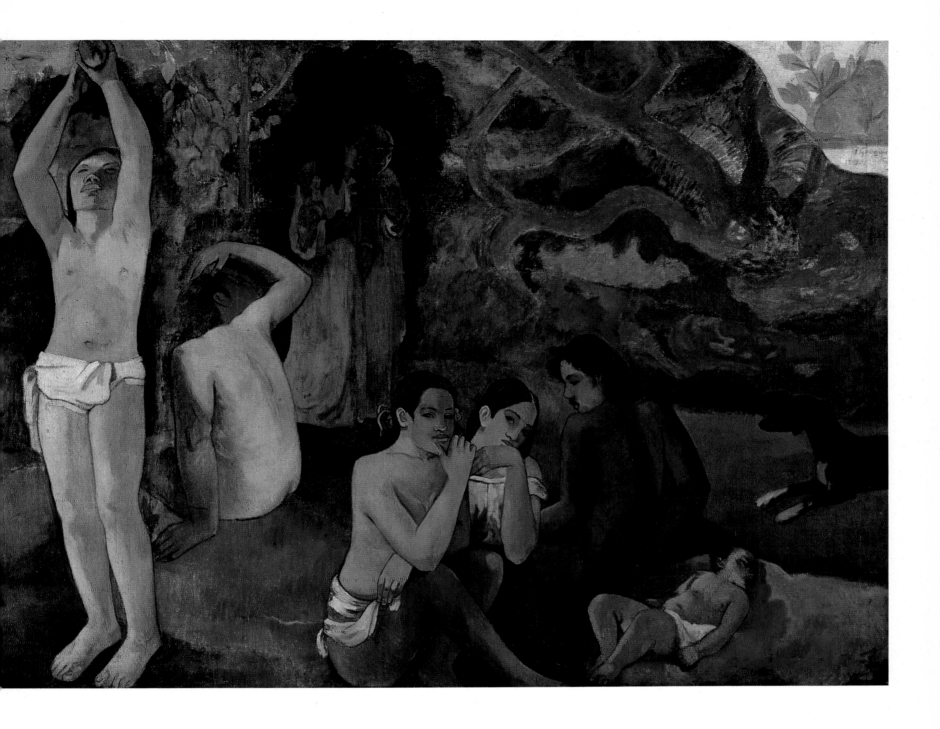

its potential as a 'final statement', heightening his attempts to portray himself as an artistic martyr. The suicide story may well be a fiction, and there are certainly inconsistencies in his report of his working methods. A remarkably finished and intricate full-scale sketch for the work exists, casting doubt on the whole story.

The work is intended to resemble a large decorative wall-painting and is meant to be read from right to left, contrary to normal

practice. The narration opens with the recumbent baby who corresponds to the first question in the title 'Where do we come from?', and then the work progresses through the central figure, larger than the others, who plucks the fruit from the Tree of Knowledge, in an attempt to answer the query 'What are we?' The final image is of the crouching white-haired woman, close to death, who was derived from the Peruvian mummy which Gauguin had used

several times before in his work (page 7).

Despite its clear program, the figures in the work, both those with some apparent narrative function and the many subsidiary figures, are remarkably self-contained and the sense of isolation is strong. In a letter to André Fontainas, Gauguin explained the pictorial role of the idol: 'The idol is there not as a literary explanation, but as a statue, perhaps less of a statue than the living figures. . .'

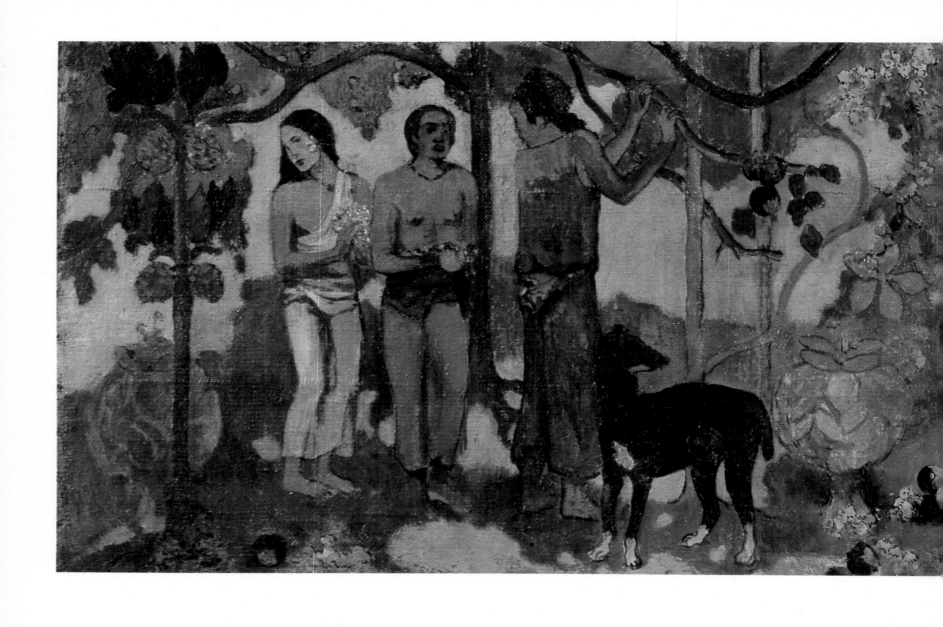

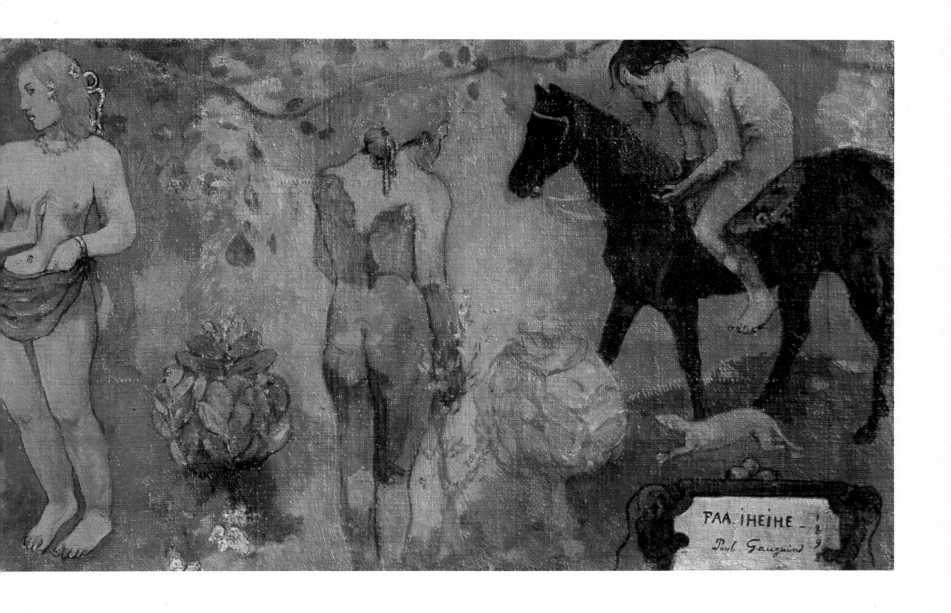

Faa Iheihe (Tahitian Pastoral),
1898
Oil on canvas
21¼×66½ inches (54×169 cm)
London, Tate Gallery

The mural-like appearance of this work is heightened by its greatly elongated shape and the sense of monumentality in the full-length figures. The decorative quality makes it similar to *Where do we come from?* (page 160), as does the gathering of the figures into three discernable groups, each quite separate from the others. The work's ornamental quality is strengthened by the limited palette of oranges and yellows.

The genre scenes which had characterized Gauguin's earlier Tahitian works have disappeared by this time and he has attempted to suggest a complex ritualistic work, partly inspired by his reading of Moerenhout. The hieratic poses of the figures draw on photographs of Javanese sculptural friezes, several of which featured in other paintings (for example *Three Tahitians*, page 164). The lack of any native art pertaining to ancient religious rites forced Gauguin to manufacture a vision of Polynesia which relied on a number of disparate sources, chosen for their apparently 'primitive' quality. Coupled with a contrivedly naive paint application, often on coarse canvas or sackcloth, which he hoped would give the works an authentic feeling, Gauguin has thus created an enduring vision of a tropical paradise which had little to do with reality in late nineteenth-century Tahiti.

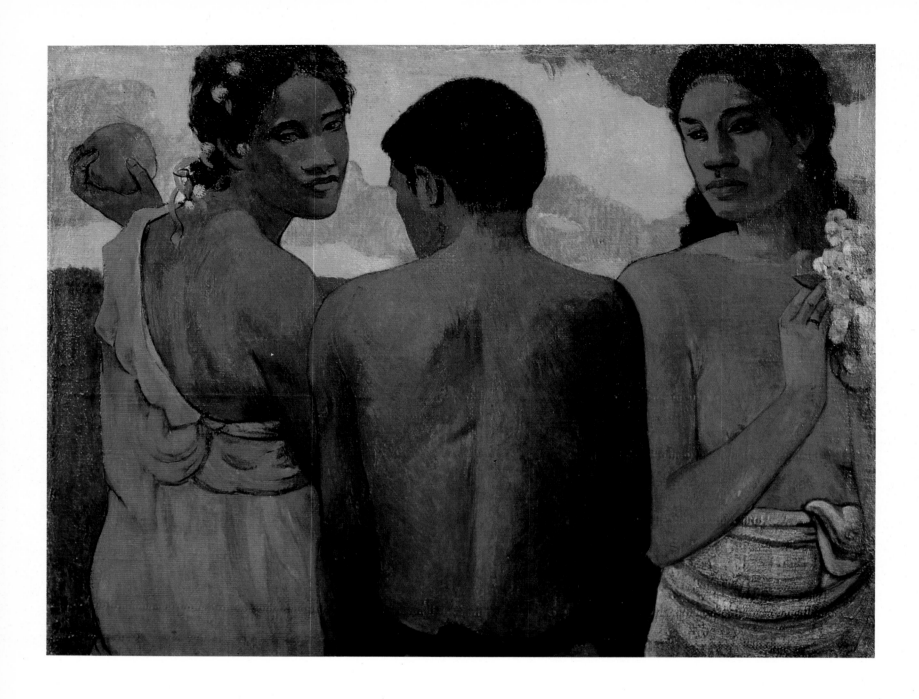

Three Tahitians, 1899

Oil on canvas
28¾×36 inches (73×91 cm)
National Gallery of Scotland

Gauguin has here used the format of three nude or semi-nude figures, one presented from behind and the two outer ones facing inwards, to rework the traditional subject of the Three Graces. The rhythmic interplay between the figures and the undulating line which locks them together helps reinforce this allusion. The subject is subtly altered in this version, however, by making the central figure male and by depicting only the upper halves of the bodies. *Three Tahitians* also recalls the allegory of a young man faced with the choice between virtue and vice personified as two female figures, one dressed in red and the other in white, who try to lure him with symbolic objects. The hesitant nature of his pose suggests indecision.

On a more mundane level, the work is a magnificent genre scene with the rather weak youth sandwiched between two Tahitian women. The abundant flowers and the fruit in the hand of the left-hand woman may be references to fertility and the work may chronicle some part of a marriage ritual, which Gauguin treated in a number of other works and which he had read about in both *The Marriage of Loti* and Moerenhout's *Voyages aux Iles du Grand Océan.*

The painting becomes quite monumental in effect because of the sculptural quality of the figures. The use of a young Tahitian man in such a prominent position is quite unusual for Gauguin, and the pose may owe something to the famous painting of *The Large Bather* by Ingres, in the Louvre. The work suggests a dissatisfaction with the flattening, contrived, 'primitive' aspect of earlier paintings and shows Gauguin's interest in a more classical handling of the human form.

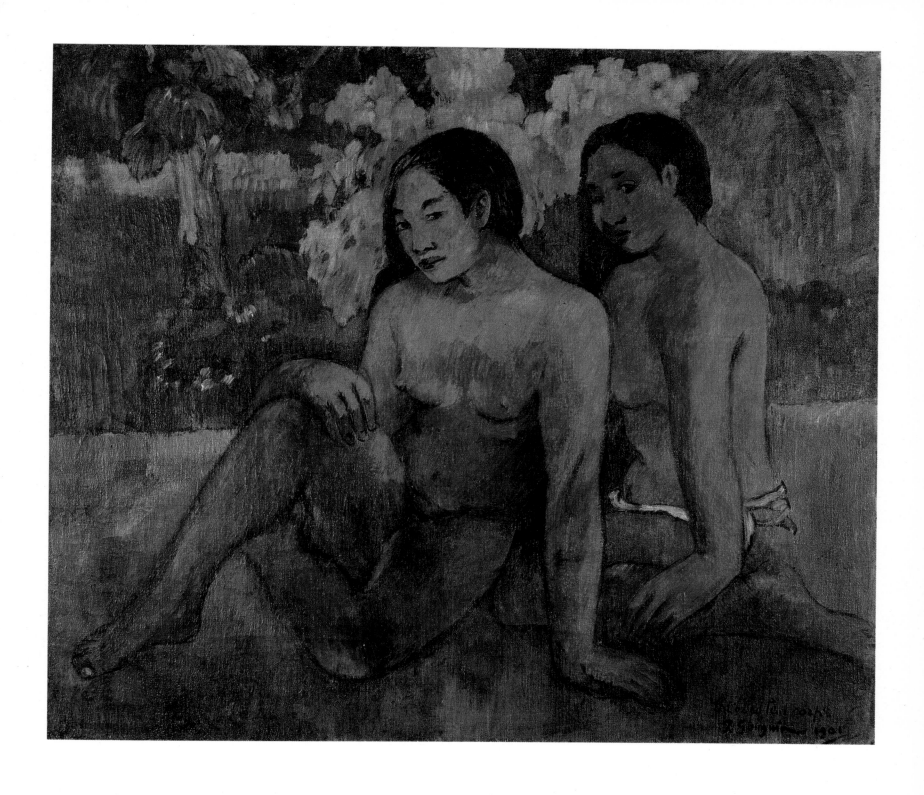

And the Gold of their Bodies,
1901

Oil on canvas
26⅜×31⅛ inches (67×79 cm)
Musée d'Orsay, Paris

In 1900 Gauguin apparently painted no works because of ill-health, and in 1901 he produced only about a dozen canvases, including this one. In it he returned to the subject of two Polynesian women seated on the ground, the solidity of their bodies contrasting with a fairly schematic and flat background. Here the two women gaze provocatively at the spectator; the use of a full-frontal nude is quite rare in Gauguin's oeuvre. The rather dark tonality is enlivened by the patch of brilliant vermilion behind the women's heads while the decorative quality of their bodies, with the repetition of poses, is exploited at the expense of anatomical accuracy. The right-hand woman's arm seems to be welded onto the front of her body and her hand is strangely contorted; the leg of the other woman is curled under her body in a cramped fashion.

Like many of his other works, the figures in *And the Gold of their Bodies* derive from the friezes of the Javanese temple at Borobudur, a photograph of which Gauguin had with him in Polynesia and which was found in his possession after his death. The poetic nature of the title inscribed on the bottom of the canvas above his signature demonstrates the importance of titles for Gauguin. By assigning mysterious and complex labels to his work he effectively added a further layer of meaning to his paintings.

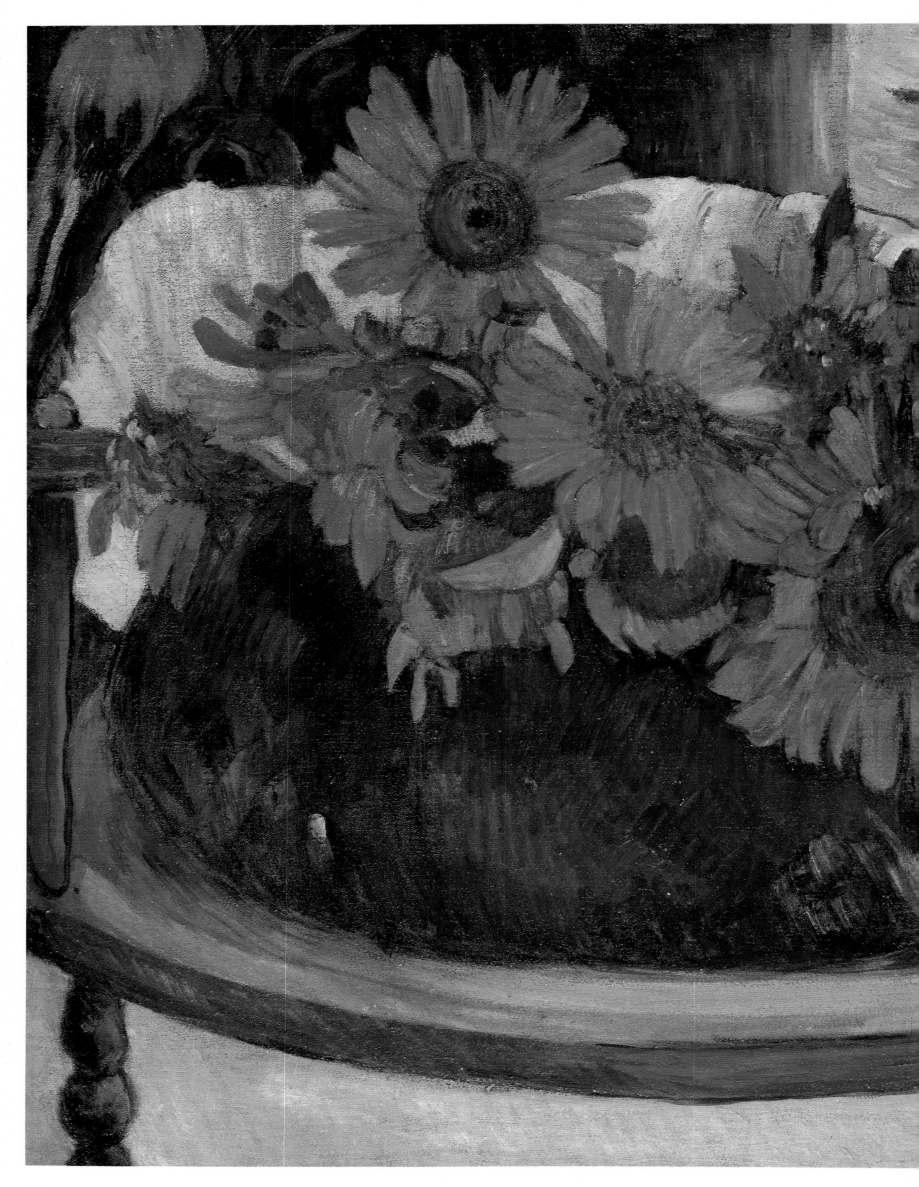

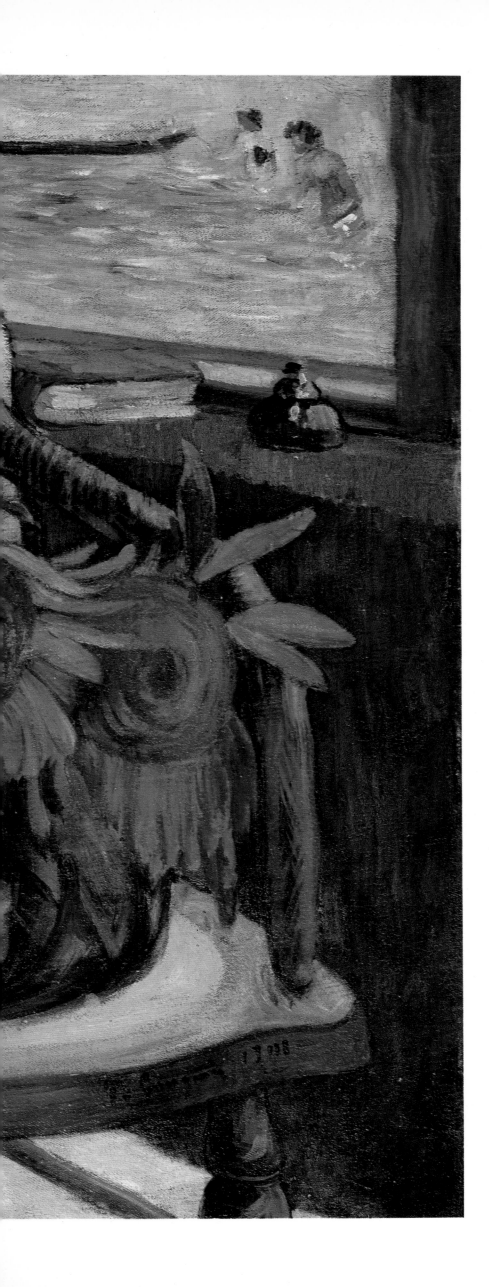

Still Life with Sunflowers, 1901

Oil on canvas
26×30 inches (66×76 cm)
Private collection, Switzerland

Gauguin had written to Daniel de Monfreid in 1898, requesting that he send him some flower seeds including 'dahlias, nasturtiums, sunflowers, flowers which can stand a hot climate . . . something to add beauty to my little plot of land, for as you know I adore flowers' and by the following summer he started work on a number of still lifes, using flowers from his garden. When the dealer Ambroise Vollard requested that he paint a number of these flower pieces for sale in Paris, however, Gauguin replied that Tahiti was not really '. . . the land of flowers' . . . and besides:

I do not copy nature, today even less than formerly. With me everything happens in my crazy imagination and when I tire of painting figures (which I prefer) I begin a still life and finish it without any model. . .

This work, and an almost identical version in the Hermitage Museum in Leningrad, is an overt homage to Vincent Van Gogh, who had killed himself in 1890 and whose suicide continued to haunt Gauguin. In 1902-3 in Hivaoa Gauguin worked on the important autobiographical text *Avant et Après*, which included a long section devoted to his version of events in Arles with Van Gogh. The memory of Van Gogh's sunflower paintings which had decorated the Yellow House in Arles was central to his image of the other artist, whose portrait with these very flowers he had painted in Arles (page 82). The choice of the sturdy seat on which the flowers are placed may be a reference to Van Gogh's painting of Gauguin's empty chair, which was itself a kind of symbolic portrait.

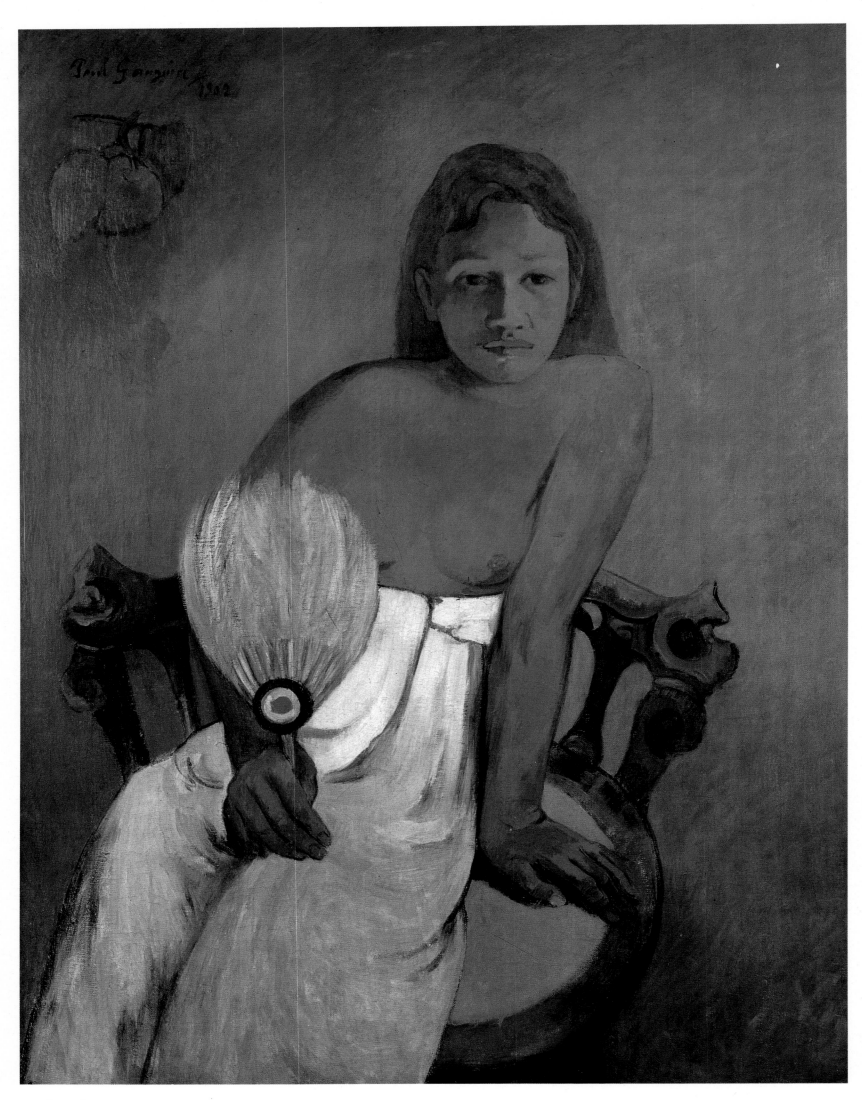

Girl with a Fan, 1902

Oil on canvas
36¼×28¾ inches (92×73 cm)
Folkwang Museum, Essen

After Gauguin's death the effects of his
studio were sent to Daniel de Monfreid in
Paris and these included a photograph of a
young woman, Tohotaua, who was notable

for having naturally red hair, seated like
the figure in this painting. In the photograph, taken in Gauguin's studio in
Hivaoa, the model is holding the large

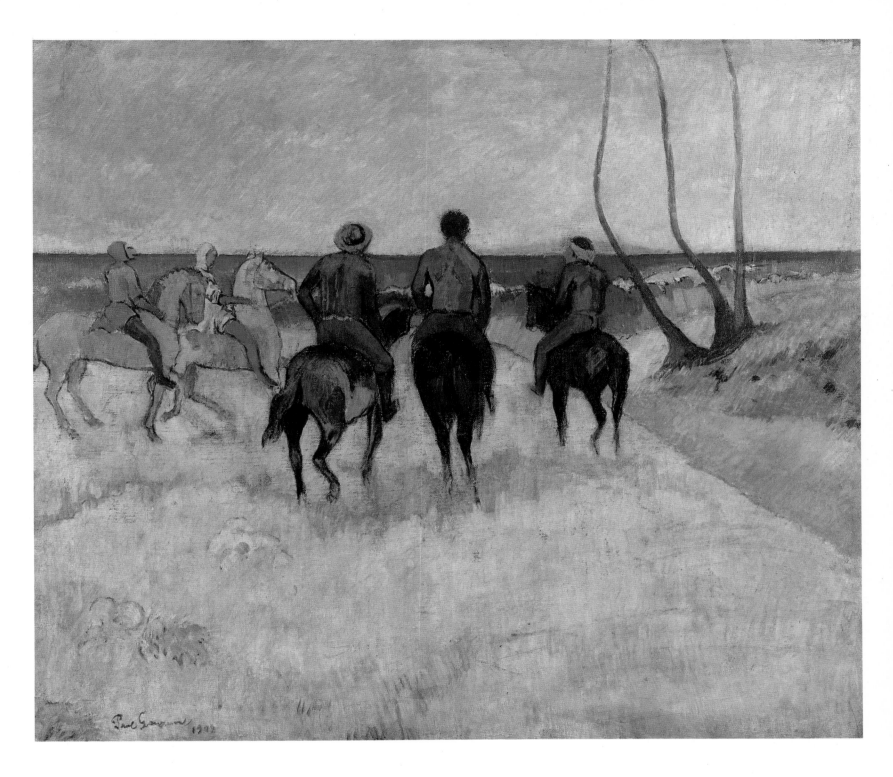

white fan, which in Polynesian culture had aristocratic connotations. In the background, a number of reproductions of Old Master paintings and a photograph of a Buddha decorate the wall. In the finished painting, however, Gauguin has made a number of alterations, and the wall is reduced to a delicate harmony of light tones. The model, who in the photograph was wearing a dress, has her breasts bared and Gauguin has placed her in an ornate chair, which was presumably the product of his imagination.

The coloring is notable for its softness; whites, grays, rose and a warm orange. The changes which Gauguin has introduced in the setting, and the simplification and close harmonies of the finished painting, demonstrate the extent to which he would enlarge upon a simple photograph. While he made use of a large number of pictorial sources, he did not do so indiscriminately and the final image achieved an existence independent of the original inspiration.

Riders on the Beach, 1902

Oil on canvas
26×28 inches (66×76 cm)
Folkwang Museum, Essen

In September 1901 Gauguin moved to the small island of Hivaoa in the Marquesas. After buying some land in the village of Atuona Gauguin began building his 'House of Pleasure', where he painted his last works. In 1902 he painted two versions of *Riders on the Beach* which use the same non-naturalistic colors. The beach is reduced to a pink ground and the figures are painted in hot oranges and deep blues, while the sea is reduced to Japanese white-tipped waves like those used in *Woman in the Waves (Ondine)* (page 106). In both versions a group of male riders are placed strategically along the shore, which is punctuated by slender tree-trunks.

The obvious source for both works is the horseracing pictures of Degas, which Gauguin particularly admired. The group of three horses seen from behind in this work are derived from Degas's *Races at Longchamps* of 1873-5, with his jockeys transposed into Marquesans. In the painting by Degas there are the same large open areas in the foreground and the same interest in the graceful anatomy of the horses. Just why Gauguin should have turned to the work of Degas for inspiration at this stage is difficult to say. In other works painted in Polynesia he sought inspiration from the works of Cézanne and Van Gogh, both of them influential on Gauguin at particular stages throughout his career, and the use of a Degas painted thirty years earlier is perhaps symptomatic of Gauguin's regard for the artist and his continual reference to the French capital after he had left it for good. The blending of East and West is perhaps more successful in this work than in previous paintings, such as *Manao Tupapau* page 136), but the world which Gauguin has painted is no less fictional for all its apparent authenticity.

Contes Barbares (Primitive Tales), 1902

Oil on canvas
51¾×35⅝ inches (131.5×90.5 cm)
Folkwang Museum, Essen

This is a slightly larger work than normal in Gauguin's oeuvre and he has returned to the practice of naming his canvases, which he had largely abandoned by this time; both these facts highlight this as one of his most important late works. Two of the figures in the work are identifiable. The exotic red-headed woman is Tohotaua, who had served as the model for *Girl with a Fan* (page 168), while the odd, crouching, dwarf-like figure in the background is Jacob Meyer de Haan, Gauguin's painting companion from Brittany, whose portrait he had painted in *Nirvana* (page 98). Meyer de Haan resembles a fox, the animal Gauguin had referred to as the 'symbol of perversity' and his feet have become menacing claws. His character contrasts sharply with the tranquillity of the two women, who derive from Gauguin's photographs of the temple of Borobudur in Java. The dark-haired woman is seated in a classic Buddha pose. The contrast between a fictionalized East and a half-remembered West is particularly evident in this work, which is also sometimes seen as a dialogue between Knowledge and Innocence. This is perhaps too sharp a distinction to draw, however; the suggestion of Knowledge, as represented by Meyer de Haan from Europe, being a corrupting force and Innocence as being exemplified in these two serene women fails to take account of earlier works. Meyer de Haan was always associated by Gauguin with the 'primitive' and 'savage' Brittany and had already been linked with eastern philosophy in *Nirvana*, in which work, too, his features took on a diabolic aspect. Similarly, the duality of women was one of Gauguin's favorite themes in Polynesia, where he explored the ambivalence of the Eve figure, simultaneously innocent and pure and riddled with the guilt which results from Knowledge.

The title is as complex in its allusions as the content of the work. It is not clear who, if anyone, is relating the primitive stories. The contemplative poses of the three figures and the way in which they look out towards the viewer suggest that they may in fact be listening.

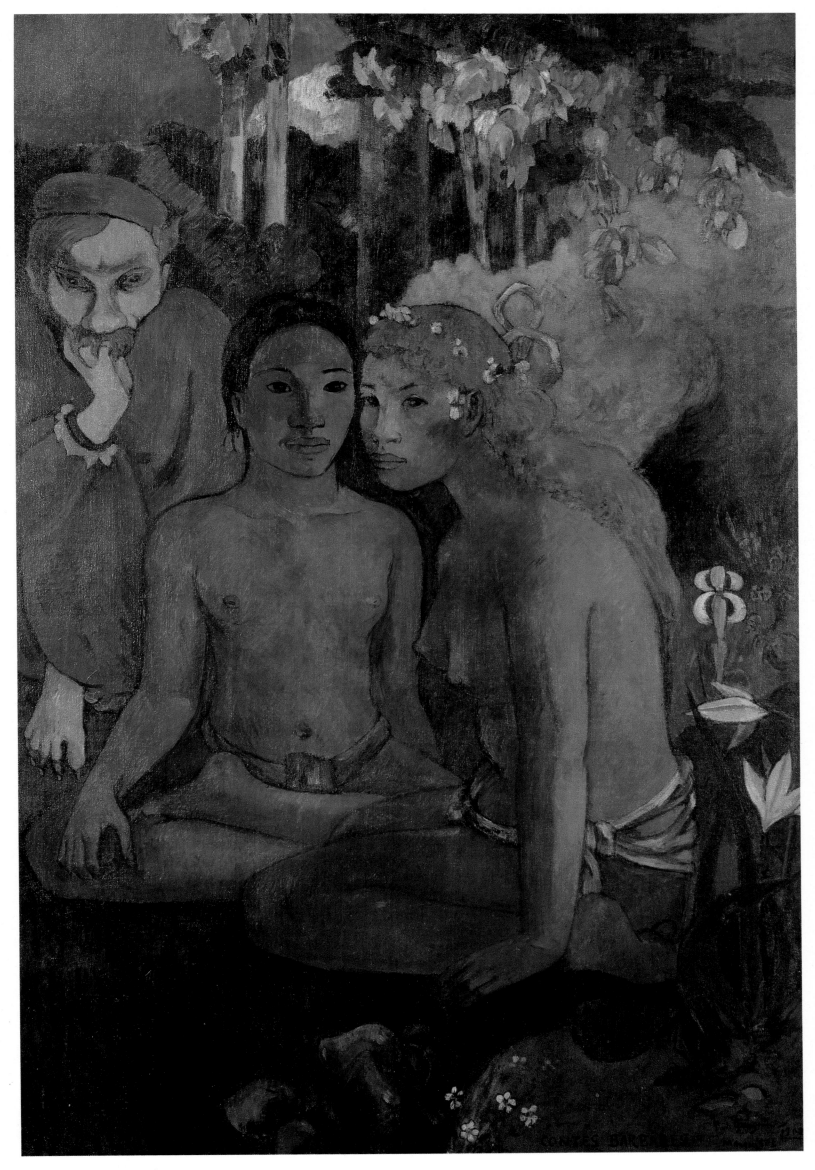

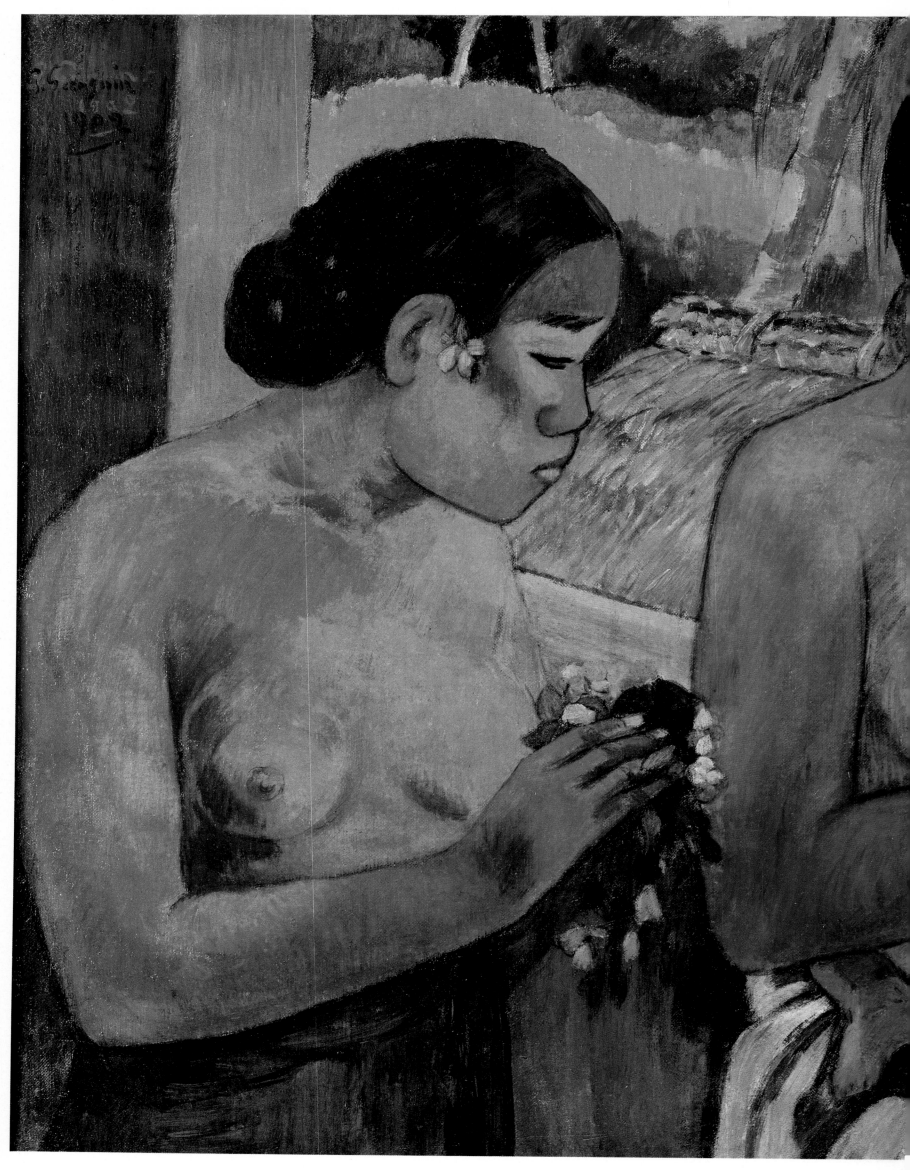

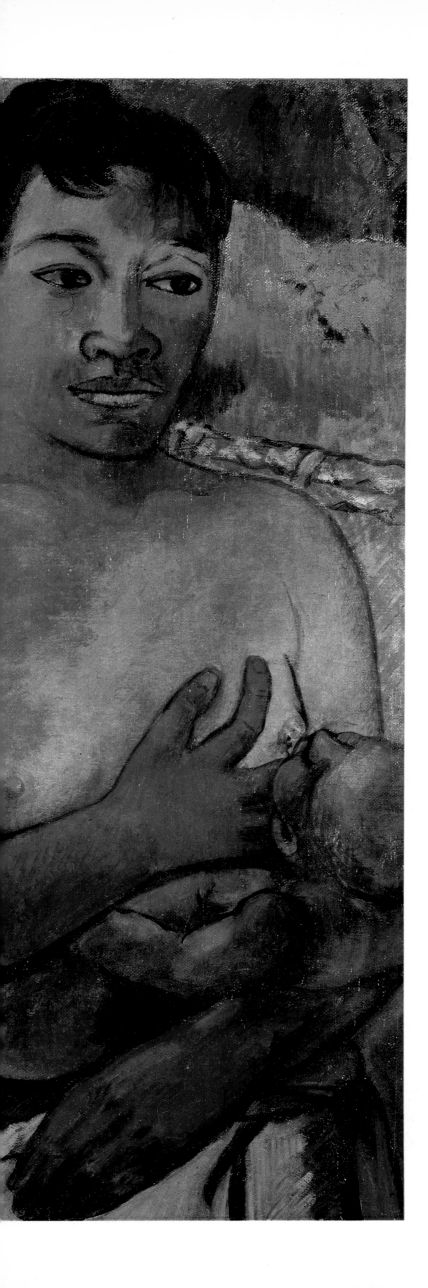

The Offering, 1902

Oil on canvas
27×31 inches (68.6×78.7 cm)
Foundation E G Bührle Collection,
Zürich, Switzerland

In its classic simplicity and the heavy
sculptural forms of the figures, *The Offering* is related to the half-length figures in
Three Tahitians (page 164). It is a Mar-
quesan genre scene with two women, one
of whom nurses an infant. However the
similarity to the religious theme of
Madonna and Child should not be overlooked. The models have not been identified but the theme of maternity was particularly relevant for Gauguin in 1902. His
most recent 14-year-old *vahine*, Vaeoho
Marie Rose, whom he had taken from
school in November of 1901, had become
pregnant with his child. In the middle of
August, 1902, she went to her parents'
home to have the baby and never returned
to live with Gauguin. Their daughter
Tahiatikaomata was born in September.
Whether this work was painted during the
earlier part of Vaeoho's pregnancy, and
should therefore be construed as embody-
ing an optimistic message, or as a result of
feelings of bitterness after losing both wife
and child is difficult to say. Certainly the
canvas was reworked at some point, to
judge by the two, virtually superimposed,
signatures.

The painting has a feeling of joyousness
far removed from the dark, brooding
nature of much of Gauguin's final paintings, such as *Contes Barbares* (page 170).
The two women are set against a rich and
tropical landscape, which is probably
viewed from an upper-storey window
rather than being one of Gauguin's paintings. If this is in fact a view onto the external world, then the work was probably
painted in Gauguin's house, one of the
very few buildings in Hivaoa with an upper
storey.

Index

Figures in *italics* refer to illustrations; all works of art are by Gauguin unless otherwise indicated.

Aha oe Feii 23, *130*, 135
Alyscamps, The 86-87
Ancien Culte Mahorie, text by Gauguin 23, 24, 144
And the Gold of their Bodies 165
Annah the Javanese 24
Arearea (Pranks) 138-39
Arles 14, 17, 19, 69, 72, 75, 80, 82, *84-85*, 86, 87, 87, 88, *90-91*, 91, 95, 100, 113, 167
Arosa, Gustave 6, 8, 26, 29, 155
Aurier, Albert 15, 16, 19, 20, 77, 104
Avant et Après, Gauguin's autobiographical text 167

Barbizon school 7
Bathers at La Grenouillère by Monet 8, *8*
Be in Love and you will be Happy (wooden sculpture) 19
Belle Angèle, La 96-97, 125
Bernard, Emile 14-15, *14*, 16, 17, 18, *18*, 19, 20, 22, 75, 78, 79, 80, 82, 84, 91, 104, 112
Bernard, Madeleine 15, *18*, 78-79, *78-79*
birth and family background of Gauguin 6
Blue Roofs (Rouen) 42-43
Bonjour Monsieur Courbet by Courbet 18, *18*, 100, 111
Bonjour Monsieur Gauguin 18, *100-01*, 147
Boys Wrestling 70, 72-73
Breton Girl, The 14, 24
Breton Girls Dancing, Pont-Aven 13, 68-69, 70
Breton Shepherdess, The 56-57
Bretons in Gauguin's paintings 13, 14, *15*, 16, *24*, *56-57*, *58-59*, 59, *68-69*, 69, 70, *70-71*, 72, *72-73*, *90-91*, 91, *96-97*, 97, 108, *108-09*, *110-11*, 111, 112, *112*, 113, *113*, 114, *114*, 148, *148-49*
Brittany 12-13, *14*, 17, 19, 20, 22, 24, 59, 62, 77, 82, 87, 88, 95, 113, *113*, 114, *114*, 117, 119, 121, 129, 151, 170, *see also* Le Pouldu, Pont-Aven
Bruyas collection, Montpellier 18, 100
Buckwheat Harvest, The by Bernard *14*, 15
By the Sea, Martinique 14, 62-63, 65

Café Voltaire 21
Cassatt, Mary 9, 11, 37
Castle at Médan by Cézanne 9, 10, *10*, 48, 66
Cézanne, Paul 7, 8, 9, *9*, 10, *10*, 11, 12, 19, 20, 30, 37, 39, 42, 44, 47, 48, 49, 53, 60, 66, 67, 88, 104, 116, 117, 123, 125, 169
Chardin, Jean Baptiste 39, 92
Chazal, Aline-Marie, Gauguin's mother 6, 119
Christ in the Garden of Olives (Agony in the Garden) 20, 104-05, 108
Contes Barbares (Primitive Tales) 99, 170-71, 173
Copenhagen 11, 12, 13, 21, 23, 40, 42, 48, *48*, 49, 66, 104, 137
Corot, Camille 7, 26
Côte des Boeufs by Pissarro *12*, 30, 66
Courbet, Gustave 7, 18, *18*, 100, 111
Cows in a Landscape 50-51

Dagnan-Bouveret, 13, *14*, 19, 56, 59
death of Gauguin 25, 168

Degas, Edgar 7, 8, 9, 11, 23, 40, 54, 59, 60, 70, 79, 99, 133, 144, 169
Delacroix, Eugène 7, 12, 16, *16*, 100
de Monfreid, Daniel 127, 131, 158, 159, 167, 168
Denis, Maurice 19, 79
Durand-Ruel, Paul 9, 11, 12
   one-man show of Gauguin's work, l893 23-24, 100, 135, 138, 141, 144, 147

Ea Haere Ia Oe? (Where are you Going?) 144-45
Eclair, L', periodical 24-25
Entrance to a Village 44-45
exhibitions
   Copenhagen, 1883 137; 1885 12; 1889 104
   Exposition Universelle, 1889 18-19, 20, 129, 143
   Impressionist Exhibitions, 1874 7, 26, 29; 1879 9; 1880 9, 30, 40; 1881 9, 32; 1882 11, 34, 36, 39; 1886 12, 48, 50, 54
   one-man show of Gauguin's work given by Durand-Ruel gallery, 1893 23-24, 100, 135, 138, 141, 144, 147
   Salon system 7, 8, 9, 10, 13, 19, 21, 26, 32, 59, 69, 151
   Volpini, 1889 19, 69, 95, 107
Exposition Universelle, 1889 18-19, 20, 129, 143
Expressionist art 21

Faa Iheihe (Tahitian Pastoral) 162-63
fan painting 12, 49, *49*, 138
Fèvre, Henry 50
Flowers, Still Life or *Interior of the Artist's House, Rue Carcel 34-35*, 36, 125
Forain, Jean Louis 79
Four Breton Women 14, 16, *58-59*

Gad, Mette Sophie, Gauguin's wife, *see* Gauguin family
Garden in the Rue Carcel 37
Gauguin family
   Aline-Marie, mother 6, 116, 119
   Clovis, father 6, 119
   Fernande Marceline Marie, sister 6, 116
   Mette Sofie, wife 7, 8, 9, *10*, 11, 13, 20, 21, 34, 37, *37*, 40, *40-41*, 47, 48, 49, 66, 95, 147, letters from Gauguin in Tahiti to 22, 23, 24, 121, 123, 127, 133, 137
   Mette's children 8, 11, 21, 34, 37, *37*, 40, *46-47*, 95; Aline 11, 37, 47, 160; Clovis 11, 12, 37, 47, 48; Emil 9, 37; Jean-René 37, 47, Pola 11
Geffroy, Gustave 50
Ginoux, Madame 18, 84, *84-85*, 87
Girl with a Fan 168-69, 170
Grape Harvest at Arles, Human Anguish 90-91
Green Christ (Breton Calvary) 110-11, 127
Guillaumin, Armand 53

Haymaking 114-15
Haystacks series by Monet 88
Henry, Marie 103, 117
Hina Tefatou (The Moon and the Earth) 144
Hivaoa 25, 167, 168, 169, 173
Huet, Juliette 119, *119*
Huysman, J-K 9-10, 15, 32
Ia Orana Maria (Hail Mary) 126-27, 155

Impression Setting Sun by Monet *11*
Impressionist Exhibitions
   First, 1874 7, 26, 29; Fourth, 1879 9; Fifth, 1880 9, 30, 40; Sixth, 1881 9, 32; Seventh, 1882 11, 34, 36, 39; Eighth, 1886 12, 48, 50, 54
Impressionists 6, 7, 8, 10, 11, 12, 15, 16, 17, 19, 26, 29, 34, 37, 47, 48, 49, 53, 59, 65, 77, 144, 147, 151
Ingres, Jean 164

Jacob wrestling with the Angel by Delacroix *16*
Japanese prints, influence of 16, 22, 72, 77, 80, 95, 103, 107
Java 22, 127, 163, 165, 170

Krohn, Pietro 49

La Grenouillère by Renoir 9
Landscape 7, 26-27, 29, 44
Landscape at Le Pouldu 117
Landscape near Arles 88-89
Large Bather, The by Ingres 164
Laval, Charles 14, 60, *60-61*, 62, 66
Le Pouldu 20, 24, 91, 99, 103, 117, *117*, 148
Leroy, Louis 8
Loss of Virginity or *The Awakening of Spring* 20, *118-19*
Loti, Pierre 20

Madame Mette Gauguin 40-41
Mahana no Atua (Day of the God) 24, 138, 147
Man with an Ax 130-31
Manao Tupapau (The Spirit of the Dead Keeps Watch) 23, *136-37*, 146, 147, 159
Manet, Edouard 8, 19, 20, *21*, 22, 54, 116, 119, 137, 155, 159
Mango Pickers, Martinique 14, 64-65, 66
Market Gardens at Vaugirard, The 9, 30-31
Marriage of Loti, The fictionalized account by Pierre Loti 20, 23, 24, 133, 135, 164
Martinique 14, 19, 20, 60, 62, *62-63*, *64-65*, 66, *66-67*, 67, 77
Martinique Landscape 66-67
Matete, Ta (The Market) 140
Meal, The 124-25, 131
Merahi Metua no Tehamana (The Ancestors of Tehamana) 142-43
Meyer de Haan, Jacob *98-99*, 99, 103, 117, 170
Mirbeau, Octave 109
Moerenhout, J-A 22, 24, 137, 143, 144, 147, 163, 164
Molard, William 25, 147
Monet, Claude 7, 8, *8*, 10, 12, 19, 26, 49, 88, 133
Moréas, Jean 15
Morice, Charles 24, 25
Morisot, Berthe 7, 9
Mountains at l'Estaque by Cézanne 9, *9*, 12 49

Nafea Faa Ipoipo (When will you Marry?) 134-35, 140, 144, 158
Naked Breton Boy 112
Naturalism 12, 15, 16, 32
Nave Nave Mahana (Wonderful Days) 156-57
Nevermore O Tahiti 158, *159*

Night Café, The by Van Gogh 17, *17*
Night Café at Arles (Madame Ginoux) 18, *84-85*
Nirvana, Portrait of Meyer de Haan 98-99, 103, 170
Noa Noa, text by Gauguin 23, 24, 129, 133, 137, 138, 141, 144, 147, 148

Oestervold Park, Copenhagen 12, *48*, 49, 88
Offering, The 172-73
Old Women at Arles 87, 91, 100, 125, 155
Olympia by Manet 20, *21*, 22, 116, 119, 137, 155, 159

Pahura, Tahitian companion to Gauguin 25, 155
Panama 14, 60, 62
Pape Moe (Mysterious Water) 141, 144
Papeete 22, 23, *23*, 25, 121, 123, 140, *140*, 152
Papyrus of Ani (Theban Book of the Dead) 20, 140
Pardon in Brittany, The by Dagnan-Bouveret 13, *14*, 19, 56
Paris 6, 7, 10, 11, 12, 13, 14, 15, 16, 17, 18, 19, 20, 21, 22, 23, 24, *28-29*, 29, 48, 49, 59, 60, 62, 69, 87, 91, 95, 107, 117, 119, 129, 135, 137, 138, 141, 146, 147, 148, 151, *151*, 156, 167, 168
Paris in the Snow 151
Peasant Women from Brittany 148-49
Pension Gloanec, Pont-Aven 13, *13*
Peru 6, 116
  mummy from 7, *19*, 91, 161
Pissarro, Camille 7, 8, 9, 10, 11, *12*, 16, 19, *21*, 26, 29, 30, 37, 39, 42, 44, 53, 56, 66, 116
Poe, Edgar Allan 159
Polynesia 13, 22, 23, 112, 121, 133, 137, 143, 144, 147, 151, 159, 163, 165, 169, 170, *see also* Papeete, Tahiti
Pomare V, Polynesian king 23, 123
Pont-Aven 13, *13*, 14-15, 16, 17, 18, 24, *25*, 56, 59, 60, *68-69*, 75, 77, 78, 99, 108, 111, 114, 117, 148
Pontoise 10, 30, 37, 53
Portier's gallery 14, 62
Portrait Bust of Mette Gauguin (sculpture) *10*, 40
Portrait of a Woman, with Still Life by Cézanne 20, 60, *116-17*, 125
Portrait of Atiti 133
Portrait of Gauguin by Pissarro *21*
Portrait of Madeleine Bernard 18, *78-79*
Portrait of my sister Madeleine by Bernard *18*
Portrait of Pissarro 21
Provençal Landscape (after Cézanne) 49

Races at Longchamps by Degas 169
Rarahu see *Marriage of Loti, The*
Renoir, Auguste 7, *8, 9, 9*, 10, 12, 26, 49

Rerioa, Te (The Dream) 158
Riders on the Beach 169
Rivière, Henri 36
Rouen 11, 12, 42, *42-43*, 44, 48, 50, 54

sale of Gauguin's work, 1891 20; 1895 24, 138, 156
Salon state-sanctioned system 7, 8, 9, 10, 12, 13, 19, 21, 26, 32, 59, 69, 151
Satre, Madame Marie-Angélique *96-97*, 97
Schneklud, Fritz 150, *150*
Schuffenecker, Emile 7, 12, 13, 16, 19, 34, 49, 65, 75, *94-95*, 95, 117
Schuffenecker Family, The 94-95
Seine at the Pont d'Iéna, Snow, The 28-29, 151
Self-Portrait (at Golgotha) 152-53
Self-Portrait (Les Misérables) 17, 47, *74-75*, 79, 97, 104, 111, 112, 147, 152
Self-Portrait for Carrière 24
Self-Portrait for his Friend Vincent by Bernard 17, 22, 75
Self-Portrait Wearing a Hat 146-47
Self-Portrait with Halo 20, 99, *102-03*, 152
Sérusier, Paul 17, *17*, 87, 99, 103, 116
Sisley, Alfred 7, 8, 9, 29
Sleeping Child 46-47
Still Life Fête Gloanec 79
Still Life with Compotier by Cézanne 60, 117
Still Life with Fan 92-93
Still Life with Mandoline 52-53
Still Life with Oranges 22, *38-39*
Still Life with Profile of Laval 60-61
Still Life with Sunflowers 166-67
Still Life with Three Puppies 80-81
Strindberg, August 24-25, 156
Study of a Nude or *Suzanne Sewing* 9, 15, *32-33*, 53, 107
Suhas, Aristide 133, *133*
suicide attempt by Gauguin 23, 160-61
Suzanne Bambridge 23, 34, *122-23*, 133
Symbolist movement 12, 15-16, 19, 20, 24, 65, 75, 77, 99, 104, 107, 119, 135, 138, 146, 147, 158, 159
synthetism 16, 20, 103, 108, 111, 117

Tahiti 6, 20, 24, *122-23*, 148, 151
  Gauguin's first stay in, 1891-93 21, 22, 23, 62, 100, 121, 123, 127, 133, 137, 138, 140, 143, 144, 155, 163
  Gauguin's second stay in, 1895-1902 25, 117, 129, 159, 160, 163
  native companions of Gauguin 23, 25, 112, *132*, 133, *136-37*, 137, *142-43*, 143, 155, 173

Tahitian Landscape 120-22, 158
Talisman, The by Sérusier 17, *17*, 87
Tamari no Atua, Te (The Birth of Christ, Son of God) 154-55, 159
Tassaert, Octave 155
Tehamana, Gauguin's native bride 23, *132*, 133, *136-37*, 137, *142-43*, 143
Three Tahitians 163, *164*, 173
Tiare Farani, Te (The Flowers of France) 129
Titi, Anglo-Tahitian companion of Gauguin 23
Tohotaura, Tahitian model 168-69, *168-69*, 170, 170-71
Tropical Landscape on Martinique 66

Upaupa Schneklud 150-51

Vaeoho Marie Rose, Tahitian companion to Gauguin 173
Vahine no te Vi (Woman with a Mango) 132-33
Van Gogh, Theo 14, 16, 17, 18, 20, 54, 59, 62, 65, 69, 82, 84, 86, 87, 91, 97, 100, 104
Van Gogh, Vincent 14, 17, *17*, 18, 19, 20, 54, 62, 69, 72, 75, 77, 82, *82-83*, 84, 86, 87, 88, 91, 92, 97, 100, 104, 111, 113, 167, 169
Van Gogh Painting Sunflowers 82-83
Vase of Flowers 36, 39, 53
Vase with Breton Girls (ceramic work) 14, *15*, 16
Vaugirard 30, *30-31*
Vision after the Sermon or *Jacob Wrestling with the Angel* 15, 16, 20, *76-77*, 79, 103, 108, 111, 127
Vollard, Ambroise 167
Volpini Exhibition, 1889 19, 69, 95, 107
Voyages aux Iles du Grand Océan, book by J-A Moerenhout 22-23, 137, 143, 147, *164*

Where do we come from? What are we? Where are we going? 25, 156, *160-61*, 163
Woman in the Waves (Ondine) 54, 99, *106-07*, 119, 169
Women Bathing 54-55
Women Bathing, Life and Death 99, 107
writings of Gauguin 6, 22
  Ancien Culte Mahorie 23, 24, 144
  Avant et Après 167
  Noa Noa 23, 24, 129, 133, 137, 138, 141, 147, 148

Yellow Christ 20, *108-09*, 111, 127
Yellow Haystacks 113, 114
Young Bretons Bathing 70-71, 72, 112

Zola, Emile 15, 32, 133

Acknowledgments

The publisher would like to thank Martin Bristow who designed this book; Jessica Orebi Gann, the editor; and Moira Dykes, the picture researcher. We would also like to thank the following museums, individuals and agencies for the illustrations:

Albright-Knox Art Gallery, Buffalo, New York: page 109 (General Purchase Funds 1946); page 136-137 (A Conger Goodyear Collection 1965)

The Art Institute of Chicago: page 147 (Helen Birch Bartlett Memorial Collection, 1926.198); page 87 (Mr and Mrs Lewis Larned Coburn Memorial Collection, 1934.391); page 116 (The Joseph Winterbotham Collection, 1925.753); page 142 (Gift of Mr and Mrs Charles Deering McCormick, 1980.613)

The Baltimore Museum of Art: pages 2, 132 (The Cone Collection, formed by Dr Claribel Cone and Miss Etta Cone of Baltimore, Maryland); page 150 (Given by Hilda K Blaustein in memory of her husband Jacob Blaustein)

British Museum/Photo C M Dixon: page 20

Foundation E G Bührle Collection, Zurich/Photo W Drayer, Zurich: pages 166-167; 172-173

Photo Bulloz: page 16

The Burrell Collection, Glasgow Museums and Art Galleries: pages 10(below); 24(top)

The Chrysler Museum, Norfolk, Virginia: pages 118-119

The Cleveland Museum of Art: page 106 (Gift of Mr and Mrs William Powell Jones, 78.63)

Courtauld Institute Galleries, London (Courtauld Collection): pages 10(top); 115; 158; 159

Fitzwilliam Museum, Cambridge: pages 26-27

Folkwang Museum, Essen: pages 168; 169; 171

Photograph Giraudon/Weidenfeld Archive: page 21(top)

Glasgow Art Gallery and Museum: page 46

Hamburger Kunsthalle: page 69

Hermitage Museum, Leningrad/Photo SCALA: pages 129; 145

Hulton-Deutsch Collection: page 6

Indianapolis Museum of Art: page 86 (Gift in Memory of William Ray Adams)

Josefowitz Collection: pages 14(below); 44-45; 59; 71

From the Collection at the Laing Art Gallery, Newcastle upon Tyne, Reproduced by permission of Tyne and Wear Museums Service: pages 54-55

The Metropolitan Museum of Art: page 14(top) (Gift of George F Baker 1931, 31.132.34); page 126 (Bequest of Sam A Lewinsohn 1951, 51.112.2)

The Minneapolis Institute of Arts: pages 120-121 (The Julius C Eliel Memorial Fund)

Montpellier, Musée Fabré/The Bridgeman Art Library: page 18(top)

Musée d'Albi: page 18(below)

Muséu de Arte de São Paulo, Brazil: page 153

Musée des Beaux-Arts de Lyon: pages 156-157

Musée des Beaux-Arts, Rennes/The Bridgeman Art Library: pages 22(below); 36; 38-39

Museum Boymans-van Beuningen, Rotterdam: pages 48-49

Courtesy Museum of Fine Arts, Boston: page 19 (Arthur Tracy Cabot Fund, 57.582); pages 42-43 (Bequest of John T Spaulding); pages 160-161 (Tompkins Collection Purchase, Arthur Gordon Tompkins Fund 1936)

Musée de Grenoble: page 76

Musée de l'Homme, Paris: page 7

Musée Marmottan, Paris/The Bridgeman Art Library: page 11

Collection, The Museum of Modern Art, New York: page 81 (Mrs Simon Guggenheim Fund); page 144 (Lillie P Bliss collection)

Musée d'Orsay/Photo RMN: pages 17(top); 21(below); 28-29; 50; 86; 92-93; 94-95; 96; 124-125; 138-139; 146; 148-149; 165

Musées Royaux d'Art et d'Histoire, Brussels/ Privately Owned: page 15(below)

Musées Royaux des Beaux-Arts de Belgique: pages 110; 122

Narodni Gallery, Prague: page 101

Nasjonalgalleriet, Oslo/Photo Jacques Lathion: pages 34-35; 40-41

The National Gallery, London: pages 8; 12

National Gallery of Art, Washington: pages 24(below); 66-67; 117 (Collection of Mr and Mrs Paul Mellon); page 102 (Chester Dale Collection)

National Gallery of Scotland: pages 65; 74-75; 164

National Museum of Wales: page 9(below)

The National Museum of Western Art, Tokyo, Matsukata Collection: pages 52-53

Neue Pinakothek, Munchen/Photo Artothek: pages 1; 56-57; 64; 154-155

Norton Gallery of Art, West Palm Beach, Florida: pages 104-105

Ny Carlsberg Glyptotek: pages 33; 37; 47; 60-61

Ordrupgaard Collection, Copenhagen: pages 90-91

Orleans, Musée des Beaux-Arts: page 77

Oskar Reinhart Collection 'Am Römerholz', Winterthur: pages 9(top); 41

Private Collection/The Bridgeman Art Library: page 128

Pushkin Museum, Moscow/Photo SCALA: pages 84-85; 130-131

Rudolf Staechelin Family Foundation, Basel/Color-photo Hans Hinz: page 134

Smith College Museum of Art, Northampton, Massachusetts: pages 30-31 (Purchased 1953)

State Museum Kröller-Müller, Otterlo: page 133

Tate Gallery, London: pages 162-163

Vincent van Gogh Foundation/National Museum Vincent van Gogh, Amsterdam: pages 22(top); 62-63; 72-73; 82-83; 151

Collection Viollet: pages 23; 25(below)

Harlingue-Viollet: pages 13; 25(top)

ND-Viollet: page 15(top)

Wadsworth Atheneum, Hartford: pages 98-99 (Ella Gallup Sumner and Mary Catlin Sumner Collection)

Yale University Art Gallery: page 17(below) (Bequest of Stephen Carlton Clark BA, 1903)